AF488184

WALK, RUN, FLY AGAIN

A COMBAT PILOT'S RETURN TO THE COCKPIT

LISETTE ALVAREZ

JOHN ALVAREZ

PRAISE FOR WALK, RUN, FLY AGAIN

"Powerful, deeply personal and inspiring beyond words! Walk, Run, Fly Again *will give you hope that no matter what setbacks you face in life— you can overcome them with grit, love and faith. Let John Alvarez show you how!"* - Admiral William H. McRaven, US Navy (Retired)

"A must read! A story of resilience, faith, and family. From a helicopter incident, John was tested to beat the odds. With his pursuit of excellence, he had an opportunity to fly the Chief of Staff Air Force (CSAF) to prove his tenacity. On the way to the Pave Low, I told the CSAF that he would be flying with a 'prosthetic' leg pilot. He immediately responded—'Who approved that?' I replied—'Let's discuss that after the flight.' When he landed, we adjourned to the Hurlburt "Houch" where the CSAF partici-pated in a post-flight celebration. As we departed, his only comment was: 'We need to do more of this.'" - General Charles "Charlie" Holland, USAF (Ret.), Former AFSOC and USSOCOM Commander

"John's story of courage and determination has been an inspiration for all of us who flew with him for a long time. I was thrilled to see it captured in a truly well-written book, and I know that it will inspire countless others for years to come!" - Lt Gen Tom Trask, USAF (Ret.), Former Vice Commander, US Special Operations Command

"The Spirit of a Warrior. Lisette Alvarez beautifully illustrates the embodiment of this by relaying one year (albeit a significant one!) in the life of her father, Col (Ret) John Alvarez. I've known Johnny for many, many years. He possesses the "never quit" mindset; and so, after the devastating event of September 1996, Johnny charts a course to overcome all obstacles with courage, resilience and persistence. Simply put, he set unprecedented goals for himself and then proceeded to crush them! Walk, Run, Fly Again *is an inspirational book for service members; but honestly this is a great*

TABLE OF CONTENTS

FOREWORD

This book recounts a remarkable story of courage, grit, and determination. Of an aviation mishap, the lengthy recovery, and a pilot's return to flight. But even more, it is a love story, the ultimate achievement, between a worthy father and an equally accomplished and admiring daughter.

Read on!

Norton A. Schwartz, Gen (ret), USAF
    19th Chief of Staff

A MESSAGE FROM THE AUTHOR

There is very little more that defined my childhood than my father's accident, survival, and recovery. Parents usually define childhood. It is their legacy. We are utterly reliant on our parents, or on facing life without them.

But (as many military brats will tell you) having a parent in the United States military is a unique experience. Military brats are told: "They are going away for a while," or sometimes, "No, we can't know where they went." "They'll be back soon, I promise." Five sleeps. Ten sleeps. Thirty sleeps.

Don't feel sorry for us. More often than not, this was our normal. I don't recall mourning the absence of my father or feeling like I was missing out. My dad still coached my soccer team and took the time to improve my art projects. He accompanied me to theater auditions and gave me advice on my college essays. He made the most of the time he was around, which was plenty.

This was before 9/11 and the subsequent wars. My dad took on plenty of missions in the nineties of my early childhood, but I also have a feeling my siblings and I were lucky. He was around a lot, and we moved with him for the extended missions in Italy, Argentina, and

Bolivia. The other missions were comparatively short until he was tapped to help in Iraq, too. Even then, his Iraq tour was not the long months and sometimes years some mothers and fathers spent overseas, away from their kids. I know we were lucky for other reasons, too.

I don't remember how many services for fallen soldiers I attended, but there is one I will never forget. Brian Downs was one of the brave and competent men who saved my father's life. Brian Downs helped my father stick around to watch my sister and me grow up. Brian Downs was, for whatever reason, not given the same opportunity. At his service, I was looking at his kids—Brian's kids—across the room. Chandler, Ella, and Bailey were around my and my siblings' ages. I could see myself in them. I count myself lucky because death was always at my father's front door. My ongoing fear was potent. Not only was my father nearly taken from me, but I saw the impact of that possibility turned reality. Brian's kids experienced, and now live with, a cruel reality that too many military brats contend with: a loved one stolen in an act of violence.

Despite my current reservations about the realm of the United States military and the political choices behind placing people in harm's way, I don't believe my childhood was lessened by being a military kid. When you have a parent in the military, most of your understanding of their work comes from what we as a society call them. Heroes. Defenders. Protectors. My father was my hero, my defender, my protector.

What happens to this image when it is shattered? What happens to you when your father falls, human, and can be broken? What does it do to a five-year-old? How does a kid, barely coming into their own consciousness, process that kind of trauma?

Maybe unwittingly, my father gave me those answers in the most incredible way. He found the best in himself. He rose from the ashes, not only for his own sake but also for everyone he loved. Through his fight to attain what seemed nearly impossible—first to survive and then to fly—my father taught me so many things about what I needed to know to get through this strange thing called life. I know he gave me the right tools because I've used some of them and survived a few things myself. What he has taught me has helped me more than I probably realize and for more that will come.

John Alvarez has taught me that a calling is not as simple as just being good at something. A calling comes from something ineffable and indefinable, and almost holy. You might not be the best pilot, or the best actor, or the best entrepreneur, or the best nurse, or the best engineer. A calling doesn't care if you have natural talent. A calling reaches into you and gives you what nothing else can: a purpose. John Alvarez made sure his life had a purpose. Whether the military would have taken him back, he would have stayed true to his calling and his purpose against any odds.

As a self-described storyteller, I have learned a lot on this journey into my father's story. I have learned a lot about the people who know him. I have learned a lot about all the weird and wonderful "coincidences" and miracles that make up such a harrowing time in my family's life. I am grateful for these lessons.

To John, from your eldest child, thank you for being a role model and a hero. Thank you for setting an example for me to carry with me for the rest of my life. I am grateful to have your love and support no matter what crazy adventures I get myself into.

Yes, this is my father's story. But by being a child of my father, this is my story too. My father's choices and his legacy have made a mark on me as deep as blood. His struggles, his failures, and his victories were mine, too. They were mine in the way my parents were my entire world, and so what happened to them happened to me.

This is a story not told from a child's eyes, but from an adult who experienced this story as a child. This is a story of hope, faith, and love. This is a story of finding the core of the self and the places you turn to in your darkest hour. This is a story about family: the one you are born into and the one you create. This is a story about the strength that comes when you are true to your calling and you've got people to back you up.

This is a story about walking, running, and flying into the unknown. This is a story about flying into the brilliant light of our destiny and our choices, which shape our destiny. This is a story, too, about the preciousness of life and the inevitability of death.

This is the story of John Alvarez. This is also the story of Lisette Alvarez.

And neither story is finished just yet.

INTRODUCTION BY JOHN ALVAREZ

This story was originally meant for our family only. This book was created so my future grandchildren could understand their grandfather's journey. About how a terrible and almost unbelievable tragedy became a gift: a blessing for me and my family. My wife's cousin stated that our little family was *"forged after impact"*.

Discipline. Self control. Grit. Never giving up. Those concepts were already part of my life long before the crash. Instilled in me through the stoic principles taught to me by my father, later honed and ingrained by my coaches, my mentors, and by my military training. But there came a moment when those things were not enough. In my darkest hours, I was led to something greater: the strength of faith, the power of love, and the grace of others who stepped forward when the odds seemed impossible. There were no coincidences on our journey. Call it serendipity or divine intervention—not coincidence.

We also honestly deal with the emotions of fear, doubt, and even despair. We deal with the act of admitting that we need help to succeed. We understand, in practice, the title of Lieutenant Commander Frank Ellis's book: *No Man Walks Alone.*

In 1996, a helicopter crash mangled my legs, took one of them and nearly ended my life—it also stripped me of my identity. What followed was a journey few believed possible. The true story of this journey is not just about overcoming injuries, disabilities, or even returning to the cockpit. It's about the people, the faith, the love, and grace that made the impossible possible.

So what's the point of this story? Even in your darkest hour, you can tap into a power much stronger than yourself to rise again, to overcome, and to transcend.

When Lisette offered to chronicle my/our story, she promised that this would be about Love, Faith and Transcendence. Thank you, my "Little Miss Magic".

Forged after Impact—Tempered by Grace!

DEDICATIONS

For Shelley and our Duckies.
My reasons for living.
- John

For my Daddio.
My first hero.
- Lisette

This is true love – you think this happens every day?
– Westley (The Princess Bride)

PART I

Every difficulty in life presents us with an opportunity to turn inward and to invoke our own inner resources. The trials we endure can and should introduce us to our strengths. Prudent people look beyond the incident itself and seek to form the habit of putting it to good use. On the occasion of an accidental event, don't just react in a haphazard fashion: remember to turn inward and ask what resources you have for dealing with it...
– Epictetus

One of the inescapable encumbrances of leading an interesting life is that there have to be moments when you almost lose it.
– Jimmy Buffett

1

BREAK

"Need me to break anything?"

John looked at his wife and her threat with a grin. The girls had already been swept off to their respective caretakers for the day: Lisette at kindergarten and Nicole at daycare. Even with just the trunk open, the smell of their shampoo lingered in the air around the van. He already received their tiny kisses goodbye. Shelley had first offered to maim him then, when he had his hands on his girls' soft brown curls.

When deployed, John often daydreamed of dancing with Shelley and the girls. John had brought his CD player in order to listen to Jimmy Buffett's *Boats Beaches Bars and Ballads* whenever he felt homesick. He left a copy behind for his girls to dance to in his absence. And to remember him by, if he never made it back home.

Dealing with an injury to keep him home? Yeah, it was tempting. John inhaled and laughed, turning towards his wife.

"Not this time," he told her lightly. "Good to go?"

"Yep," Shelley replied. She had already strolled to the driver's seat, precise and businesslike.

Before he closed the trunk, John ran through his checklist again. Getting into the right mindset was key, especially if he was expected to share it with others.

His fingers danced over his bags mechanically, as he had done for years. Logging his inventory and pulling zippers shut, snapping the snaps snug, crisp, and ready to go. The deployment to Ecuador was to only last about a month, but they had already been delayed once by government bureaucracy.

He was scheduled to embark that morning on the MC-130P Shadow, piloted by Captain Brian Downs and Major Mike Wercinski from Eglin Air Force Base to Ecuador. Technical Sergeant Charles "Butch" Lesley, the loadmaster, had thought it was a novelty to have a pilot from the Navy onboard. John was excited to finally get on with the mission.

John closed the trunk and moved towards the passenger side of the car. As he slid into his seat, Shelley started up the car. He leaned forward to turn on the A/C. The morning was already warming, and he would shortly be without such creature comforts in the heat and humidity of the jungle. As Shelley pulled out of the driveway, he turned his thoughts away from home and his girls and back to the mission.

It had been a long road with a lot of hard work to get to this point. People were counting on him.

"THEY NEED SOMEONE WITH YOUR SKILLS," his commander had told him. "You're the right guy for us to send to fly with AFSOC. You need to go there instead."

It was 1994. John was scrambling to get his application for the Navy's Test Pilot School (TPS) in order. He was nearly finished with his second year at the Navy Postgraduate School (NPS) in Monterey, California, in their Master's degree program in Aeronautical Engineering.

While discussing his options with his squadron and wing

commander, John was pointed in the direction of a newly agreed upon Naval Aviation/Air Force Special Operations Command (AFSOC) exchange program. His commander had said that the program could use John's skills and research on night-airborne mine warfare.

John ended up applying to both the TPS and the exchange program. He was selected for the exchange, pulled his TPS application as the Navy assignment office worked out the details of his assignment. Upon graduation from NPS and waiting for official orders, he attended the Navy aviation safety school. In the meantime, he had to pass a fitness test, an interview, and a psychologic evaluation for placement in a special operations unit.

In the early spring of 1995, the Alvarez family had packed up and moved to Albuquerque, New Mexico, where John was assigned for training at the 551st Special Operations Squadron (SOS) at Kirtland Air Force Base. There, John completed the MH-53J Pave-Low transition course and finished his NPS Master's research thesis simultaneously.

By Christmas 1995, John had checked into Hurlburt Field Air Force Base, home of AFSOC and the legendary 20th SOS.

The 20th SOS was designated as the premier helicopter special operations aviation unit. The unit handled the infiltration, extraction, and resupply of elite Special Operations Forces (SOF) at night and in adverse weather.

John had met the commander, Lt. Colo Tommy Hull, when Hull was the operations officer of the "Green Hornets". Tommy had two exchange officers: one Marine, Captain Brooks Gruber, and one Navy pilot—John. John was the first Navy officer in the 20th SOS, so Hull had made good use of him.

In the spring of 1996, John had deployed with the 20th SOS on several missions. He had taken part in the operations in Bosnia, Croatia and then-Yugoslavia. He had worked with elite SOF teams, including for the recovery of the downed U.S. Air Force T-43, which had been carrying U.S. Commerce Secretary Ron Brown and 32 others.

John had also deployed to Sierra Leone during a break in its own civil war, where he took part in the evacuation of United States Embassy personnel, partner nation diplomats, and foreign nationals from Liberia. There, John's callsign changed from 'Frito' (a holdover from when he was the only Hispanic pilot on his team) to 'Klepto'—for 'liberating items' from those war-torn regions.

Besides shipboard operations, the 20th frequently leveraged John's Cuban background and Spanish language skills for interviews. The 6th SOS, inevitably, heard about John's Spanish capability and asked to borrow the pilot and train him as a Combat Aviation Advisor (CAA).

The 6th was a newly re-established squadron with roots in Special Ops—the original force was part of WWII secret missions in the China-Burma theater, then recommissioned again conducting counter-insurgency and unconventional warfare in Vietnam and Laos. One of the founders of the 6th was Lieutenant Colonel Jerome "Mr. K" Klingaman, a legend of a man who wrote the often-circulated 'Coyote Rules'. The 'Coyote Rules' served as a set of guiding principles for combat aviation advisors. The first rule was: "*If you run with the pack, play by pack rules, but keep your options open.*"

Despite the counter-drug and budding counter-insurgency efforts throughout Bolivia, Colombia, Ecuador, Peru, and Venezuela, which made up the 'Andean' region, Ecuador was fairly unfamiliar territory for Air Force Special Ops. The 6th SOS was the spearhead.

Tommy Hull had called John into his office earlier that summer to talk about the opportunity.

"Is this something you would be interested in?" Tommy had asked.

"Yes, sir!" It was the kind of mission John knew he could sink his teeth into, especially compared to the missions in Europe and Africa. There was something powerful about getting to work with and teach fellow warriors and pilots in a way that felt a little closer to home. It was maybe that much more meaningful, and it just made sense that his country would call him to do what he did best: share the calling of flight.

"The 6th's operations officer will be commanding a Joint Special Operations Task Force in Ecuador," Tommy told him. "The JSOTF will equip the Ecuadorian Army and Navy with the skills they need to operate and support each other in a jungle riverine environment. Call for fire, communications between teams on the ground and in the helo, that kind of thing. It is going to comprise two 'A-Teams' from AFSOC: one fixed-wing team with a MC-130P Shadow and a blended Helicopter/Air Ground liaison team. Operational Aviation Detachment—OAD. That's you."

"A-Team, huh?" John prodded with a smile. Tommy nodded, smug. Tommy Hull was regularly referred to as 'Hannibal' from the hit series. He loved it when a plan came together.

"You know it, dude. In addition, you're going to be working with a Navy SEAL platoon from SEAL Team 4, and a riverine special boat team from Special Boat Unit 26." He had leaned forward to emphasize the next part. "There is a significant amount of planning, coordination, and preparation to do to get you integrated with the 6th and the entire team. There's not a lot of time between now and deployment. Are you confident you want to be loaned out?"

"Yes, sir."

John had been on his way out when Tommy left him with one last piece of advice.

"We still have elite customers that need your skills," the squadron commander reminded him. "Just remember that you're on loan. So be careful out there."

"Always, sir. Good to go!"

Tommy just sighed and laughed. "I told the 6th. You can borrow him, just don't break him."

John thought about Tommy's comments as Shelley drove him to Eglin. There was a massive tribal mentality between the SOF squadrons. John felt compelled to shrug the warning off. Folks never like sharing their toys. Tommy was just being possessive.

～

SHELLEY KEPT up the facade of normalcy as they made their way east on Highway 98. Occasionally, the twinkle of the Gulf of Mexico beckoned out the passenger side of the van. John chatted with her about his new colleagues as he fiddled with the radio and the A/C, and any other buttons he could get his hands on. It was as if he were already in the cockpit.

"Oh, you'd appreciate this," John said between button-pushing. "So you know Joe Basinger–"

"Your flight surgeon, right?" What little John could talk about regarding his missions, Shelley would at least get some of the stuff that sounded medical. As a nurse, it was nice that her husband felt the need to include her in on the fun anecdotes. Not that she was particularly in the mood for fun anecdotes. At least, what she knew of Joe, she liked. Shelley tried to focus on John's voice, and not the tightness in her chest as he spoke.

"I told you he was from the 16th?"

"Maybe."

"So just last month we were with the 6th up in Eglin, doing a live-fire range exercise–"

"Oh lord, should you be telling me this?"

"Well," John continued, "Joe and I are the only folks who know each other well enough to be considered friends, right? So we were doing general field training: orienteering with compasses, small team tactics, disengagement with hostile forces, how to put up temporary shelters, live call-for-fire. That is...okay, that's when you got air-to-ground fires from helicopters and fixed-wing attack aircraft..."

"Get to the point, Johnny A," Shelley intoned.

"Anyway, one night we were operating overnight on the firing range, and an AC-130 gunship from the 16th and Pave Lows from the 20th started firing simultaneously. Our team started doggin' on Joe, like, *'Basinger is that your aircraft? Tell them to stop firing!'*"

"So you never got blown up?"

John was smug. "The target we were marking for them did."

"Just for my sake...you *are* going to avoid friendly fire in the jungle, right?"

They pulled into the base and showed their IDs at the gate. Shelley followed John's directions to park in front of the 9th SOS hangar, where the MC-130 and Captain Downs were waiting to take her husband to South America.

Shelley took a breath as she turned the car off and decided she would try to offer him an out again. One last time. The third time was a charm, right? Maybe it would be different. It felt different this time.

Was it different, though? She should be used to his Navy and SOF deployments after almost ten years. But she hadn't felt this weird when he left for Colombia. Bosnia, Yugoslavia, Liberia. Or his Pacific countermine deployments prior to that. Or even when she was pregnant with Lisette, with John deploying at the beginning of the Gulf War. She would pout and complain about missing him, but then send him off with a sweet mix of trust and love. Maybe this was something that came to a head every dozen deployments, an unscheduled anxiety that was just part of being a military wife.

"I *can* break your fingers, you know."

John gave his wife a look. She knew that look. In other circumstances, he would have taken offense. After all, it was the third time in an hour she had suggested this particular form of spousal abuse. The look on his face told her that John felt his wife was overreacting.

"I'm serious," she said. Her fingers flexed on the steering wheel. Shelley could not quite voice the unexpected desperation that gripped her. This whole military thing wasn't exactly new to her. She was also an intensive care nurse. Shelley had experienced the ICU for adults, and now she had to deal with neonates and the trauma of tiny lives in her hands, plus the emotional turmoil of their parents.

Shelley knew the psychology of this crap. She ought not to be so anxious about his deployment. Usually she felt sad and supplemented this with healthy doses of concern and prayer.

But this was different. There was something about letting him out of her sight this time around that triggered a storm of barely restrained terror.

"Just one," she told him. "Your pinky. Nothing too serious."

Shelley glanced at her husband's face. She had tried to shake the feeling, but it persisted. *You're not supposed to be there,* she wanted to tell him. But she did not know how to justify the feeling in her gut.

"Very funny. But no. I've gotta go."

"You started training with them a month ago. You guys had to come back from Panama just to re-deploy now because the Secretary of Defense didn't sign the deployment orders on time! And–*and...*" She cut her husband off before he could rationalize at her some more. "You did not have to joke around about friendly fire!"

"I've been training with them for two months. And hey, I don't question you on what to do when the girls get sick."

"Oh, yes you do!"

John reached out to her hand. "I trust these guys to have my back. C'mon, Shel."

"I'm not even going to be able to talk to you to know you're okay." Which was nothing new; she was used to radio silence when he was deployed. That was a security measure. It just sucked.

"It's just a couple of weeks. Thirty, forty-five days max," John grinned. "You better throw me a great birthday party after this."

"Just...be careful," she told him.

"As you wish," he responded, pulling her into him as he had done dozens of times before. John repeated the phrase from their favorite movie as he pressed his face into the curve of her neck, breathing her in as if he wanted the familiar scent to sink inside his soul. *The Princess Bride* had provided a lot for them over the years–and not just romantic catchphrases. They had even selected the movie's end credits song, "Storybook Love", as their first dance at their wedding.

Shelley leaned into his kiss as always, but could not force down the fear. But not just fear. Another emotion bubbled up, one that she had never felt in the face of her husband's deployment. Helplessness.

Helplessness threatened to overwhelm her entirely.

2

BITTER LAKE

"Damn, I hate these Mae West LPUs," John said to Technical Sergeant Ramon "Lobo" Acosta, his gunner, as they looked over the list of aircrew and deployment equipment in the life support shop along with some of the other 6th SOS teammates. The vests weren't even stocked yet in the newly re-established unit. "But we have to get one for each of us."

"Damn straight, sir," the technical sergeant agreed.

Acosta was also a combat-hardened aerial gunner instructor/evaluator in the MH-53J and MH-60G Pave Hawk, and a 20th SOS veteran. He was a member of the OAD-A Team. The OAD-A Team also included Captain Mike Hargis, who was a 'plank-owner' of the 6th SOS who helped re-establish the unit two years earlier. He was the OAD-A Team leader and an experienced helicopter instructor pilot. Master Sergeant Dan "Labby" Labrador was the OAD-A Team maintenance advisor—and a fellow Cuban-American. The A-Team ground members were Pararescue Jumper Master Sergeant "Iggy" and Jack, their Combat Controller (CCT).

Captain (Dr.) Joe Basinger, the deployment's flight surgeon, was the only guy John knew well other than Acosta, who was his helicopter gunner on several previous Pave Low missions. The doc had been busy assessing the mission's medical evacuation (MEDEVAC) plans and other medical procedures. John had to try to the best of his ability to make sure the team wouldn't need him.

"Why?" one of the other teammates questioned. "You don't need them when you're flying over the jungle."

As a Naval Aviator, John knew better. "You can crash into a *pool* and drown."

He wasn't keen on the Mae Wests, but they were better than nothing at all. The 20th issued life preserver units (LPUs) along with combat survival vests for combat and water survival as part of their extensive shipboard and over-water mission requirements. The Air Force and Army LPUs looked like bras and were comically bulbous when inflated, earning them the nickname "Mae West" vests after the well-endowed actress. It clipped in front, and lobes inflated under the armpits. In contrast, Naval and Marine Corps aircrew survival vests included integrated inflation devices and beaded handles in two locations so a person could reach them even in the fetal position or when pinned in an awkward position.

Still, John insisted on bringing them to Ecuador. "Does the 6th even have LPUs besides Army-style survival vests?" John asked as he surveyed their pre-deployment checklist. The life support technician and logistician on the team jumped into the argument.

"Do we really need them?"

"Christ, LT...it's just another thing to keep track of and maintain. Why don't we just take two, and you share them when it's your turn to fly?"

"You're only going to be over the river a few seconds at a time, anyway."

"No," John insisted. "We're flying over water. We're conducting riverine operations. We *will all wear* an LPU any time you get into a helicopter with me or Captain Hargis. Do you understand?"

"Yes, sir," was the immediate response, however begrudgingly.

Hargis, on the spot, made the LPUs an official requirement and ordered them to be part of their pack-out.

John arranged for extra LPUs, survival vests, Helicopter Emergency Egress Device (HEEDs) bottles (mini scuba tanks with regulators which provide precious extra minutes of air if trapped underwater), helmets, and enough spares on loan from the 20th SOS. The flyers on the team were each assigned a dedicated Mae West and HEEDs bottle with their combat survival vests.

26 AUG 1996 // LAGO AGRIO, ECUADOR // 1555L

Florida was hot and humid in the dog days of summer, but the rainforest was worse. Flight suits grew damp at a rapid pace, and John tended to overheat even on balmy days. Shelley complained all the time that her husband was built like an overactive furnace, but at least she didn't have to deal with him and a dozen other guys packed into an Army truck with no A/C. John swiped off the sweat pouring into his eyes as he helped unload the C-130.

After an eight-hour flight, the MC-130 had landed at the U.S.-supported airstrip in Lago Agrio, Ecuador while the JSOTF leadership team flew to Panama in order to in-brief the SOCSOUTH commander. This time, the SECDEF had signed their deployment orders.

Upon arrival, their logistician and a MILGRP advance party greeted the OAD. The OAD A-team quickly got to unloading their gear, weapons cases, ammo for the helicopters, and personal bags from the C-130 pallets and trans-loading it all into a M35A2 2½-ton truck (nicknamed a *deuce-and-a-half)* on loan from their soon-to-be host command in the Amazon jungle.

In Spanish, Lago Agrio means "Bitter Lake". The name was not a pleasant omen, especially considering their convoy would drive through the infamous Sucumbios Province to Coca, Ecuador. In 1995, U.S. Special Forces almost launched a rescue mission for four Americans and three foreign oil workers whom kidnappers had taken hostage in the region. However, after they paid a ransom, the kidnappers released the hostages, and the rescuers called off the operation.

On the same road to Coca, just months prior to John's deployment, a U.S. Army Special Forces team of advisors was involved in a firefight with an armed group that had hijacked a bus full of civilians. The SF team killed several captors, but the SF team and all civilians remained unharmed. The incident directly shaped the rules of engagement for all U.S. SOF personnel involved in any Foreign Internal Defense missions throughout the Andean region. It also served as an example of how quickly a so-called training or advisory mission, like the one John was about to embark on, could escalate.

The MC-130P crew reconfigured their bird, refueled, and were almost ready to depart for the Mariscal Sucre International Airport in the capital of Quito, where they would operate from for the rest of the deployment.

"You fixed-wing boys are lucky," John told Brian as the A-Team was preparing to load into a convoy of trucks headed into the jungle. "I bet you plan to do some shopping, napping in your nice five-star hotels..."

"Got *my* Gucci bag all packed!" Wercinski called back to him from within the plane.

"... ordering room service while the helo bubbas have to eat ants off the jungle floor?" John finished.

"Just call us when you need us," Brian told John with a smug grin, "We'll be here to give your sorry asses a ride home."

Captain Brian Downs, Major Mike Wercinski, and their fixed-wing team in Quito were to be on call. They would not have time to interact with the JSOTF too much other than by satellite radio or landline phone. The fixed-wing team was to conduct re-supply air drops to the riverine team and to the jungle dirt strip in Coca. They could not land on that airstrip, according to the pre-deployment survey. The paltry oil-packed dirt runway could not support the weight of its wheels if they tried to land and park; it would sink. The

150,000-pound beast was just too heavy and a mismatch for the short jungle strip.

John smiled and clapped the Captain on the shoulder before joining the rest of A-Team by the trucks. Go time.

As John loaded his bag onto the truck, the team's Combat Controllers walked up to him. Jack was a former Marine who had been cross-trained into the Air Force. Air Force Combat Controllers (CCTs) are elite, highly trained Special Tactics airmen who operate and deploy alongside our most elite SEALs, Rangers, and Special Forces, and are experts in calling in precision airstrikes and raining lead and destruction down on the enemy. In addition, these special operations airmen are certified air traffic controllers adept at coordinating and controlling complex air operations from major airports to remote, austere landing strips.

According to the brief, Jack replaced another combat controller who was Puerto Rican and a fluent Spanish speaker. The other CCT had to back out because his wife was pregnant and due to deliver. Jack volunteered to take his place because he reported that he was also bilingual. Jack would train the other fledgling forward air controllers within the blended Ecuadorian team.

"Hey L.T.! Do you have a second, sir?"

"Sure! What's up?"

The CCT shifted from one foot to the other. "You speak Spanish, right?"

John's brow furrowed. "Yeah?"

"Well. You see, sir, uh. I really wanted to get assigned to this mission," Jack mumbled. "You can count on me for the call-for-fire, for sure, sir. But...I don't actually speak it fully. Spanish."

John stared at the CCT. "Seriously?"

"I mean, I know some phrases!" Jack insisted. "I'm just not, like, fully bilingual."

"You are assigned to do the Close Air Support briefings," John told him. "To the Ecuadorians. In Spanish."

"Right, which is why I came to you, sir. I could really use your help with that."

John wanted to throw his hands up and, instead, prayed for patience. They were already in the country; it wasn't like they could call for another Air Force CCT who spoke fluent Spanish. Besides, Jack had already spent the last two months training with them. It would break the cohesion of the group to send him back. Their best option was for John to pick up the linguistic slack.

"Fine. I'll do your briefings for the Ecuadorian combat controllers–"

"Oh," Jack cut in. "And the call for fire lesson plans."

John growled, "Right. Good to go, *Airman*?" He let the words hang, recognizing how they would land, knowing that Jack was a former Marine.

Jack at least had the decency to look a little ashamed.

ONCE THE TRUCKS WERE LOADED, the A-Team gathered to conduct a vehicle movement brief. The brief was a concise but essential review of the route, their roles, communications, and contingencies if something went wrong. Every person in the vehicle had a defined responsibility to stay alert and protect one another as a coordinated unit. No one was just a passenger. They also reviewed their immediate action drills, how the team would respond to enemy or violent contact, breakdowns, blocked routes, and so on.

They would improvise nothing; they brought up the SOF incident on the road earlier that year. John and the rest of the team had to keep their weapons at the ready during the long, bumpy trip through isolated miles of jungle.

As the armed convoy worked its way to the outpost in Coca near the border of Colombia, John got an eerie feeling. He was mentally prepared and trained for a possible attack by human enemies. As a South Florida boy, John was not squeamish about the kinds of critters that stalked the jungle. In fact, he found that the Ecuadorian jungle was actually quite beautiful. The late summer marked the shoulder season; a little drier than normal in the rainforest but still verdant.

As John watched out the window of the truck, however, a thought at the back of his head took root like the rain-soaked vegetation surrounding him. He could not shake the impression that he had taken this road before.

John was superstitious and not particularly ashamed of it. He grew up in a household that was not only spiritual but profoundly esoteric. His mother and father, Carmen and Juan, ran a New Age store in Miami. Although his parents raised him as a Catholic, they also encouraged John to trust his intuition. His mother always reminded him to pray; for help, for health, for protection...for everything.

He struggled with the concept of past lives and the notion of karma. But on that road from Lago Agrio, he could not help but think about his ancestors. John's family descended from Spanish settlers. His family had been a part of multiple political upheavals in the Old and New World since the late 1800s: the Spanish-American War, the Spanish Civil War, the Cuban Revolution. His uncle was an army veteran who served in Korea.

As much as he loved his family and was proud of his history, John was not a fool. He was aware of the darker historical context associated with his Spanish ancestry. He was also aware of his nation's grim past. He knew that to many Ecuadorians, the U.S. military presence in Ecuador was unwelcome. He wondered if they might even have a good reason to think so.

He thought about the Spanish conquistadors, conquerors trampling this precise forest in an often violent search for glory, gold, and God. He reflected on guilt and the transmission of curses through bloodlines. He thought about a land and lakes ripe with bitterness and vengeance.

He tried to ignore the feeling of wrongness. He tried to attribute it to his own wariness of the jungle, the narcos, and the guerrilla fighters who sought violently to kick out the U.S. influence from their country.

Instead, John concentrated on running through his own preparation checklist. He found comfort in knowing where things were and how he could use them.

The feeling of an angry jungle would linger.

27 AUG-7 SEP 1996 // COCA, ECUADOR //

"¡Ay, Chamo!" the Ecuadorian pilot barked in Spanish, sharp and dismissive. "Go get my helmet."

The enlisted mechanic stiffened, nodded, and hurried off.

John observed the exchange. The word itself wasn't obscene, but the tone was unmistakable. It was demeaning; a reminder of the presupposed hierarchy. John was familiar with the racial and class dynamics in Latin America. The Ecuadorian officers were mostly of Spanish European descent, and the enlisted were primarily of *mestizo* (mixed) or indigenous descent.

John and his team were guests of the Ecuadorian 19th Jungle Brigade, at their base in the jungle town of Coca. Coca, officially named Puerto Francisco de Orellana, was in the Amazon rainforest at the junction of the Napo and Coca rivers. Francisco Orellana was a 16th-century Spanish explorer and conquistador with a patch over his left eye. Orellana was famous for one of the most improbable voyages in history: sailing the entire length of the Amazon River. The 19th Jungle Brigade had been at the epicenter of *selva* (jungle) warfare and counterinsurgency operations for years, and for years to come.

A human rights briefing had been a part of the U.S.'s require-ments for coordination with foreign militaries. There was to be respect for enlisted expertise, and they had to listen when a mechanic grounded an aircraft. Safety depended on trust, not fear.

Later that first week, John stood with the U.S. OAD-A mainte-nance chief, Labby, reviewing maintenance coordination principles. As they talked, John noticed the same Ecuadorian officer near the maintenance area. He was leaning toward one of the enlisted men, raised his boot slightly, and mimed kicking him in the ass to get him moving.

The enlisted man smiled tightly and said nothing.

The officer suddenly backed off. He didn't make eye contact, but John could tell that he and Labby were visible to the officer. He knew they had seen him.

John lowered his voice. "Asshole. He's self-aware enough to know better," he muttered to Labby.

Labby nodded. "It's self-defeating. Maintenance won't speak up if they're afraid."

"Exactly," John said. "And that gets people killed."

Those conversations became part of the rhythm of the day. Formal instruction paired with informal modeling. How do you talk in an aircraft? How do you talk to the people who keep it flying? Concise and clear communication was mandatory. Using disciplined and agreed-upon specific terminology was crucial to avoid misunderstanding and disaster.

But it was impossible not to notice the deeper currents at play. The officers were dismissive, if not outright nasty, to the enlisted men.

Except for Javier Perez.

John noticed him almost immediately. It was not because the Ecuadorian pilot was loud, but because he wasn't. Perez moved easily among the enlisted men. They spoke to him without hesitation. They laughed around him. There was no edge to their interactions, no flinch when he approached. Perez was shorter than most of the pilots, stocky and broad through the shoulders. His features marked him clearly as indigenous. He had also been enlisted infantry before becoming an officer, and still carried himself like one.

John and Javier exchanged a firm, respectful handshake at their formal introduction.

"Good to have you here," Perez said.

The Ecuadorian pilots coordinated with John and Mike on how the Ecuadorians flew the two-seated Gazelle. John and Mike would share how the Americans would structure the introduction rides.

"Sure, it is built for two, but we usually fly single pilot," Perez explained. "It's an attack helicopter."

"That works," John said. "As long as we agree on terminology. Miscommunication is the easiest way for things to go wrong."

They went over the basics together.

"If I say 'break left,'" John said, "it means now. Immediate."

Perez nodded. "Same for us."

Over lunch, they talked more easily. Perez asked about John's kids. About home. He talked about his own life—newly married, recently back from operations.

"I was infantry," Perez said. "Before flight school."

"Where?" John asked.

"Along the border last year."

Ecuador had experienced a war with Peru in 1995. It only lasted a month, a bloody month, and ended with both sides claiming victory in exchange for a mediated ceasefire.

John nodded. "That'll change how you see things."

Perez smiled faintly. "Yes."

John and Javier exchanged wings, unit t-shirts and flight patches. It was a gesture of respect between warriors. Like the way athletes swap jerseys, it was a small ritual of brotherhood forged around the roar of engines and rotor wash.

THE A-TEAM JOINED two other groups that made up the JSOTF in Coca. The Navy SEAL "Golf Platoon" was on a six-month deployment attached to the Naval Special Warfare Unit based in Panama. Howard "Rico" Lenway, a 'mustang' Lieutenant and former enlisted Navy SEAL led the platoon. The platoon was from SEAL Team 4, based out of Naval Amphibious Base (NAB) Little Creek in Virginia Beach, Virginia. Special Boat Unit (SBU) 26, based out of Panama and comprising special operations sailors, also rounded out the JSOTF. These sailors were the predecessors to modern Special Warfare Combatant-Craft Crewmen (SWCC). The JSOTF commander had set up a tactical operations center (TOC) along with LT Rico and the joint communication experts from the OAD and SEAL platoon. The OAD also provided an intel captain, Ed.

The OAD-A team, the SEAL platoon, and the SBU/SWCC sailors all bunked together. The barracks were an open bay: rows of cots under mosquito nets, gear stacked wherever space allowed, the air alive with insects and sweat. There was no privacy and little relief. Everyone slept, worked, and waited in the same space.

John worked closely with Rico in the planning. Two of the SEALs, Matt and Jeremy, also got to know John quickly. Hull Maintenance Technician Fireman (HTFN) Jeremy Trump was the youngest SEAL on the team—not yet 21—and bunked next to John. He was the platoon's machine gunner and boat mechanic. Jeremy's ambition was to become a sniper, but he ended up training as a SEAL Corpsman. He went to the Special Operations' grueling 18-Delta medic course and, at the very end, flunked it along with another SEAL on a dare. Jeremy also brought a box of Milk Bones dog treats for extra calories and protein because they were easy to pack, indestructible, and wouldn't rot in the jungle. The joint team all tried it.

Jeremy was under the watchful eye of the platoon's most experienced senior Petty Officer Boatswain's Mate Second Class (BM2), James Martin. John got to know Martin earlier during the workup in Panama. Martin considered Jeremy one of his problem kids. Jeremy was not too keen on him either.

Matt had played football for the University of Washington and wanted to join the Navy SEALs to test himself. John connected with Matt over football and singer-songwriter Jimmy Buffett.

In their downtime, they would play soccer or basketball with the Ecuadorians. Soccer matches would quickly deteriorate into chaotic pseudo-football matches as the Americans kept getting shown up by Ecuadorian foot skills. At night, they would trade stories as John played his beloved Jimmy Buffett music. They slept on cots under nets. Camaraderie grew.

Breakfasts were informal and telling.

One morning, the U.S. team sat together with trays of tripe, eggs, and rice.

Jack poked at his plate. "Ooh… What is this? Chicken skin?"

Matt laughed. "No. It's tripe."

"What's tripe?" Jack asked.

Joe B leaned over. "It's intestine."

Jack grimaced. The doctor reached into his pack and produced Tabasco. "Here," Joe said, shaking it generously over his food. "This'll kill anything."

They all laughed and ate. Carefully.

John settled quickly into a routine. The JSOTF ground and riverine elements joined with their Ecuadorian counterparts that were going to be trained: Ecuadorian Rangers, Naval Infantry (Marines), and Coast Guard small craft mechanics and drivers. The helo OAD-A team joined up with the helicopter aviation assets from the 43rd Attack and 44th Combat Transport Group of the Brigada de Aviación del Ejército 15 (15 BAE) or 15th Army Aviation Brigade. Before the helicopters and aviation teams were cleared for flight, several joint and specialized ground briefings were necessary. The bulk of the week involved morning training and afternoon preparation for introduction flights.

John and Mike rotated the two flights per day, flying familiarization runs. During the briefs, John noticed how carefully Perez listened, how he tracked radio calls, how he checked in with his crew. Every morning began the same way: a full operations order with ground units, riverine teams, and aircrews present. They established which frequencies they would communicate on. Ran through safety checks and emergency plans. Afterwards, John would lead the aircrew briefs and debriefs, walking through both sorties for the day and the call-for-fire procedures.

The Americans joined the Ecuadorians in a shortened version of their jungle survival course called *selva* training, or "jungle" survival training. It was considered one of the toughest in the world. The Ecuadorian Army maintained three jungle troop units and a training school for jungle operations; the Escuela de Selva. John's team went through only a portion of the training. They spent a few days deep in the jungle, navigating through the triple canopy, catching and cooking piranha, eating lemon ants, and drinking chicha—a questionable fermented drink made of chewed-up yucca. Upon their return, as is customary for all graduates, they leaped from the bridge near the base into the Rio Napo. Each graduate then received the SELVA embroidered tab; a symbol that Ecuadorian graduates proudly display on the right shoulder of their uniforms.

Between selva training, basketball, and soccer matches, an easy bond formed between the Americans and Ecuadorians. One night, one of the SEALs provided a special form of entertainment. He stripped down to his jockstrap, poured the liquid from their industrial-sized chemlights onto his body, and danced around the barracks.

This particular SEAL remains unnamed to this day.

12 SEP 1996 // NAVARRE, FLORIDA //

Ever since John left, unease followed Shelley like a shadow. It was background noise at first; easy enough to talk herself out of. This was his work. He was trained. He had done harder things than this.

Still, something about him leaving felt wrong.

It was a Thursday. Shelley was at home with the kids, trying to create a sense of normalcy. Lisette and Nicole bounced from one small adventure to the next. She told herself this was good. This was grounding.

When the phone rang, she almost didn't answer it.

"Hey, Shelley."

The moment she heard John's voice, something inside her broke open. It wasn't fear, the way she understood fear. It was sharper. A violent twist in her gut, like a warning her body had issued without consulting her mind. Tears surged before she could stop them.

"Here," she said too quickly, handing the phone to little Lisette. "Daddy wants to talk to you."

She turned away before anyone could see her face.

The girls chattered happily, their voices light and oblivious. Shelley pressed a hand to her mouth and tried to breathe. She needed just a few seconds to pull herself back together. She needed time to keep herself from saying the thing that was clawing its way up her throat.

Get out. Please. Don't stay there.

When the phone came back to her, she had composed herself as best she could.

"How are you?" she asked.

John sounded tired. Not just exhausted, though. There was something else. He sounded burdened.

"This place makes me sad," he said. "I don't know why. It just does."

Her stomach clenched. She listened as he tried to explain it, verbally circling the feeling instead of naming it. He talked about the jungle, about its history, and about how old everything felt.

"Maybe I was here in another life," he said. "Maybe that's why I'm here now. Doing good instead of... you know." She heard what he meant between the lines–a kind of multigenerational guilt. "I'm protecting people this time."

Shelley closed her eyes.

That was it. That was the thing she couldn't say out loud.

You're not supposed to be there.

She didn't argue with him. She didn't challenge the idea. She realized he was trying to convince her that he was there for a reason, that he was right to refuse her offer to break his finger. She also understood how dangerous it would be to encourage the conversation.

Instead, she remained quiet. She just listened, let him talk.

When he told her he did not know if he could call her again before the mission ended, her throat tightened.

"I just wanted to hear your voice," he said.

"I'm glad you did," she replied.

When the girls came back on the line, John's voice softened in a way that made her chest ache.

"Don't forget to ask Mommy to play the Cheeseburger song," he told Lisette. Parrothead forever, that man. "For you and Nicole."

They laughed. Shelley held herself together by sheer will.

After the call ended, she sat very still. She thought about his deployment to Panama in early August. How something had felt off then too, even before Ecuador. From the beginning, she hadn't wanted him to go with the 6th. She'd told herself she was being irrational, that she was letting imagination get the better of her.

She remembered watching him leave and feeling powerless. Standing there, forcing a smile, telling herself to stop hounding him. To respect his judgment. To trust that he knew what he was doing.

Suck it up, she had thought. *Hope for the best.*

But now, sitting there with the echo of his voice still ringing in her ears, she understood what that feeling had been.

Her mother had always said some people could step outside themselves. She believed there were ways of knowing that didn't fit neatly into logic or science. Shelley had grown up with a healthy skepticism, but also respect, because not everything real could be tested or measured.

This was one of those things.

She would think back to this moment again and again. The sound of his voice. The way she'd broken the instant she heard it. The way her body had known before her mind was ready. She had ignored the message.

Trust your gut.

12-18 SEP 1996 // 19TH JUNGLE BRIGADE, COCA, ECUADOR //

John found himself back on the water instead of in the air, riding a long, narrow cayuca upriver with the A-Team and Ecuadorian army civil affairs soldiers. By the first week of September, the team was finally flying tactical sorties with the Ecuadorian Army. These were low-level familiarization flights that followed the river as it cut through the jungle. The mission no longer felt theoretical. They were in it now.

The dugout canoe rode low, burdened with people bound for the village market near the jungle base. Swollen from the rainy season, the river was fast and unforgiving; its brown water beat against the hull as they progressed upstream. This visit to the market was more than a convenience; it was part of the "hearts and minds" outreach. The villagers depended on the cayucas to bring goods to sell; the Ecuadorian Army depended on the relationship. Everything moved by river.

Coca weighed on John. There was something about the place—the air, the river, the sense of being watched by history—that pressed against him in a way he couldn't explain. It wasn't fear, exactly. It was heavier than that. A sadness. Maybe more than a little Catholic guilt. A feeling that lingered no matter how busy he stayed.

Later, as the team explored the market, John was approached by a tall man with a sunburned face and an American accent. His shirt was damp with sweat; his manner open but weary. They struck up a conversation when the gentleman recognized John's U.S. military uniform.

"You're an American military pilot?" he asked.

"Yes, sir," John replied. "We're here training with the Ecuadorians."

The man nodded. "I'm here as a missionary with the Baptist Church. I work with the villages and coordinate some of the civil affairs stuff with the base."

Then the missionary glanced back toward the river, his expression tightening.

"One of their cayucas sank last week," he said.

John frowned. "That's unfortunate. Did it hit something?" He was worried that there was some kind of violence they hadn't heard about.

"It's the rainy season, which means high water and strong currents," the missionary said. "Normally the cayucas are secure on shore, but the rainy season came early, and the banks overflowed. The river took it."

He explained that the boat belonged to one of the indigenous villages upriver. Without it, the families had fewer reliable ways to reach the market or the base. No trade meant no income.

"They can't get it out themselves," the missionary added. "They don't have any equipment if it's lodged somewhere, and no way to really find it."

The river surged behind them, opaque and powerful. Perhaps even more unforgiving than insurgents. Whatever had gone under wasn't coming back up easily.

After a moment, the missionary leaned forward, "Is there any chance you could look for it? It would be so much faster to find it from the air."

John didn't answer right away. It wasn't totally up to him, but now he felt like there was a reason he met the missionary.

"I don't fly alone," John said. "But I'll ask."

Back at the base, he raised the issue with the Ecuadorian pilots. Perez was there, along with the other captain. When he suggested that they try to find the cayuca, the response was immediate.

"No hay tiempo," one of them said. *No time.* "We don't have the fuel."

John stared at them. "We're already flying over that river every day."

The senior pilot crossed his arms. "We're not a search-and-rescue service."

John felt his patience snap. "These people don't have much," he said. "And right now, we're their only chance to get that cayuca back."

The pilots exchanged looks, unconvinced.

"Let me ask you something," John said, his voice hardening. "If your helicopter goes down in the jungle, who do you want to find you first?"

That got their attention.

"The villagers you helped," he continued, "or the ones you ignored? And who do you want them to turn you over to? The base?" John leaned forward. "Or to the FARC?"

Silence followed.

Finally, the senior pilot exhaled and shook his head. "Okay," he said, reluctant but resigned. "Fine. We'll keep an eye out."

The next day, John flew with Perez on a familiarization run. Within the first ten minutes, they crossed the river. John leaned forward, scanning the edges where debris was collecting after the floods.

"There," he said suddenly.

At first, it was just a shadow beneath the surface. But as they circled, the shape became unmistakable. Something wooden; long, narrow, partially submerged. It was pinned near the riverbank.

Perez nodded. "That's it."

John marked the location on his handheld GPS, locking it in.

That afternoon, after they landed, John briefed the SEAL platoon.

"There's a submerged cayuca," he told them, passing along the coordinates. "It belongs to one of the villages. It's their livelihood, and they don't have any other means of getting it back."

"Then let's go get it," one of the SEALs said. There was no hesitation. The SEALs were all over it.

They deployed with the Ecuadorians in Zodiacs, hauling ropes and gear upriver. By evening, they had raised the cayuca and dragged it back to the village docks, coordinating directly with the grateful locals.

Watching the operation come together, John felt a quiet sense of satisfaction. He felt as though a debt had been paid.

Please God, he thought. *If there's any way to account for the sins of my ancestors, let this be a start.*

THE US and Ecuadorian pilots huddled over laminated tactical maps and satellite imagery. Both banks of the river had their trellises highlighted, and the river was delineated using erasable marker. John stood with his arms folded, Mike and Jack beside him, while the Ecuadorian pilots studied the route.

After the first few missions, John and Mike had noticed the Ecuadorians had an alarming tendency.

"You all keep flying too low over the river," John said. "And with the SAS off? It's dangerous."

"We have to drop below the treeline," one of the Ecuadorian pilots said.

"Why?" John asked.

"Guerrilla scouts," the pilot replied. "If they're out that far, they'll see us."

Mike shook his head. "If they're out that far, they already know you're there."

John and Mike were still getting used to the Ecuadorian aircrew procedures and the Aerospatiale SA342L Gazelle gunships and AS 332 Super Puma transport; the two helicopters they were using for the training missions. The official training exercises for the Ecuadorian marines started with call-for-fire training from the Gazelle gunships. Familiarization flights for the US pilots and crews were supposed to happen earlier, in the original deployment, but the delay forced them to spend more time getting used to the aircraft. In the final stage of their deployment to Ecuador, John was slated to take the lead in piloting, instructing, and advising the Ecuadorian aircrews who flew the Puma, a helicopter designed for troop transport. The Puma training was planned for over-water insertion and extraction of Ecuadorian marine and riverine forces.

The French-made Gazelle gunships were, on the other hand, a single-piloted (in practice) aircraft with basic instruments for flight in clear conditions where the pilots could clearly see and navigate. The Gazelles were not equipped to fly in Instrument Meteorological Conditions (IMC), nor were their pilots allowed to fly where they might have to rely solely on instruments to fly and navigate in weather conditions with poor visibility. One Ecuadorian Gazelle was armed with 2.75 mm rockets, while the other had twin 7.62 mm machine guns. There was barely enough space for someone to sit behind the pilot and co-pilot seats. In fact, in the Gazelle cockpit there was only one instrument panel in front of the pilot's seat on the right side. The left seat was unobstructed and could be removed.

John and Mike would fly in the left seat and act as safety observers, translators, and advise the pilots so that the ground controllers in training would learn their new craft. The U.S. communications headsets were not properly adapted to the French helicopter, so for the first two flights someone (often Joe, who was also filming on some of the first training missions) had to hold the plug in place between the pilots. Labrador and Acosta eventually devised a MacGyver-style fix.

John leaned in and tapped the map. "We're talking about maintaining no less than fifty feet above the water," he said. "The air control training teams need to see your flight path."

"It's too exposed," another pilot said. "The FARC will see the aircraft."

"With respect," John said evenly, "between two armed helicopters and an armed riverine team, you outgun anything operating out there."

"And the churning river and trees are a bigger threat than guerrillas," Mike added. "You dip too low, you're done."

Jack spoke up from the far end of the table. "Also, my controllers need more time," he said. "They have to see the aircraft before they make the radio calls."

"They should already be ready," one of the Ecuadorians said.

"They're training," John replied. "That's why we're here."

There was a pause.

"And the SAS?" John continued. The Stability Augmentation System was key to a safe flight; it keeps the aircraft level and dampens inputs. Some people also referred to the SAS as *Suicidal Aerobatics Suppression*. For the training missions? It was a non-negotiable. "We need to keep it on."

"We usually fly with it off," the pilot argued. "You feel more at one with the aircraft."

John nodded once. "I get that," he said. "But for this, we need you trimmed and stable."

The Ecuadorians spoke quietly among themselves.

Finally, the senior pilot looked up. "All right," he said. "We'll stay above the treeline while over the river."

"And…" John said, making it clear he wasn't asking.

"And we'll fly with the SAS on," the pilot added. "Stable."

John nodded. "That will work." Then in English, "Good to go!"

DURING ONE OF the daily JSOTF US team members-only stand-up briefings, John finally let Joe get a word in about medical contingencies. Regular morning training and afternoon preparation for introduction flights occupied most of the week. They had a lot to cover: coordination with the Ecuadorian Rangers and Marines, small craft operations, ground insertions, and prep for the afternoon flights. Lives were on the line, sure, but dragging the briefing for every contingency every day felt excessive. He told Joe to keep his talk on medical evacuation short.

Joe's urgency cut through the room. "Alright, team. Before you guys get on with the brief, I need to run through the MEDEVAC plan…"

John noticed a few operators exchanging glances behind him. He knew Joe meant well, but the medical contingencies always felt redundant at these daily stand-up briefings. Matt, in fact, kept trying to buck Dr. Joe Basinger off the missions for the chance to try out the Gazelle. He begged John, for days at a time, to get the space in the back to observe the call for the call-for-fire missions from the aircraft. He argued that since he was the platoon Air Operations petty officer, it was one of his collateral duties.

John let the doctor finish a little beyond what they agreed to before he stepped in.

"Great. Thanks, doc," John said, taking back control of the brief again. "We'll circle back if we've got time. Let's get back to operations."

"Thanks, Doc!" chimed in the peanut gallery, all in unison.

Joe sighed. "Just trying to make sure no one, you know, dies of sepsis in the jungle."

John caught the edge in his tone and felt a flicker of guilt. But he had seen the crew's eyes glaze over at long-winded updates before and he needed them alert for the rest of the briefing.

In the evenings, they watched several warrior-friendly movies on old-school VHS tapes, including some John Wayne films John brought from home, *Apocalypse Now*, and *Predator*. The team was particularly tickled by the scene in *Predator*, where a female guerrilla fighter warns the heroes after an alien hunter snatched their comrade.

"La selva se lo llevó," she tells Arnold Schwarzenegger's team.

The SEALs and Helo team would toss the ominous phrase at each other in jest.

"La selva se lo llevó!"

"The jungle took him!"

3

F.U.B.A.R.

The morning was spattered with rain clouds before their mission. Mike Hargis was scheduled to fly the early morning sortie and the second early afternoon flight, but there was a delay as the second Gazelle was called off on an Ecuadorian priority mission along with the two Pumas elsewhere. Mike approached John as he, Lobo, and Labby were playing basketball with some of the Ecuadorian maintainers.

John was intimately familiar with and had led the brief for Hargis's mission early in the morning, so John agreed to take over the second flight.

John turned to Acosta. "You wanna suit up?"

Lobo paused for a moment. A strange look came over him, and he responded quietly. "No boss, I'm good."

John thought little of it. Someone else would probably volunteer. "Roger that."

He left to change into his flight suit, still wearing Javier's sweat-stained squadron t-shirt. He grabbed his helmet bag, his combat survival vest, inserted his issued Beretta 9mm side arm and ammo, and LPUs. On his way to the Gazelle, Matt caught up with him.

News traveled fast.

"Please, L.T.," Matt said. "I'm the Platoon's air ops guy, I need the experience."

John rolled his eyes at the overgrown kid, but relented. "Fine. Go get the mission commander's helmet and bring your combat diver's vest." When Matt returned, John took the SEAL out to the aircraft and showed him how to operate and secure the Gazelle doors. He briefed him about emergency egress and had Matt practice getting out of the Gazelle in case they crashed in the river. He reviewed their Navy Helo egress procedures.

"Remember," John told Matt, "wait for all violent motion to stop before trying to egress. Identify a hand-hold reference point now, before we even take flight." The process was a deeply ingrained habit for them, a direct result of their grueling hours of dunker training.

John, Matt, and Lt. Perez briefed the flight and assigned close air support (CAS) mission once more, and then headed out to the Gazelle to strap in. John, Javier, and Matt hopped into the helicopter as it was getting fueled. Jack, the CCT, and his riverine team of sub and host nation FAC trainees departed after the early morning brief and were already out on the river range miles away.

As John strapped in, a sharp pang shot through his chest. He winced and rubbed his chest. The feeling sat there briefly, right in his heart. Something felt wrong. John shook it off. It was probably just heartburn. John quickly refocused. Fangs back again and in the game. Ready to head out to the riverine weapons range along the Napo River.

Good to go, John told himself.

19 SEP 1996 // RIO NAPA, ECUADOR // 1150L

They took off without incident. It was a beautiful day, despite a few clouds. They flew through a light rain shower. Just before the first gun run, they got in contact with Jack, the combat controller on the ground. They reviewed their brief over the radio. They then orbited and visually confirmed the position of "friendly forces under simulated fire" and visually cleared the range before heading to the predesignated hold-point. The flight path over the river was an oval pattern, similar to a NASCAR track.

They reviewed the 9-line close air support (CAS) procedures with the predetermined or canned data the controllers on the ground are expected to be repeating for each of their turns. The "9-line" is a standardized and very exact briefing format transmitted primarily by radio communication. It provides the attack helicopter crew with all the critical targeting information in nine concise and precise lines, ensuring deadly accuracy and speed, and minimizing the risk of fratricide during the chaos of combat.

After flying dry runs for all the forward air controller trainees, Javier, John, and Matt headed back out to the initial point for live fire. After going through their internal combat ingress and pre-CAS checklists, John reached down and instinctively turned the gun control box on.

Upon egress from the target and as they turned away after their first live fire pass, John secured the gun control box.

"You're still too low," John chastised Javier in Spanish as the belly dipped just below the treeline towards just a few feet above the river. "Pull up."

"Roger," Javier said, reluctantly pulling up to the agreed fifty feet. He did not seem to appreciate the reminder.

They prepped for the second gun run over the northern bank of the river. After firing and peeling away from the target, Javier turned the helicopter aggressively away after they fired the machine gun. He came back down towards the water. They were heading north, away from where they had been shooting towards the south.

John frowned, noticing the helicopter blades were once again level with the treeline. Javier straightened over the river and descended to just three feet above the water. He was moving fast to go around and hide behind the mangrove island ahead of them, impatient and clearly frustrated. As they skimmed the surface, John quickly glanced at the set of too-basic flight instruments in the cockpit in front of Javier. He noticed they were past 150 knots and accelerating.

"Come up! Climb!" John repeated.

The water was close, rippling just underneath the skids of the helicopter like a giant serpent's scales. John realized, with a jolt, that the water was much closer than it was supposed to be.

Did he hear me? John thought wildly before reaching out to take over the controls. Wind whipping around and through the Gazelle, he snapped at the pilot.

"Come up *now*," John barked. He looked left, leaning into his harness, then scanned back towards the nose as the helicopter continued to accelerate. Through his peripheral vision, he could see the churning river rushing by in a blur just beneath the skids. Just as he was about to notify Javier he was "clear left", Javier glanced his way, nodded and said, "O.K."

John never got the chance to reply.

The nose of the helicopter lurched down. Hard.

In a heartbeat, the black jungle river roared up to meet the cockpit.

*This can't be happening...*a small voice whispered to him as reality smashed through the bubble-shaped windshield. *I can't believe this is happening...*

John braced for impact.

〜

19 SEP 1996 // RIO NAPO, ECUADOR // 1205L

Everything turned black. He couldn't see a thing; the churning darkness of the river obscured his vision. Water crushed metal. The helicopter was not flying anymore; it was disintegrating and being consumed by the river. Violent sounds, explosions, muffled and chaotic, roared in his ears. It was as if he, Javier, and Matt were falling and tumbling into the wet mouth of a dragon—a massive beast that plucked the helicopter out of the air and swallowed, crushing it between massive teeth.

Blinding flashes of light alternated with suffocating, wet darkness. John needed to remain calm. He needed to wait for all violent motion to stop, his survival training kicking in. Years of brutal practice had silenced the small, screaming voice in the back of his head to a mere whisper. Panic was no longer his first reaction. Panic was not an option.

He waited.

He still could not see a thing, but the violence eventually subsided, his breath suspended along with the rest of reality. His lungs burned. He reached to his waist to undo his restraints, his fingers ready to seek traction and pull him out of the helicopter. He needed to locate a reference point. He would reach hand over hand until he found an exit. His mind had already conjured a model of the interior. He was trained to memorize helicopter interiors while blindfolded in dunker training. The mental map would clue him in on where he was and the location of the closest exit. He knew the drill—the training was ingrained as muscle memory. He would first reach with his pre-rehearsed hand and hold the window frame near the door handle on his left side, then his seat frame underneath him, then in each direction around him, under him, over him. He was ready.

In the surreal darkness that still enveloped him, John reached out...

...and found nothing but water.

He reached out further, his arms stretching painfully. He had to have hit something by now. The roof of the aircraft. The seat. His harness buckle. Anything.

Nothing.

Okay, so he must have been ejected out of the aircraft through the canopy. He was surrounded only by dark, churning water. He moved his arms and willed himself to kick and swim to the surface. He was a strong swimmer. He had grown up near the ocean. Fishing, swimming, surfing, snorkeling, scuba diving, lifeguard training in Miami, the Everglades, and the Florida Keys. Anyone with his kind of upbringing had to be a strong swimmer. Anyone with Naval Aviation water survival and Special Ops training was even better at it.

John barely moved in the dark water.

He reached, painfully, for his HEEDs with his right hand. The mini scuba tank was supposed to be tucked into the left side of his vest. But to his dismay, he came up empty. It must have been ripped from his vest.

John's lungs were beginning to protest. A sharp burning pain spread across his chest. He stroked his arms harder, forcing himself to glide up to where he *hoped* the surface would be. After an eternal, excruciating moment, his head broke the surface. He gasped for a breath before purposefully going back under again. He just needed enough air to calm himself and think. *Checklist!*

He methodically removed his flight gloves for dexterity. Frustration replaced panic. It shouldn't be so hard to swim. Something was wrong.

His legs weren't working. *His legs weren't working.*

His chest and ribs hurt.

His mind ran through the next steps. He couldn't tread water. He needed to inflate the life preserver. His hands shot to his trusty Navy vest inflators and their beaded handles near his waist. Well, his hands reached towards where he *thought* they were. He reached for the beaded handles near his chest this time. They weren't there.

Goddamn Air Force LPUs! John cursed, frantically creeping his fingers towards his armpits. He continued to bash the Air Force and their stupidly designed "Mae West" vests in silence. His left side protested as he stretched to grasp the unfamiliar tabs, but he finally inflated one lobe of the vest.

His head broke the surface of the river once more and stayed there. He inhaled gratefully. His mind cleared enough for him to take the next step: take stock of his injuries.

Checklist, his brain supplied helpfully. *Run through your checklist.*

The first, obvious injury he could assess was the stabbing pain along his left ribs. Broken, almost certainly. He then looked down at his lower body to see what had kept him from swimming. The right leg of his flight suit was ripped open at the knee. John felt a wave of disbelief as he saw the inside of his knee splayed open: the mess of muscles, sinew, cartilage, and femur sticking out of the shreds of his flight suit.

His right leg was bent at 90 degrees, as if he was still sitting in the cockpit, but it was also bent out to the side at a very *unnatural* 90 degrees. He tore his gaze from his right leg to assess his left. The pant leg was intact, but the shin underneath was clearly broken, bent and twisted in a way that looked deeply unnatural. *Probably broken. But the boot!* The boot, and his foot, were probably unscathed.

Man, this is going to hurt soon...

"L.T.!"

John strained to face the direction of Matt's voice. The Navy SEAL was gripping the side of the submerged Gazelle. Blood streamed down Matt's face.

"Are you okay?" Matt called.

"I'm alive," John shouted. "I think I'm okay." He refused to look down past his torso and let out a groan. "But my legs are all fucked up!"

"Can you make it to the helicopter?" Matt yelled. "Paddle! Can you make it to the shore?"

The current of the river was moving fast. They weren't in any rapids, but the river was churning and persistently dragging John along. John tried to paddle towards Matt. He saw his left boot flopping lifelessly in the current. Worried about the boot falling off, he took a hold of his leg to guide it back to the center of his body. His right knee was beginning to hurt. A lot.

"Are you okay?" John shouted back at Matt as he drifted further away. "What about Javier? Lieutenant Perez?"

"Sir, he's pinned underwater. I'm trying to get him out!" Matt said. *Shit*, John thought, looking towards the wreckage of the helicopter's tail jutting out from the water. He automatically fumbled for his HEEDs tank again. Maybe if Matt could get the tank to Javier, it would buy the Ecuadorian pilot a few more minutes of oxygen for the SEAL to pull him out.

Muscle memory kicked in. This time he found the HEEDs. It had, in fact, not been totally ripped away from his body. A lanyard still attached it to his vest.

"Matt, I have a HEEDs bottle," he told the SEAL. "You gotta get it in his mouth! I'm going to throw you my HEEDs." He pulled the lanyard, drawing the HEEDs towards him. By the time he pulled the tank into his hand, however, Matt's voice was fading. He tried paddling backward, trying to remain in one spot in order for Matt to reach him. Eventually, the pain in the left side of his chest kept him from fighting the current. John did not know the extent of the SEAL's injuries or the extent of the Ecuadorian pilot's. Either way, he was of no use to either of them. He just hoped that Matt could get to Javier.

It was quiet.

The vest and its lobes were now both inflated and holding him nearly immobile, upward-facing and prone. This positioned him so that the only thing he could really see was the sky. The heavens were forget-me-not blue and speckled with clouds. Ironically, it was a perfect day for flying.

John's left flank was beginning to flare, and every breath hurt with a vengeance as the initial shock faded. Going by the state of his legs, the pain was going to get worse very, very soon. *Tunnel vision setting in...checklist! Prep myself for rescue.*

John fumbled at the left side of his survival vest again, feeling for the med kit tucked away in its pocket. Back in his deployments to

Africa and Yugoslavia, he knew they had packed something for pain. He got the waterproof baggie in front of his face. *Focus!*

Only once he was looking at the plastic-sealed little pills did he remember they had only packed aspirin and Imodium for this deployment.

Neither would do shit for his mangled body. He swore, tossing it into the water to join the now equally useless HEEDs tank still tethered to his vest.

The black, muddy water of the river was cool, but not cold. It did not really feel much like anything. He did not want to miss his chance if his hands became numb. His mind was now preoccupied with one mission: preparing himself for his own rescue. John grabbed for his radio. He recognized the severity of his situation. The PRC-90, the emergency radio, only worked on an emergency frequency. No GPS beacon either. There were no rescue helicopters out there. The other helicopters were nowhere near; they had been assigned out of the region on other host-nation missions. The 19th Jungle Brigade base was too far away.

He was an American military pilot in an environmentally and politically hostile territory. His ingrained training and discipline had kept his panic at bay. He kept going back to his mental checklists. *Prepare yourself for recovery.*

No one is going to hear me, John thought. Despair welled up as he tried connecting with someone, anyone, on the radio. He waited, but there was no response.

Finally, he let the radio go, too.

Years of well-honed survival training found themselves spent. The river dragged him unrelentingly away from the wreckage and from any hope of rescue. He was at the mercy of an unforgiving jungle and the pace of blood draining out of his shredded legs into the dark river.

The military had a phrase for this. SITUATION: F.U.B.A.R.

Fucked Up Beyond All Recognition.

A week prior to their ill-fated flight, the squadron took a few photos after *selva* (jungle) survival training. Doc Joe had joked about how John was the only one smiling after their jungle exercises with the Ecuadorian Special Forces. Everyone knew the "L.T." was a reliable go-to teammate. John Alvarez was someone his team could consistently turn to for leadership, camaraderie, and support.

But now, in the muddy river, he was not smiling. He was not joking. He was out of options. His training, his discipline, and his checklists were spent.

John Alvarez was alone.

PART II

My own true love
10,000 miles or more
And the rocks may melt
And the seas may burn
If I no more return
– Traditional English Ballad

And whatever you ask for in prayer with faith, you will receive.
– Matthew 21:22

4

ON A WING AND A PRAYER

19 SEP 1996 // RIO NAPO, ECUADOR // 1230L

*J*ohn, *you idiot. You're going to die here.*

He was going to die alone, in pain, and bleeding out in a river.

The world around him was quiet.

The controllers had to have heard the crash. But there would be no way they could get the Zodiac close enough to the wreck to help Matt and Javier. It was too dangerous. They couldn't risk possibly puncturing the inflatable boat. The only way to get to the wreckage was to get the Zodiac close, anchor it, and then swim, and that would be stupid. Flammable gas in the water, who knows what else is swimming in the river with them...

The dark water of the fast-flowing river seemed to stretch on and on. John had already gone through all his mental checklists and only became more exhausted as he bled out into the river. The pain was growing, too. His breath hitched at the difficulty of breathing against his broken ribs. Tunnel vision was setting in. Death was still a strange concept to consider. Maybe it was true, what they said about pilots and an invincibility complex.

There was really only one thing left to do. John took a shaky breath and began to say the Lord's Prayer.

"Our Father who art in heaven, hallowed be thy name. Thy kingdom come, thy will be done, on earth as it is in heaven..."

He thought of Shelley, her fear and helplessness in warning him not to go on this mission. Their girls. He thought of the pain in his gut that very morning, a warning that he had so quickly blown off. He felt the sting of regret for his hubris and cockiness in not listening to his intuition.

Maybe God would forgive him for his pride.

"Give us this day our daily bread and forgive us our trespasses—"

Hopefully he would reach unconsciousness soon and let death take him quickly. Would they find his body afterwards?

"As...as we forgive those who..." John choked on the words.

Would his body go home? Back to his family, to Shelley? To the girls?

He tried to continue. "...forgive those who trespass against us. And lead us not into temptation, but deliver us from evil."

What's the point of begging now? John's inner voice screamed out at him. *You're going to die here.*

"For thine is the kingdom, the power and..."

God! Wait. What about Shelley? I can't do this to her! What about the girls? They were only five and four. The guilt struck him, sinking its fangs deep into his chest. Sharper than the injury to his side, the grief sent him visions of a life extinguished. His mind conjured images of Shelley, heartbroken and alone. Lisette and Nicole, their faces lost and confused. His baby girls struggling with the concept that Daddy was never coming home.

My girls are going to grow up without a dad...

∽

16 JUN 1996 // NAVARRE, FLORIDA // FATHER'S DAY

"Kill da wabbit!" John sang to the tune of Richard Wagner's opera "Ride of the Valkyries" as the little girls giggled. He chased them around the coffee table, and they shrieked.

"Again!" Nicole giggled.

"Again, again, again!" Lisette chimed. John exaggerated his panting, but it *was* turning back into a makeshift workout routine. He started this simulated dance-slash-chase with them when they lived in Monterey, and then in Albuquerque. They weighed more now, but he did not mind.

He bent his knees deep and hoisted his girls, one in each of his arms, as the next *Cartoon Classics* song burst from the speakers. They shrieked as he dashed around the living room; vocalizing, bouncing, and bounding in time to the *William Tell Overture*.

His girls were happy. Johnny A was happy. As a child in South Florida, his family's life revolved around the vibrant sounds of music and the energetic rhythm of dancing. During the day, classical music soothed and focused the mind. But when the occasion called for parties, whether for rallying the team or boosting morale, the soundtrack was a lively mix of rock, Motown, funk, and disco. Young Johnny would constantly see his parents kiss and dance to Neil Diamond. Cuban jazz, salsa and merengue, even country music. Every child learned to dance early on. They had no choice. They were told to dance with their mothers, grandmothers, aunts, and cousins.

For Christmas the year before, Santa/Shelley replaced John's trusty portable cassette player that had seen him through his seaborne deployments with a new, rugged, state-of-the-art portable CD player. He could now more easily share his music with Shelley and the girls. It went with him on every deployment after that. Long nights in places most people couldn't pronounce or even find on a map. Places where his music was the only thing that felt like *home*. That little CD player ended up in more places in the world than most people ever will.

The larger home CD player then changed to Jimmy Buffett's

Boats, Beaches, Bars & Ballads. John, Lisette, and Nicole continued to dance and sing to "Cheeseburgers in Paradise", then "Volcano". Growing up in South Florida and the Keys, Jimmy Buffett's music also followed Johnny through his childhood, college, the military, and Shelley, then to their kids. The "Alvari Parrotheads"!

As the music faded into "Stars Fell on Alabama", John shimmied over to the kitchen.

"May I have this dance?" John asked his wife, who was elbows deep in dishes.

"My hands are wet!" Shelley protested as he reached out for her.

"I'll dance you dry!" he insisted, pulling her out of the kitchen and into the living room to slow dance with him. She laughed and swayed with him.

"As you wish..."

Just like the first time they met, at a Texan bar in Corpus Christi. John had approached the Canadian nurse, and it was love at first dance. As he recalled that moment, he nestled his face against hers. Their embrace tightened, and John breathed in Shelley's familiar fragrance. His home. His soulmate.

Nicole, the jealous three-year-old as she was, squeezed between them to regain her father's affections. Finally, he scooped her up, and Lisette joined as the four of them waltzed around the small kitchen once again.

19 SEP 1996 // RIO NAPO, ECUADOR // 1232L

"I can't," John choked aloud to the sky, "I can't do this to them. God, *please.*"

But how? He was dying as his blood drained into the river. He had nothing. But in the haze of pain and grief, another voice answered from the depths of his memories. His mother's.

You have to pray. Ask for miracles, mijo.

Besides the discipline, mindfulness, and stoic principles

ingrained in him by his father, John's mother taught him to believe in miracles and to pray. Carmen Alvarez Mori was not a believer who thought God looked askance on people who asked for miracles. John sometimes brushed her off when she told him to pray to God, to pray for whatever he needed. He was a grown adult. John didn't see himself as someone who needed help. He had everything he needed: a dream career, a healthy family, a wonderful partner. What else could he possibly ask God for? No, leave the miracles for those who really need them.

Pray for a miracle, he thought. *God, if this is the one thing I ever ask for in my life... please... let me go home to Shelley and the girls.*

What would life be like if only God would let him stay? His legs were fucked. He imagined himself as an old veteran. Grizzled, graying. An unkempt beard. A wheelchair, his trousers rolled up to reveal nothing more than two short stubs instead of legs. No longer flying and no longer able to walk. The kind of person you would see at war memorials and feel sorry for.

Okay, so maybe he would never be able to walk again. He would never be able to run. He would never be able to fly again. But he could see his girls once more. He could watch them grow and watch them dance. He could hold hands with the love of his life and breathe her in. He would be grateful. He could do it. He had to.

"I can still be a good husband," John begged. "I can still be a good father. Please, God. *Please.* You can have my legs, Lord. Take both of my legs, but just bring me back to my girls. Take my legs, just don't take me away from them, *please...*"

John prayed once more. This time, to Mother Mary.

"Hail Mary, full of grace, the Lord is with thee; blessed art thou among women, and blessed is the fruit of thy womb, Jesus..."

It was the only thing that tethered him to reality as the pain grew and his vision became blurry.

"Holy Mary, Mother of God, pray for us sinners..."

Now and at the hour of our death. He struggled to finish the prayer out loud in his haze. He was not afraid of dying. He was, however, terrified of the pain he'd leave behind. His wife and girls being forced to bear a burden he could not shield them from. *Now and at the hour of our death. C'mon! Finish the prayer, John!*

"...pray for us sinners..."

Now and at the hour of our death. Amen.

John never finished the prayer. Something distracted him; in the distance, moving towards him through the water.

No one could blame him when he thought the oncoming canoe was a hallucination.

John blinked away the haze and tunnel vision—whether they came from his pain or guilt, he was not sure—and tried to dispel the image before him. But the more he blinked, the more he was certain about what was coming up the river, against the current.

A canoe... he realized. *A canoe?!*

John shook his head and almost laughed in disbelief. He could not believe his eyes. "No way," he breathed. "A friggin' canoe?"

The sunken cayuca flashed across his mind, the one he and his team had found and recovered exactly a week prior. Had it really been only days? It felt like he had been in this river for an eternity.

Two men were in the canoe. As they grew closer, clearly aiming towards where he was floating, he could see they both wore shorts and one was shirtless. They were also clearly Indigenous, likely Kichwa, Shuar, or any of the other fourteen nationalities in Ecuador. He noticed the electric trolling motor on the dugout canoe. His disbelief quickly turned into distrust. It was very possible that the only way they could afford a motor would be if they were drug runners. Possibly for the FARC.

Trying to ignore the pain in his ribs, John began to reach for his nine-mil. The Beretta M9 nine-millimeter had been issued to him by the 6th SOS—and it was not his preferred weapon. He wished it was his "nineteen-eleven": a non-standard 45-caliber 1911 Colt he usually packed in his Pave Low missions.

A thought, however, stopped him.

Hell, he winced, *at this point it doesn't matter whether I die here or at the hands of FARC guerrillas. They don't really look like FARC, anyway.*

Instead, he waved his one arm that was not in pain at them. "Auxilio! Help!"

The canoe came right up to him. One man reached over to his side of the river and took a hold of John's arm.

"My legs, they're badly injured," John told him in Spanish. "There's a helicopter in the water over there. A crash."

"Legs, your legs, yes," the man replied in halting Spanish.

"Via la base, si?" John prompted.

"La base?"

"Si!"

John realized that the man's Spanish was a second language to his native one. The second man could not speak to him at all. Regardless, the two men labored to get him into the canoe. The pain in his left rib cage and legs was now excruciating. They nearly capsized the boat in the effort. They spoke to each other frantically in their native language as one placed a bait bucket under John's right knee. His arms rested over the sides of the canoe, hands dragging in the water. The piranha they had caught flopped in the bottom of the canoe.

Maybe it was the fact that some part of his brain registered 'possibility of rescue', but his pain was hazing his mind. The man who could speak Spanish sat by his heel, pressing his hands down firmly on his left leg. John was confused. His right leg was the one which was clearly the worst off of the two.

"It's my right leg..." John protested, pointing at the carnage of his knee.

"Sangre. Mucha sangre, señor."

John let him be for a while. It seemed like a lot of time had passed. He was not entirely sure how long, but he was realizing they had not seen the wreckage of the helicopter yet.

"Stop... stop! My friends are right over there," John said, waving frantically downstream. He could not see the wreckage from his position in the boat, but he was sure they must have passed it by now. Matt had just been around the bend... right? Or did the current take him farther?

The brown, muddy water at the bottom of the canoe was turning red as the fish the natives had caught earlier flapped around. He could see his HEEDS bottle rolling in the bloody pool as well.

Shit! Javier must still be pinned. He needs my HEEDS!

"Apurase, por favor!" John urged in Spanish. *Hurry, please!*

"We'll get to your friend, don't worry," his rescuer told him.

Time passed—maybe minutes, maybe hours. He laid back. He tried to keep from screaming every time the canoe rocked and jostled his body. Breathing hurt. Everything hurt. Maybe it was good he had not had lunch yet—he probably would have thrown up twice by now. He thought about how the river was probably infested with piranhas. He thought about how he and the team had recently eaten piranha. How ironic. *A good revenge, maybe, if they wanted to eat me now.*

Finally, he heard voices. English voices. They were faint, but slowly became clearer. John lifted his head and saw two people bobbing in the river. The canoe was a few feet away from the crashed helicopter. From his perspective, it looked like his two teammates were wrestling in the oil-stained water.

"No, you've gotta get into the canoe!" Jack was yelling at Matt. His Boston accent was unmistakable and aggravated by stress. "You gotta get the Lieutenant back!"

"Perez is pinned in the cockpit," Matt sputtered, flinging Jack's hands off of him. There was still blood matting his hair. "I need to—"

"Perez is dead, don't you get it?" Jack shouted. "Perez. Is. Dead! Forget about it! You need to get into the canoe and get the Lieutenant back before he dies, too!"

At the mention of Perez, John's pain-fueled mind snapped back into focus. "Jack, my HEEDs bottle, it's between my legs!"

The next thing John could register was a face hovering over him. Jack's face. Jack filled John's blurry field-of-view.

"Sir, you okay?"

"Jack! My HEEDS bottle is..." Before he could finish, Jack grabbed him.

"What the hell are you talkin' about?"

"For Javier. Goddammit, Jack," John flailed about for the tank, "it's here in the canoe!"

Jack's face twisted in a snarl, and he yanked John forward by his vest. The violent jerk knocked the wind out of John. He wheezed in pain as the combat controller growled in his face.

"Sir! Shut the fuck up! Perez is dead, forget about the fuckin' HEEDs. You're gonna live, do you understand me? You're gonna live."

"What the hell are you talking about, 'I'm gonna live'," John panted, on the verge of unconsciousness. "Jack, listen, my HEEDS bottle—!"

Jack released him. "Goddammit! Matt, get him back to the base. Now!"

John looked down between his mangled legs and looked at his HEEDs bottle. His heart sank. *Javier...*

The next few moments were a blur as Matt tried to get into the canoe. However, four grown men could not keep the canoe afloat. Instead, Matt clung to the canoe's side as they made their way back up the river to the base. John's pain had ticked up a couple more notches. His hands hung over the edge, dragging in the river water. John stared at the clouds and tried to keep breathing. His father's voice echoed in his mind, guiding him to control his breath with practiced calm. John even tried the Lamaze breathing exercises he had helped Shelley through when she was pregnant. He gave up after a few breaths. The stupid exercise was about as effective now as it was back when Shelley was in labor.

Man, at some point you've gotta pass out, right? he thought, his head spinning. *Okay. God? Please? Just let me pass out.*

"Sir! Uh-uh. No. Stay with me, John. Hey! Stay with me, sir!"

John, still in a prone position looking skyward with his peripheral vision blocked by the inflated orange LPUs, could not see Matt but could see and feel his heavy-knuckled fist rubbing hard on John's sternum. "Sir, talk to me. Look at me. Hey, tell me again how you danced with your girls! What was their favorite Jimmy Buffett song? The one you guys dance to all the time? Cheeseburger in Paradise! Let's sing it!"

John groaned. *Damnit, Matt!* A part of John knew what the SEAL was doing and appreciated it. But, on the other hand, Matt was also an asshole.

He spent the rest of the ride back to the makeshift marina wrestling with the overwhelming need to pass out and a bitter internal monologue aimed at Matt, whom he resented for not allowing him the oblivion of unconsciousness. The pain surrounded him on all sides. John tried to focus on staying still, relieved knowing Matt was by his side clinging to the canoe.

There were more voices. Matt swam away from the boat. John heard Daisy, one of the SEAL corpsmen, Rico, and James. Air Commandos Mike and Ed. Another face pushed through the haze into John's limited field of view. Rough and grainy, but there was something solid in it too, like he'd already decided his brother wasn't going anywhere on his watch. Jeremy. He had a big wad of chewing tobacco in his mouth as he stared down at John, wide-eyed and probably a little frantic.

"Sir, don't worry, we're gonna get you outta here. We've got ya brother! You'll be just fine!"

Great, John thought, *the first guy to work on me is the guy who flunked corpsman school. At least he flunked on purpose...*Later, John might joke about that. But not today. Voices and pain drowned out the rest of his thoughts.

"How are we going to get him out?"

"Here, shit, get into the—"

"—but first we need to—"

"Fuck!"

"—losing blood. Should we start a tourniquet?"

Then John heard another voice.

"How long has it been?" Dr. Joe Basinger demanded as he waded into the water.

One of the SEALs repeated the question in Spanish to the owners of the canoe. One of them replied in Spanish.

"They found him about twenty minutes ago," the SEAL translated.

Joe did the mental math and exhaled. "We're at the end of the golden hour," Joe said, sounding grim. During the critical "golden hour" that immediately follows a traumatic injury, prompt medical care offers the best chance of preventing death. Doc B knew that the next couple of minutes and hours, and the next few days were going to be harrowing for John if he made it that far. He looked around at the wet, muddied team. They were looking to the doc for guidance.

Golf Platoon had already lost a teammate to a diving accident earlier in their deployment to South America. They had also been questioned about their medical decisions. This time, however, Petty Officer David Scott, the platoon's comm specialist, started recording via videotape recorder to document their actions. Doc B allowed himself half a second to let the grim reality sink in. And then he went to work.

John could sense the heat of more bodies around him and multiple hands frantically working on him, feeling and scanning his body and limbs for injuries. Through this buzz of activity, he struggled to see what was happening to him through his diminished field of view. He realized and acknowledged it as 'gurney vision'. Someone then deflated and cut away John's orange LPUs with a combat diver's knife. Someone else was cutting away John's flight suit and the unwashed t-shirt underneath that Javier had given him. His flight suit sleeve was gone; he felt the cold shock of a wet alcohol wipe applied to the inner crease of his elbow, just above his forearm.

Yes! John thought. *Morphine!*

Then Doc B, Joe, came into his field of view, and he struggled to focus on Joe's face. "These are antibiotics. I'm sorry, John. I can't give you anything until we know if you have a spinal cord injury."

John spat out a couple of choice expletives at that revelation. Again, he resigned himself to the pain.

"You gotta get to Javier. I'm okay, get to Javier," John insisted as Joe inserted two needles, one for the antibiotic and one for an IV. Joe ignored John's half-hearted protests and applied bandages where he could.

The team continued to cut John's flight suit away and then the left pant leg. They all winced as John let out another shout of pain. The leg was almost completely severed about eight inches below the knee and above his boot; it hung on by a string of calf muscle and flesh.

Joe organized the effort to get John into a stretcher so they could take him to the battalion aid station. There, at least, he could start working on putting the pilot back together.

When the group debated how to get him out of the canoe, John decided on two last things. He mustered all his willpower to focus. He grabbed Joe by the front of his medical vest. "Doc—ID! Left breast pocket." That small, rectangular plastic card would identify him as "one of ours". John had dark skin and a subdued flight suit with no patches, no rank—just a US flag and a basic black Velcro name tag with his name and blood type to identify him. He just hoped that this would help get him home to Shelley and his girls.

John then grasped for the second thing: a chain hanging around his neck. He lifted it up towards Joe.

There, his wedding ring hung, the chain looped through it with his dog tags. Wrapped around and tucked in between the rubber silencer of one of his dog tags was a piece of Nicole's safety blanket— a ratty thing his daughter had offered to him before he deployed to Yugoslavia.

To keep you safe, Daddy, she had told him with all the seriousness a toddler could muster.

"Doc, these have gotta go home to the girls," John told him. "Joe, you've gotta get me back to Shelley and the girls." He then zoned out again. He closed his eyes for a bit as he was so very done with his gurney vision. For now.

Tag, you're it.

Joe looked at John like he was stupid. He probably was; pain and massive blood loss did weird things to logic. "You know I'm not planning to do anything else," the doc promised. He then handed the ring and tags to Acosta for safekeeping.

John breathed in and let go. He watched in a darkening haze as the SEALs pulled out their weapons and shooed the Indigenous men away to establish a secure perimeter.

"We need to get him to the battalion aid station," Joe told the SEALs. "He needs blood, and he needs it now."

Petty Officer James Martin, one of the most experienced of all the platoon, cursed almost as violently as John as they tried to extract the pilot from the canoe. John and James had become friends during the work-ups in Panama prior to going to Ecuador, which ended up with John snapping pictures of the SEAL taking a "bead" on a U.S. submarine from his sniper's perch from the side of a Night Stalker MH-60 helicopter they were in.

The team eventually maneuvered around the canoe; half in the river, half on the bank. The SEALs were so agitated, trying to coordinate themselves over John's groans of pain, that at first they did not think to get the stretcher over the bow of the canoe rather than sideways. But they figured it out and got John onto the stretcher.

Joe, Daisy, Rico, James Martin, Mike Hargis, Jeremy, Ed, and the rest. They moved in formation around John's stretcher as he was carried to their battered 4x4 pickup truck that served as a makeshift ambulance.

No one is touching this guy, his teammates seemed to tell the jungle. They were keeping the faith with one of their own.

My brothers are here, John thought as he zoned out. *They got me.*

5

MAKING CALLS

19 SEP 1996 // 19TH JUNGLE BRIGADE, COCA, ECUADOR // 1315L

The battered 4x4 barreled down the dirt roads of the base, engine screaming as they raced to keep their brother alive. Every second counted. With every pothole or divot, John writhed in pain. Jeremy, Mike and Daisy held him down as best they could on the flatbed. It seemed to drag on and on, and John couldn't even get morphine to knock him the hell out. He felt their hands on him, both keeping him awake and, he presumed, trying to keep him alive.

"Are we there yet?" John rasped. He really wanted that morphine.

"Nearly, John. We'll get a blood transfusion started as soon as we get there. We've got two liters of saline in you already," Joe said, apparently misreading John's concern. "You've lost a lot of blood, but that's keeping things moving—heart pumping, oxygen flowing."

God, John mused, thinking about the canoe full of blood. He had read somewhere about how much blood someone can lose before dying. He couldn't pull the factoid forward just then, but if the doc was worried about things 'not moving', he must have lost enough to stop his heart. *How the hell have I not passed out yet?*

"Where's Matt?" John asked. "He was with me...he kept me awake. Is Matt okay?"

"He's okay. He's got some injuries, nothing serious. Let's get you sorted for now, okay?"

When they arrived at the aid station, the team carried John into the aid station while Joe approached one of the terrified-looking Ecuadorians on staff.

"We need to get a blood transfusion and a morphine drip set up," Joe told him.

God, finally, please...

"Morphine yes, but..." The man stuttered for a moment. "The blood. It is just for inspections, señor."

"I'm sorry, *what*?"

"We only have power for three hours a day," he explained to the disbelieving doctor. "The blood is just for inspections."

Joe inhaled and took a step back. They had misled his physician's assistant months earlier during the medical capabilities assessment visit as part of the pre-deployment site survey (PDSS).

John closed his eyes. The morphine delay was one thing. But he wasn't about to have *rotten blood* hooked up to him, right?

"Sir, hook me up for a direct transfusion," Jeremy offered. Like popcorn, the rest of the SEALs volunteered to give blood to John.

"Hold on!" Joe snapped. "You guys clean?"

By the looks on their faces, they had no clue.

"Have you been taking your antimalarials?"

They at least had the decency to look a little ashamed of themselves.

"There's no way I'm letting John get an infection or God knows what else on top of what he was already dealing with," Joe said. "Besides, the transfusion unit looked like a rusty coffee can. Get me more IV fluids. You've got to swell to live. If you don't have blood, we need to keep giving fluid in order to keep the heart, the veins and arteries open and moving. Medic, get saline to flush the left leg. We need to reduce the dislocation of the right."

"Sir." Petty Officer Scott—the SEAL team's communications expert—popped into the room. He was talking to Joe. "Medevac Plan with the Ecuadorian team to Lago Agrio has failed. I'm moving to the next one."

"Tell them time is not on our side here!" Joe ordered. The doc sighed, apparently steeling himself. "Thank you, Petty Officer Scott. Keep us updated." He turned to John again.

"I'm making a bolster for your left leg, and we need to test your capillaries there."

"Alright," John breathed. Not that he was in any position to argue.

"Doc, why aren't we getting a tourniquet on the left leg?" Daisy asked after a few minutes.

"The left foot has passed a capillary refill," Joe responded. "I'm hoping there is a vessel still working well enough to save the leg. The fluid will stabilize him for now. We will get blood as soon as we get to Quito, but we have to get there first. Where the *hell* is Scott?"

As they worked to stabilize the legs and get on top of the bleeding, Scott ran back and forth from the ops room. Every time he came back into the aid station, he listed which step of the flowchart for medevac had failed.

"What the hell is going on out there?" Daisy growled.

"Ecuadorians are probably unwilling to take part in John's extraction," Joe said, face tight. "Probably too shaken up about the accident. Scared about an international incident."

"Don't want to have the American pilot die on *their* plane."

"Jesus," John groaned, as the rest of the team erupted in protest.

Finally, Petty Officer Scott came in and announced that they had a workable medical plan.

"But," he said, "they want us to take him to Panama."

"Panama?" Joe demanded. He didn't sound happy about it.

"They said it's Army procedure," Scott said. "According to procedure, major casualties in South America were to be taken to Gorgas Army Hospital."

"All of this simply to trade vascular surgeons? On a plane which would have no proper medical equipment to help?" Joe muttered. "The L.T. is at risk of kidney failure without a blood transfusion! Gorgas does not have US-trained vascular or ortho surgeons either. Metropolitano does. We did the damn survey ourselves." Joe looked around the room. "That procedure was written for wartime, not for one guy."

Someone piped up. "What does Newt know about this?"

The JSOTF commander, Lt. Col. Rick "Newt" Newton was incredibly even-keeled. For a new squadron, it was a beneficial temperament to have. Building a team was a skill that required seasoned leadership and a whole lot of patience.

"He's supporting the Doc for this one," one of the SEALs said. "Man, that was the first time I ever saw the Colonel lose his temper, when Doc Joe told him about the crash at the river." He mimicked Newt's affect, but with red-faced fury. "*Why are you still standing here?! Why is there not a hole in the air where you are?!*"

John could hardly imagine the normally calm, mild-mannered commander roaring at people. Granted, the situation probably called for it.

PO Scott pulled Jeremy aside as not to interfere and informed him of his last transmission.

Jeremy called out to Doc B. "Hey sir, okay, here's the deal. You think he's stable enough to make it to Panama? They rather get him to Panama. You got to make the call now—Quito or Panama?

Joe looked up, frowning.

Scott sounded urgent. "You make the call, Doc—your opinion, man!"

Another voice chimed in, "It's at least another hour and a half of transit time."

"Okay," Joe broke in. "Who wants to take him to Panama?"

All the SEALs spoke immediately, with Jeremy the loudest, and threw their hands up. "I'll go!"

The SBU operator on John's left pressed the oxygen mask down on John's face, and held down John's right hand; partly to reassure him but also to stop John from tearing the mask off.

"Okay," Joe started slowly, "What I see—and I'm gonna ask for a little help with this...Medically, I got the facts straight. However! Transportation. The way I understand it–C-130 into Quito will likely get him there in forty minutes."

Scott chimed in. "Versus two and half, three hours to Panama!"

Joe threw up his hands. "No, no, no. Who is driving the boat to Panama?" After a while with these guys, Joe had obviously picked up some of the SEALs' language. Translation: *Who the hell made that stupid decision?*

"You make the call."

"What?"

Jeremy blurted out, then the team joined in unison, "You make the call, Doc, it's your decision."

"Alright. We're not going to Panama," Joe declared. "Hospital Metropolitano, Quito."

The room was a flurry of movement again, and John bore down on the pain. *Relief was coming soon.* He repeated that to himself with growing urgency as the Ecuadorian nurse approached him with the morphine. He extended his arm to her, eager to get the roar of pain down to a whimper. Instead of the needle he expected, she started messing with his IV bag. *What the hell is she doing?*

It dawned on his pain-soaked brain that it was going to take too long for him to get the morphine if she put it in with the fluid.

"Doc...tell her where to fucking put it," John shouted through his oxygen mask. Joe was busy flushing his leg. The inferno engulfed him as someone did something to his right knee. Joe stood and faced the nurse. The nurse was saying something about not having the right port, but John had lost his patience. He snapped. "Joe, just put it in the right fucking place!"

"Okay, okay, here. Here we go. We got you, brother. Hold on."

A prick on the inside of his arm, and a few breaths later...sweet relief. The tide that threatened to break John's mind receded.

"Get some, L.T.!" Jeremy blurted out.

John could finally simply observe, almost calmly, the scene unfolding before him.

Finally, Petty Officer Scott ran back into the aid station, this time with good news. "We finally got a hold of the MC-130 crew in Quito through the embassy and the front desk at their hotel," he said. "Captain Downs just so happened to be running back into the hotel to grab a sweater as the embassy operator patched us through to the front desk." Scott huffed in disbelief. "Thank God, because they were all packed in a van out front, about to go sightseeing and gold shopping. They want to meet us in Lago Agrio. The runway is long enough there."

"I don't want to risk the L.T.'s stability on the road to Lago Agrio. Remember how much we were tossed around getting here?" Joe said. "Ask them if they can do anything else. A smaller plane? They can use the runway here. Anything else."

The petty officer ran out. When Scott got back, he was grinning. He had Jack in tow, still wet and muddied from the jungle river. AFSOC informed Special Operations Command South, which quickly approved a waiver to allow the MC-130 to make an emergency approach into Coca to get LT Alvarez out.

"The MC-130 just received special permission to land on the runway here in Coca."

"That runway can't support a C-130," Doc B protested.

He was right; not only was the airport not secured or even fenced off, but the runway was crumbling, unkept asphalt covered with oil-packed dirt patches and structurally unsound. In the 1990s, the Coca Airport was a remote Amazon oil town airport supporting exploratory operations for the oil companies. Months prior, during a pre-deployment site survey (PDSS), Air Commandos had declared the airfield unsafe and unsuitable for C-130 aircraft. In addition, it was hardly long enough and its width was marginally adequate at best. The airfield survey also highlighted that debris, wildlife, and even domesticated animals were real hazards. It would be safe for a Cessna, maybe a twin-engine airplane like a King Air, but not for a 150,000-pound aircraft. Anywhere the C-130 stopped and stayed stationary, the runway, taxiway, and ramp would crumble under its weight. The MC-130P Combat Shadow was a highly modified version of the C-130 Hercules (Herk) for special operations and weighed even more.

"Yeah, so they won't be able to stop after landing; they'll have to keep moving so the airplane won't sink into the ground," Jack told them. "We'll have to do a rolling on-load. Captain Downs is a damn good pilot, doc. If anyone could get the L.T. out of here, Downer will."

So, besides threading the needle to land in the jungle strip, the MC-130 Combat Shadow crew would have to perfectly execute a delicate combat procedure called an Engine Running On-load (ERO) to keep the aircraft rolling after landing. In order to transfer John onto the still moving aircraft, a JSOTF-improvised litter transfer team made up of the SEAL Corpsmen, Air Commandos, and Doc B in the pickup truck would have to roll up behind the taxing airplane following precise instructions given by the Shadow's loadmaster, Butch.

When cleared by the loadmaster, they would then jump off the rolling truck, walk/run with John strapped down and secured to the litter, and jump onto the rearward-facing loading ramp with John. Doc B would then run alongside the litter team and jump onto the C-130 to accompany John to Quito. The litter team would be required to jump off the ramp and return to the pickup that was rolling alongside the taxiing Herk.

All while dodging rocks, sticks, and branches and shouldering into a fifty mile-per-hour wind thrown up by four howling turbo-props just twenty-two feet in front of the loading ramp.

"And then comes the real dicey part," Jack explained.

Downer and his crew would then have to turn the plane on a dime while keeping it from sinking into the soft tarmac and then execute a maximum-performance takeoff from the cramped runway without hitting anything on the way out–especially the trees.

Once clear, they would have a thirty to forty-five minute flight up to the mountainous capital, at altitude. They'd land again at the Mariscal Sucre International Airport in Quito, taxi and shut down at the military ramp they left from. An ambulance coordinated through the US Military Group (MILGROUP) assigned to the US Embassy Quito would be waiting for them at the airfield and would then transport John and Doc B to Hospital Metropolitano; about an hour's drive away, depending on downtown traffic.

Joe rubbed his face and sighed. "Alright, how long do we have?"

19 SEP 1996 // FRANCISCO DE ORELLANO AIRPORT, ECUADOR // 1345L

They sped John from the base aid station-slash-clinic through the shanty town to the airport in their pickup truck. The sky was still scattered with clouds as the rest of the team cleared debris and any perceived obstacles from the cramped-cracked asphalt and partial dirt, oil-packed runway carved out of the jungle canopy.

Rico and his SEALs, all armed, shooed away local onlookers while Jack and part of the OAD A commandeered the control tower. Doc B and the corpsman watched and waited with bated breath from the pickup truck along the side of the airstrip. John was strapped down and could only gauge the danger from his limited worldview on the litter.

Damn gurney vision! John thought as the world blended and twisted in a haze of morphine and pain.

"There they are!" someone shouted as the telltale hum of the massive plane approached beyond the treeline. "Get ready!"

"What if a cow or goat wanders onto the runway..." Jeremy mused.

Daisy laughed nervously. Little did they know, the inbound MC-130P crew was considering that very same thing.

As the mighty Combat Shadow hurtled towards the jungle, pushed to its maximum operating speed (VMO) from its mountain top perch, Captain Downs yanked the aircraft into a 60-degree bank, and hauled back on the yoke to dissipate energy for the landing.

Butch leaned into his harness, anticipating the violent deceleration and landing. Downer told his copilot to drop the landing gear and called for full flaps, while slowing the airplane down as far as he could to shorten up his landing roll. Butch Lesley chuckled when he heard the flight engineer (F.E.) tell Captain Downs to "run over anything that's not supposed to be on the airstrip, even if it's a cow!" The FE was dead serious. Butch was Captain Downs' favorite load-master. And Downer, his favorite pilot. It was also his last deployment in the Air Force. As they approached the airstrip, Butch was deter-mined. *Failure is not an option; I'm not letting this lieutenant die on my watch!*

Jack, putting his combat controller skills to the test and acting as the tower's sole authority, couldn't stop swearing under his breath. He was scared shitless, but he made sure no one else caught on. His calm, baritone, "Chuck Norris" voice over the radio cleared Downs and his MC-130 as it barreled down towards the strip in a steep combat approach. "C'mon, Downer. This is it. C'mon…"

Downer, backed up by his crew, guided the aircraft down to final approach, nailing an impossibly slow approach speed of only 110 knots. His hands now light on the yoke, eyes flicking between his intended touchdown point, his airspeed indicator, the rotten and cramped airstrip ahead of him, Downs was getting more concerned the closer he got to it and the wall of trees right at the end of the strip. His copilot kept a steady and disciplined cadence of required calls down to the threshold, and the F.E. kept a keen focus on the engine instruments prior to landing, anticipating the short-field takeoff that would follow.

At the ramp, Butch stood at the ready, still using the tension on his restraint harness to maintain balance. Everything was prepped and space cleared for the rapid on-load of John and Doc B.

The hum became a roar as the shadow of the large plane over-head enveloped the team in the truck. They lowered their goggles over their eyes. The truck started to roll.

The touchdown was classic Downer—firm and deliberate. The plane slammed exactly on the required landing point, which had been calculated to keep the massive airplane from sinking into the rotten runway. Dirt and a dust cloud boiled up in front of the airplane as Downer slammed the throttles into reverse to abruptly decelerate to the slow, steady roll required to stay afloat. He wasted no runway.

His copilot called out tree limbs and other obstacles as they slowed to the ERO taxi speed of less than five knots. With the crew executing their duties in perfect synchronicity, Butch cracked the ramp open as the bright sunlight flooded the cargo bay and the heat and humidity engulfed the crew.

The pickup truck started to close from behind with the slowly moving aircraft as it rolled. Butch opened the ramp to level and signaled the litter team on the truck.

"Clear to on-load!"

Doc B dangled his feet off the tailgate and checked on John one more time, patted him on the chest then looked up at the litter team and gave a thumbs up. John's head and body were strapped down to the litter, and he was wrapped in a wool cocoon, eyes closed under the goggles they placed on him. The team all looked at each other and simultaneously gave a thumbs-up. They could all hear and feel the sound and heat of the roaring Herk just feet away from them. Packed gravel buckled, groaning under the impossible aircraft weight. The dirt and stones, driven backward by the props, kept blinding them and stinging any exposed spots of skin, and the roar of the four turbine engines was deafening.

Butch gave them the clear sign again and waved them on. Jeremy wasted no time and yelled, "Go! Go! Go!"

Joe B slid off the tailgate first and kept moving to clear the way. The two lead litter bearers were next, never letting go of the handles. Then Jeremy and Daisy, ensuring as smooth a transition as possible for their fallen brother. They moved in unison towards the ramp, almost running.

Butch reached down and helped pull the litter in first. He barked out clear, concise commands and directed the team, then securely strapped John's litter to the stanchions. He grabbed Doc B and directed him to sit and strap in while signaling the litter team to jump off the ramp.

They wasted no time clearing the thundering beast, and after a few running steps, they turned and saluted. Their salute was not only meant for the crew, but specifically for LT Alvarez. Butch returned the salute as he simultaneously raised the ramp. *Godspeed, brother,* rang through Jeremy's skull as he solemnly held his salute just a bit longer for the L.T.

Next, Downer needed to turn the aircraft 180 degrees on a dime while plowing through the crumbling gravel. Brian hoped that the soft ground would not degrade the takeoff performance, or that it would keep him down too long to avoid the 60-foot trees at the end of the landing zone. The crew, in perfect synchronicity, prepared for the short-field takeoff.

Downer took a deep breath as he shoved all four throttles forward. Hands firmly on the yoke and throttles, scanning the tree line out in front of them. The engines roared as the beast lunged forward. He could hear the steadily increasing airspeed calls and was waiting for that one call from his copilot that matters the most. His copilot, in a calm and clear voice, delivered the call "Rotate"; right at the precise speed they calculated with just enough runway behind them to clear the trees in front.

He felt the adrenaline surge through his body as the nose wheels dug into the runway with the power 'massively up', then Downer pulled the yoke all the way into his lap to free the nose. After ten unending seconds, he could finally feel the wings creating the lift to make the Herk lighter and lighter as it sped up down the runway. Downer then reset the yoke, and the aircraft broke free. They were now out of ground effect. He continued at maximum power through the climb, barely clearing the treeline.

"Clear!"

"After takeoff checklist complete."

Butch checked on their precious cargo and reported it back to the crew. "P.C. secure!"

The entire sequence, from touchdown to takeoff, took no more than three minutes. No drama, just calm, cool, and disciplined crew coordination and expert flying. The kind of precision expected of a special operations Combat Shadow crew, even when the margins were so razor-thin. Once airborne, Joe removed the goggles from John's face and continuously monitored his brother's vitals. John squinted at him, trying to understand what was happening. Joe sighed.

Back in the air, but not out of the woods, just yet.

6

THE CENTER OF THE WORLD

He was in a hut. It was dank. The air hung heavy with mold, dirt, and human sweat. The filth of the place clung to his skin and to his soul. He watched as his captors watched him with barely contained glee. They were bearded, wild-eyed, staring at him with hatred. Evil men.

They had nabbed him, and now they had strapped him down to this decrepit space. But the state of his capture wasn't what was keeping his attention.

No, he was focused on the red-hot pokers they were shoving into his leg. He screamed. And screamed.

They only laughed, taking pleasure from his pain.

"John. John!"

〜

19 SEP 1996 // QUITO, ECUADOR - HOSPITAL METROPOLITANO // 1616L

John gasped awake with Joe's steady voice in his ear. He was in a tunnel, lit. An MRI machine.

"I'm here, brother," the doctor told him. "We're okay."

He drifted again. The torture dreams repeated as he floated between consciousness and unconsciousness. The trauma and intensive care teams at Hospital Metropolitano were wasting no time. Orthopedics and vascular surgery—all of whom were trauma specialists—methodically and thoroughly assessed John's blood- and mud-stained body. Besides the obvious blood loss, damage to his legs and chest, he had shrapnel cuts and abrasions throughout.

John suffered through their manipulations to clean him, then for full body X-rays, ultrasounds, CT scans and MRIs in order to rule out any spinal cord and cerebral injuries, check for significant pelvic or abdominal injuries, and to look for signs of tissue death in his lower extremities.

His visions of his wrists being cut open were transposed images; medical staff carried out 'cut-downs' to get to his arterial blood for lab testing. Vascular testing of his left lower leg showed no arterial circulation below the level of the injury. John had some movement and sensation in his left heel, but not in his toes.

There were now more urgent issues to deal with. Both of John's IVs were compromised during transit and needed to be replaced. The ER team had been and was still prepping him for surgery. They had arrived at the Metropolitano Hospital at about four in the afternoon and were told the surgery would not be ready until 6:00 or 7:00 p.m. The delay was expected—the O.R. and anesthesia team needed that crucial time to prepare things—but Joe also feared they would lose too much of the 24-hour window to save a severed limb.

19 SEP 1996 // NAVARRE, FLORIDA // 4:30PM

"Hey sweetie," Shelley smiled as she picked Nicole up into her arms and gave her a kiss. She was tired from a long day at the hospital, but she was not too tired to be happy to see her youngest's smiling face.

She still had things to do, anyway. She needed to pick Lisette up from after-school care and grab groceries.

Well, she thought as she put Nicole in her car seat, *maybe groceries can wait.* After picking up a verbose Lisette (little miss Chatty Kathy, that one), Shelley forewent groceries for the day and headed straight home. Not for the first time, she missed having her co-parent around.

As they pulled up to Shearwater Drive and rounded the bend to the house, Shelley noticed a car parked at the end of their driveway. Two people were sitting in the front: a man and a woman. She recognized them from the recent change of command—the Director of Operations, second in command at the squadron, and his wife.

Huh, Shelley thought as she waved to them. *Maybe this was an Air Force thing; everyone visits the families after a change of command.* How would she know? All the Air Force stuff was still pretty new.

She parked and unloaded the girls from the car and told them to go inside. The new 20th SOS operations officer and his wife had exited their car and were walking toward her.

"Mrs. Alvarez," he greeted her. "Lieutenant Colonel Brian Johnson. This is my wife, Ranae."

"Call me Shelley," she replied. She shook both of their hands. "Please come inside." She led them through the garage to the door. When she opened it, she winced. Laundry was sorted, but had not been done. "Sorry for the mess. With John deployed, it's a bit of a hustle, you know?"

Ranae chuckled. "Trust me, I know." It struck Shelley a second time how much she instinctively liked this lady, the first time being at the change of command. Shelley ushered the two past the laundry room and into the house.

"This is the living room and kitchen," Shelley waved, leading them to the left and into the dining room, next to the front door. The girls went off to play in the open office on the other side of the dining room. "We've been redoing the bedroom, too. That's the den. We've got a pool out there, past the fence."

"It's a beautiful home. You, uh, you've been settling in well in

Navarre?" Johnson asked, standing with a hand on the back of one of the dining room chairs.

"Yeah. This is a great neighborhood," Shelley said. Johnson nodded and looked at his wife. Something unspoken passed between them, and she suddenly felt a pang of uncertainty.

Ranae smiled tightly and took a seat. Shelley automatically sat down as well.

Lt. Col. Johnson spoke first. "Shelley," he said, "we're here because there has been an accident."

Shelley's breath caught. "An accident?"

"John is alive," he assured her, "and he can move, but from what we've been told his leg is broken and his other knee is injured."

"What happened?"

"Well, we're still receiving information. From what we've been told, the helicopter he was on crashed at about noon." *About four hours ago*, Shelley's mind supplied. "The pilot died on impact, but they were able to get John out."

Shelley reached for her nurse training, covering herself with it like a cloak. "Does he have any other injuries?" she asked. "Any spinal or head injuries?"

"We can't be sure right now. We know he was responsive the whole time," he said. "From retrieval to the medevac."

Jesus, John. Wide awake during and after a major helicopter crash that killed his pilot? With a broken leg? The thought made her sick with worry. *What an awful—*

Something leaned against her leg. She looked down and saw Nicole staring up at her. *Little bat-ears,* she thought. "Is Daddy okay?

"It's okay, honey," Shelley said, thinking quickly. Crap, she didn't want a scared kid along with everything else. But what did she hear? "Daddy was in an accident, but he's okay. He just broke his leg and the doctors will put it in a cast. You can sign it when he gets back! Now go play with your sister." The four-year-old frowned, but obeyed.

"Where did they take him?" Shelley asked once she saw Nicole's attention diverted back to Lisette in the office. "Is he still at the... the crash site or—?"

"They've gotten him to the Metropolitano Hospital in Quito," Johnson replied. "Doctor Joe Basinger is with him; he'll probably call to give you an update soon."

Shelley spoke with the two a little longer, but soon gleaned they had no further medical information about John. They told her that Lt. Col. Tommy Hull had his staff set up a planning cell and assigned a squadron pilot he trusted to be the squadron liaison point of contact (POC) to Shelley. He would make sure she got whatever she needed.

They promised to stay in touch and let her know as soon as more information became available. They left, and Shelley called for pizza. She did not want to leave the phone, and she did not have the capacity to cook anything for the girls.

About an hour later, the phone rang.

"Hello, Shelley? It's Dr. Joe Basinger."

Shelley did not play with niceties. "How is he?"

Joe first confirmed what the LtCol told her: John had been in a helicopter crash in a river during a training flight.

"Any spinal injuries? Has he been in a CT scan yet?" she asked.

"We got him into a CT scan as soon as we got to Quito," Joe assured her. "No serious spinal or head injuries. But his legs..." He cleared his throat. His voice seemed hoarse, tired. Like he'd been up trying to save her husband's life. It was a relief to finally speak to another medical professional who knew exactly what had happened, but she could tell he was working overtime. "John's right femur was split, his knee was messed up, and the left leg near the calf was broken. An initial hemoglobin/hematocrit lab result was found to be 7g/dL and 20%."

Shelley inhaled sharply. A normal range was about 15g/dL and 45%.

John had lost over three-fifths of all the blood in his body.

"What kind of blood is he getting?" Shelley demanded. "Are you sure it's been screened?"

"Shelley, this hospital is top-notch, with U.S.-educated doctors. I made sure of it myself. I got on the docs to confirm their blood was HIV negative." He laughed a little. "They were pretty insulted, I think. They told me that Metropolitano *'had a first-class blood bank and tested all blood products for HIV, hepatitis, and syphilis'*. All the documentation was correct. That helps my confidence.

"Mine too," Shelley said softly. "Thanks, Joe."

"Listen, I got to go, Shelley. I will check in with you again in the morning, okay?"

After she hung up with Joe, she lingered by the phone.

I have to call Carmen.

She took a few breaths. How do you tell a mother her son was in a major accident? Juan, John's father, was on a remote spiritual trek on the other side of the globe—literally the 'roof of the world' in Tibet. Shelley chewed her lip. She did not want to break the news if Carmen was alone.

I could call Cuqui, so she could be there. Her sister-in-law was less than an hour from Kendale Lakes, Florida. But then again... *No. Crap. No, it's not right to tell Cuqui before Carmen.*

Shelley checked the time again. Carmen and Juan's store was still open. Shelley brought up *The Fairy's Ring* in her address book. When the call went through, however, the person at the register told her that Carmen was not in the store and no, she did not know where she was.

Shelley called their house instead. The answering machine picked up. The elder Alvarezes never checked their messages, but she left one anyway. "Hey, Carmen. It's Shelley. Please call me when you get this. It's important. Call me back. Love you, bye."

Maybe Carmen was visiting Lela? Lela, short for "grandmother" or "abuela", was John's maternal grandmother. She was in the hospital after a heart attack. John had called Lela before he left, so she tracked down the hospital's number and asked them to patch her through to Lela's room.

"Hello Lela! It's Shelley."

"*Hola*, Shelley, how are you?" Lela asked in her raspy, thick accent. She spoke little English. Perhaps it would make this easier. Or harder.

"I'm looking for Carmen. Is she there?"

"No," Lela said. "Is everything okay?"

"Yeah, everything's fine, thank you!"

She quickly hung up after diverting the stilted, linguistically constricted conversation. *Dammit, Carmen. Where are you? Someone has got to find her.* Shelley called the store again. Still nothing, no sign of where John's mother could be.

Shelley paced in the kitchen for another moment and made a decision. She called Cuqui. John's only sister was calm when Shelley broke the news and asked her to track down Carmen. "Can you please drive down there? I'd rather have someone be with her when she finds out."

Cuqui agreed. About half an hour later, the phone rang again. Shelley thought it might be Cuqui at Carmen and Juan's house, but it wasn't.

"*Mija*, I'm sorry I missed your call," Carmen said. "I had this horrible headache all day, Shelley. Horrible, horrible. I went to my friend to get a Reiki massage. It helped a little."

She nearly forgot she'd left a message on the answering machine. Carmen never checked her messages, anyway. Today was clearly not a typical day. "Is Cuqui there?"

"No," Carmen said slowly. "Why would she be here?"

Shelley suppressed a frustrated groan bubbling at the back of her throat. She really wanted Cuqui to be there, but she couldn't exactly hold back now.

She was surprised Carmen took the news so well. John's mother went into crisis-mode and remained calm through Shelley's explanations. When Cuqui finally arrived, Shelley felt comfortable hanging up with a promise to update them as soon as she could. She put the girls to bed and spent the rest of the evening finishing painting the bedroom and putting everything back together. She did not have to work on Friday, so she asked a fellow squadron wife, Lori Roman, whose son Tyler went to preschool with Nicole, to take care of the girls.

Shelley slept well that Thursday night, despite everything. Perhaps part of her body knew she would need the rest for what was to come.

~

19-20 SEP 1996 // QUITO, ECUADOR - HOSPITAL METROPOLITANO // 1800-0600L

Once John had regained blood flow, there were his legs to deal with. Dr. Hitra, the trauma orthopedic surgeon, helped assess the situation. An angiogram showed no arterial flow through the three major arteries that feed the left lower leg. There was some slight heel movement and sensation, but none in John's toes. Anaesthesia began at 6:00PM and for several hours, late that night and into the pre-dawn hours, the surgical team attempted to save John's severed left leg.

First, the orthopedics team cleaned and reduced the right knee, and then moved to the left leg. In order to attempt to save the nearly severed limb, they cleaned and took steps to control John's loss of blood. Two of the main arteries were "ligated" or tied off. Dr. Hitra then reduced the left tibia and fibula, placing what looked like a mediaeval torture device called an Ilizarov apparatus, a metallic "halo" of circular rings. The surgeon drove stainless steel pins into the intact part of the tibia and cranked tensioned wires through the skin, bolting what was left of John's tibia and fibula into a rigid titanium cage that functioned as a surrogate skeleton; this was external fixation. Dr. Hitra left shortly after, needing to return to his own practice to get ready for patient appointments. There was nothing more they could do either way but wait to see if the coming vascular bypass worked.

The vascular surgeon first harvested a vein from John's inner right thigh. They opened the bypass graft, tunneling into the groin, and cut open down the length of the inner side of John's thigh despite the femoral fracture and open dislocation of the mangled right knee. The extracted blood vessel was needed to bypass the shredded arteries at mid-shin and restore blood flow to the foot. Initially, the graft was successful; a pulse was felt in the left foot.

However, by the time the surgical site was sutured closed, the blood flow below the mid-calf had ceased.

～

20 SEP 1996 // NAVARRE, FLORIDA // 9:00 AM

There was something mildly satisfying about tearing tape from windows.

Tan strips littered the ground at Shelley's feet. It was odd; just yesterday she was talking casually to her husband's commander and his wife about their renovation of their bedroom. John had not been there to see it all the way through. No. Instead, he had been in a catastrophic accident half a world away.

All she could do now was strip the paint tape from their windows.

Friday morning had dawned early. Shelley was able to make breakfast for the girls before they went off to kindergarten and preschool.

Now that she was alone, with no sound but the ripping of tape and her own thoughts, worry took over. She thought about his injuries—well, at least the ones she knew—and her mind ran through all the medical procedures and checklists pertinent to a case like John's.

When she got to running down John's blood transfusions, how much he had been given, her own blood ran cold.

Oh my God! she realized. *DIC!* Disseminated intravascular coagulation frequently occurred after trauma and after a lot of blood loss. Blood would not clot, and the patient would bleed out. If it had not been caught in time, and if it had not been treated with a blood thinner like heparin, there was nothing anyone could do.

Oh my God. He's in a developing country. How much are they going to know or do about monitoring that type of stuff?

The thoughts were agonizing, but they would not stop. Finally, Joe called later in the morning. Again, Shelley did not bother with pleasantries.

"Are you checking for DIC?"

"Actually," Joe started, calm as ever. "He started to go into DIC. We've given him heparin, and he's responding well." Shelley relaxed.

"I'm calling because we have an update on the injuries to his left leg. I'm sorry to say we might have to take the leg."

"What? Why?"

No, no, it's not going to happen, Shelley thought. *John's too lucky; these kinds of things don't happen to my Johnny A.*

"We tried to establish blood-flow multiple times..."

Joe told her about the injury; details he had withheld until he was certain of the outcome. He told her about the grafts and angioplasty. Joe assured her that they were going to keep trying. He would update her when they confirmed they would have to take the leg. The Ecuadorian orthopedic surgeon needed to make the call.

Shelley tried to distract herself with cleaning and laundry, but eventually distraction came to her. The doorbell rang. It was LtCol Johnson and another man she did not recognize. He introduced himself as Joe's supervisor and the senior flight surgeon of the group. She felt tense when the man shook her hand. Something about the situation did not feel right. They sat at the dining room table, making small talk.

Eventually, the conversation turned to Joe. The doctor asked her what she knew about John's injuries and about the extent of his injuries. At first, she thought he was just making sure she had the right information. But he asked more questions, and she got the impression he was poking around.

"When was the last time you heard from Joe?" the doctor eventually asked.

"Oh, Joe? He gave me a call this morning to update me," she said. "We had spoken yesterday evening, too."

"Do you know when you're going to hear from him again?"

Shelley frowned. "No, he didn't say."

Maybe it was because a stranger was in her home and she was already tense, but something in her gut told her she did not like this man. He seemed more interested in Joe than John's situation. Wouldn't Joe be communicating with them? Part of her hoped, when she learned that this man was also a doctor, it would be great to talk to another medical person. She was wrong. It seemed as if he only paid lip service about letting her know if anything changed, and calling them if she needed anything.

She was relieved when the two finally left.

20 SEP 1996 // QUITO, ECUADOR - HOSPITAL METROPOLITANO // 1500L

John writhed in pain and at the edge of nightmares. The torture to his legs continued. *God, my legs.* The next time he remembered waking, Joe was at the foot of his bed trying to get John's attention.

He was pricking John's left heel.

"John. John, can you feel this?" Joe asked.

His tongue felt heavy. His entire world felt heavy.

"Yeah, kinda," John managed. As he zoned out into unconsciousness.

When he came to again, he could barely see Joe's face in his narrowed field of view. Joe did not look happy. In fact, his jaw was tight and his eyes were red. He looked tired.

"Everything below the trauma site is clotted," Joe was saying. "The surgeons attempted to reopen the grafted vessel this morning with an angioplasty, but no blood flow could be reestablished. They tried for two hours, but it's been twenty-four hours since the accident. We're out of time."

John's brow wrinkled. What exactly was the doc trying to tell him?

"John. I'm sorry," Joe said through his tears. "We're going to have to take your left leg. The surgery is scheduled to take place in two hours. I'm sorry."

John blinked, letting the doctor's words sink in. "What about my right leg?"

"No, we can save your right leg," Joe answered firmly.

A wave of relief swept over John. *Just one. He is taking only one.* He smiled.

"John, do you understand what I'm telling you?" Joe shifted closer, slowing his speech as if John did not comprehend what was coming out of his mouth. "We need to amputate your left leg."

"Thank you," he responded dizzily, still smiling as he closed his eyes and drifted back into unconsciousness.

Thank you, God! Thank you! Thank you! His heart felt light. *He's only taking one leg in exchange for my girls.*

Joe was ready for anger, for demands, for begging. For tears. How do you tell a guy that you have to take his leg? But here he was, watching LT John Alvarez nod at the news and fall right back asleep with a smile on his face.

It was probably the drugs. Joe did not have time to worry about the pilot's odd reaction, however, because John's DIC was getting worse.

20 SEP 1996 // NAVARRE, FLORIDA // 3:30PM

The rest of the day went by quickly for Shelley. Carmen called to let Shelley know that she and John's uncle Tevy were flying up from Miami to be with her and the girls while they waited for John to get back to the States. She fielded calls from her family members in Canada. It was emotionally draining, but it helped time move faster. Sara Lancaster, another spouse from the 20th SOS, came to visit and sat with her for a while. Joe called a second time, around late afternoon and before Carmen and John's uncle Tevy had left for Pensacola.

"We could not reestablish blood flow. We're going to have to take the leg."

"Okay," Shelley said flatly. Part of her wondered whether Joe's tone was because of an expectation of hysterics. Luckily for him, she was still in nurse mode and had another priority in mind. "So when are you going to get him stateside?"

When can I get my hands on him? her heart begged.

Joe told her he hoped John would stabilize after the amputation, but they could not be sure. The surgery was going to take place in a couple of hours. After they hung up, Shelley realized she would have to figure out how to break the news to family. She decided not to tell the kids. Not immediately, anyway. She would wait until she could have a conversation with John. *I have to get to Quito...I have to get my hands on him...I have to know he's getting the care he needs to stay alive...*

Shelley made a call to the 20th SOS operations desk and asked to speak to her point of contact (POC). Staff Sergeant Chris MacKenzie, who was on the duty desk, was an up and coming flight engineer that was recently STEP-promoted from Senior Airman (Stripes for exceptional performers).

"Yes, Mrs. Alvarez, let me find him," was the reply, even though Shelley hadn't identified herself. She realized the entire squadron had to be on alert; that acknowledgment provided a welcome comfort. When the POC came back on the line, Shelley asked if it were possible for her to get down to John if he wasn't able to be transported to the States. He chuckled.

"We were just talking about that, but it looks like there's a plan taking shape to get John to Wilford Hall Medical Center in San Antonio tomorrow. We'll arrange travel for you; there's a flight out of Pensacola early tomorrow afternoon. We'll be placing you to stay at the Fisher House."

"What is the Fisher House?" Shelley asked. The POC explained that it was a similar concept to the Ronald McDonald houses that would support families of sick children. Zachary Fisher, a New York builder, real estate developer, and son of Jewish immigrants from Lithuania, founded the Fisher House Foundation in 1990 alongside his wife, Elizabeth. They had been shocked to find out that military families were having to pay out of pocket for hotels, some even resorting to sleeping in their cars, while loved ones were in military hospitals for extended periods. They were committed to ensuring families would be treated with dignity and not have to face undue additional hardship during a medical crisis.

He assured her that they would be in good hands.

"Can we also get a plane ticket for Carmen, John's mom?" Shelley asked. "She's arriving in Pensacola this afternoon." Shelley hesitated to include Tevy in her request, unsure if it was appropriate, or even if Tevy could make the trip to Texas.

"Of course, I'll see about getting his mom's flight covered. I'll be in touch as the arrangements come together."

Shelley decided to head to Lisette's school and let her teacher know what was happening. She initially planned to tell Miss Cameron just that John had been in the accident, was being flown to San Antonio, and that they would be in Texas for an unknown amount of time. However, Shelley did not know when they would tell the girls about the amputation and realized Lisette might come to school, and to her teacher, with questions. It was best to tell the teacher about the amputation so she could be prepared to support Lisette.

Shelley was not prepared for all contingencies, however, since Miss Cameron had already heard that John had been in an accident. When she saw Shelley approaching the classroom, Lisette's teacher paled with the assumption that John had died. Luckily, Shelley cleared up *that* misunderstanding very quickly.

Shelley received a call back from her squadron POC. Flights were booked for both her and Carmen. John was being flown from Quito, with expected arrival at Wilford Hall tomorrow evening between 6PM and 8PM. *I'm finally going to get my hands on him.*

Shelley dropped off Lisette and Nicole with friends before she went to the airport to pick up Carmen and Tevy that evening. She then had to consider how to tell Carmen. The weight of it felt unbearable. She didn't understand where the strength came from, the kind that so many military commanders had to talk through bad news to family. It was one thing to talk to Carmen over the phone. But now Shelley was going to have to see her mother-in-law's face, her fears, and her tears while trying to manage her own. For a moment, the prospect was overwhelming.

During her wait, Shelley's phone rang. Unknown number.

She almost let it go to voicemail. Instead, she answered.

"Hello, is this Shelley Alvarez?"

The voice was a deep, rich baritone with a distinct accent. Controlled, but carrying the kind of authority that didn't need volume.

"Yes?"

"This is Commander Lennard King."

She blinked. *Len King?* "Oh my God, Len, how are you?

Len King had been John's first supervisor and squadron deputy of maintenance at HM-15, the airborne mine countermeasures squadron at Naval Air Station Alameda, California. Len was a former Vietnam-era decorated enlisted rescue swimmer. A larger-than-life tower of a man from Georgetown, Guyana, and New York City that no one could ever forget. John, would kid that he survived the 'Len King School of Leadership.' Len was an intimidating figure but was a wise mentor who valued grit and discipline. "No one beats my guys up but me," Len would say. Len kept tabs on John throughout his career and was frequently a sounding board for John. John had immense respect for his boss and genuine affection, and it was mutual. Somehow Commander King, through his extensive network, caught wind of what happened to one of his favorite proteges and called as soon as he could.

"I heard what happened in Ecuador," Len said. His voice softened slightly. "I'm sorry you're going through this."

"Thank you," she said, still perplexed on how Len got the news so quickly. "We're taking the news as it comes."

"He's flying into San Antonio, right?"

"Yes," Shelley said. "Tomorrow night."

"Good." A breath on the line. "I've got a nephew there. His name is Michael Stuart. If you need anything, Mike will be there."

Shelley smiled. "No, it's okay. We'll be fine."

"I didn't ask if you'd be fine," Len said evenly. "I asked if you needed anything."

She let out an involuntary laugh. "No, really! John's college friend lives there. He's picking us up. We're good."

Another pause.

"When are you arriving?"

"Tomorrow afternoon. Around four, I think."

"You sure you don't need someone to pick you up?" he pressed.

"I promise. We've got a ride."

"You shouldn't have to promise," Len muttered. Then, louder: "All right."

There was something in his tone. She imagined the man forcing himself not to pace.

"Commander King—"

"Len."

"Len," she corrected herself. "Thank you. Really."

Another measured pause.

"Okay," Len replied. "You need anything, Mike will be in contact with you."

"Well," she shook her head softly, "thank you."

"You call if plans change."

"I will."

"And Shelley? John may have gotten an earful from me a time or two." A faint smile lived in his voice now. "But you know I always took care of him."

"Oh, I know it was more than a time or two. And he probably deserved it." She laughed. "Thank you so much."

"Godspeed, Shelley, and send him my regards."

Military types, Shelley thought as she hung up. *Everything must be in order. If they can control everything they can, it's all good though. This brotherhood thing, thank God...*

Shelley then refocused on bringing Tevy and Carmen to Navarre.

As they drove and made small talk, Shelley tried to think of the best way to break the news. There really was no good way. And in the end, it probably did not matter.

Shelley took Carmen into her bedroom, John and Shelley's sanctuary, when they arrived and told her John was going to lose his left leg below the knee. Carmen tried to stay calm but broke down in tears as Shelley hugged her.

Tevy took the news only slightly better. He physically slumped, and the devastation Shelley saw in his eyes made her realize his connection to John was so much stronger than she had realized. She should have been gentler in her reporting of the news. But how was there a better way to share such tragic information?

Shelley then needed to coordinate plans with her own mother. Pat Hammond had to return to Hamilton, Ontario, Canada from Virginia and then fly to Pensacola to help take care of the girls. She still needed to confirm the time. Nicole and Lisette would stay with the Kellys—old family friends—until she got there on the 22nd.

Later that night, something else occurred to Shelley.

Oh crap, someone needs to get a medical power of attorney, Shelley thought in a rush, thinking of any number of reasons the girls would get hurt or get sick. *I don't know how long we'll be gone...a week? A month? It's a Friday night; who is going to be able to notarize a medical power of attorney before I have to leave tomorrow?*

She called the squadron again. The Staff Sergeant was, again, incredibly helpful.

"We'll take care of it, ma'am," Chris told her.

There was a JAG officer in townhouses a few blocks away from the Alvarez house. "By the way, do you have an idea for dinner?" the officer asked as he printed up the POA paperwork. Shelley paused, realizing she had not even thought about dinner for her kids.

"Oh, shoot. No. We've got pasta in the pantry, I think..."

The JAG officer smiled gently at Shelley. "We'll take care of it."

The next thing she knew, someone from the squadron had ordered pizza to be delivered.

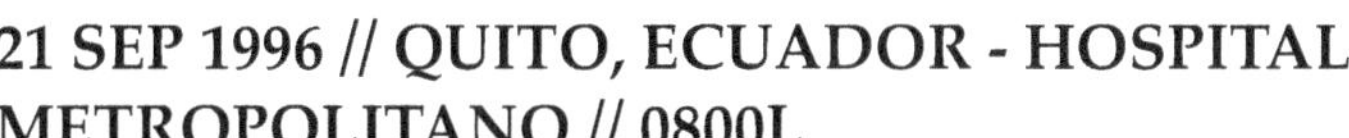

21 SEP 1996 // QUITO, ECUADOR - HOSPITAL METROPOLITANO // 0800L

The hours went by in semi-conscious flashes. John's dedicated ICU nurse came by and read him a letter from Shelley, sent in an envelope with cards and pictures via the U.S. embassy dated days before his accident.

His throat burned, still on fire from having the intubation tube shoved down his throat for so long. He could feel the tubes sticking out of his jugular on the left side of his neck. He looked down in blurred horror, seeing the tubes and wires protruding from him, his arms, sensors taped to his chest pinching at his skin. The bloodied bandages on his wrists and right elbow. His fingers looked like sausages as they came into focus.

Then his heart lifted as he was still fighting the weight of his swollen eyelids.

My sweet Shelley! My baby girls! Lisette and Nicole came into focus. His ICU nurse had pictures of Shelley, Lisette, and Nicole taped to the side rails of his bed. He found himself gazing at those, a yearning deep in his heart. He wanted, and he prayed. He even prayed in his dreams.

The pain still lingered. He wanted to go home.

He woke again to a light scraping on his cheek. The nurse was shaving him. She must have seen his bewilderment because she explained, "You have to look handsome for your wife and daughters when you get home."

John allowed it and tipped his head back as he zoned out.

"Okay, gracias, señora," he said as he smiled up at her.

Gotta look pretty for Shelley and my girls.

21 SEP 1996 // MARISCAL SUCRE INTERNATIONAL AIRPORT // 1232L

John was loaded into an ambulance and driven 30-minutes to the old Mariscal Sucre International Airport.

Joe told him how it all came together to get him to Wilford Hall in Texas. The rest of the A-Team gave him a little bit more. There were arguments he hadn't heard, decisions made while he drifted in and out of whatever passed for sleep. Somewhere in Panama, a coordination center thought it was simple. Any casualties in Latin America were supposed to be sent to the US Army Gorgas Hospital in Panama.

Joe had known better. That part came through clearly, no matter who told it. Apparently, the flight crew from Gorgas did not have the equipment to keep John stable. Joe wanted John to be flown out with proper equipment and a proper team, and then treated at Wilford Hall–the place where he learned what he knew to save John's life.

It sounded right to John, at least. Who was he to judge the man who kept him alive after losing half his blood?

Joe had pushed back against the orders, refusing to take John to Gorgas. People with rank and distance tried to turn the doc into a problem—*insubordinate*, they'd said. John tried to picture it: Joe in some cramped room with a phone, running on no sleep while trying to save the lieutenant's life, saying no over and over again while everyone else told him to *follow the chain of command*.

John was also aware of the calls to Shelley and that they had got Joe into trouble. Word of this communication got to the top operational chain of command at Hurlburt–the AFSOC commander, and then got back to Joe's superior, a Lieutenant Colonel. The LTCol had a medical degree but had not practiced medicine in some time. When Joe had given him the report of John's injuries, his supervisor only wrote down a little of what Joe told him. He reported everything about left leg, but no other injuries. Instead of mentioning the tainted blood supply, the Lt. Col. had written: *Dr. Basinger didn't give blood because the injuries weren't bad enough to require blood.*

So, when the Lt. Col. had arrived to speak to Shelley Alvarez, he was angry that she seemed to know more than he did. Joe had kept calling her anyway.

The fact that Joe was willing to be insubordinate in order for Shelley to know what was happening mattered a hell of a lot to John. Maybe more than the rest of it.

The A-Team, when they got to Quito, had backed Joe up as they tried to find John a flight home with a satellite case, calling across continents because it was easier than going through official channels. John could hear the hearty warfighters in his mind, railing against an unwarranted backlash from "non-operational *pukes*".

There was something else—something bigger—that came later in the telling. Colonel Steve Dirdack had been the one who contacted Doc Joe with an offer. Col. Dirdack had also been one of the internal medicine attending physicians at Wilford Hall when Joe was there. He was a well-respected trauma surgeon and pioneer in airborne critical care evacuation.

He had apparently cut off Joe's complaining about the lack of support with a solution.

A plane. Not just any plane. Col. Dirdack had connected with a C-141 crew in Chile. The Starlifter happened to be deployed on a sensitive national priority mission to Santiago, Chile, to deliver a propeller to a crippled U.S. nuclear fast-attack submarine that was damaged during operations off the South American coast. It would be re-tasked with a new mission to fly up to Quito instead of returning stateside.

Even now, strapped down, drifting in and out as they moved him, John tried to hold on to that part. The scale of it. The idea that somewhere, someone had moved something enormous for him. Redirected it mid-mission. There the C-21 crew would pick up LtCol Josephs to lead the CCATT, a trauma flight nurse, and required MEDEVAC equipment, then join up with two others from Howard AFB in Panama and converge in Quito with the state-of-the-art equipment. The modified C-141, now equipped for a critical medical evacuation, would soon be cleared for takeoff, its callsign altered to its urgent life-saving designation to ensure swift passage through air traffic control and expedite John's journey home.

Not Panama.

Wilford Hall. Texas. The United States.

Home.

He caught fragments of the present now—the rattle of equipment, the clear and calm drone of people who were aligned and ready. He didn't know all the names. Didn't understand the routes, the coordination, the risk.

But he understood this: Doctor Joe Basinger had committed to keeping John alive. Doc Joe had kept the faith.

As John was waiting to be loaded onto the C-141 transport, the team started to head towards the ambulance on the flight line. As they appeared in his blurred field of vision, John recognized them. The OAD-A team, then the whole extended mission team, the SEALs, and the SBU sailors, had come up to Quito to see the plane off.

They came over one and two at a time. They said their goodbyes. John was a little bewildered to see so many of these SOF operators cry.

I don't know what the hell you're going on about, John thought. *I'm going home, you guys are still stuck here!*

Yeah, sure, he was the one all messed up. They were scared for him; he got it. The damned Ecuadorian jungle almost got him. Then he chuckled to himself, remembering the scene from *Predator*.

"*La selva se la llevo!*" he said to Dan Labrador as he walked up. And Labrador's expression was hilariously scandalized, so he said it again to Daisy. "*La selva se la llevo!*"

Then a captain from the fixed-wing team headed towards him. He had something in his hands.

"Here," the captain said, placing two small, white teddy bears and a red rose on John's chest. "Get these to your wife and girls. You hear me? They need to be *hand-delivered* to your girls."

John fully understood the task. He grasped them tight with his unusually swollen hands and was *not* going to let go.

The CCATT flight medics brought a specialized wheeled gurney called an aeromedical evacuation stretcher, transferred him and strapped him down again. The loadmaster met them at the aft cargo ramp of the C-141. He assisted the team up into the cavernous cargo bay, securing the lieutenant's stretcher onto the lower stanchion. The equipment was reconnected, and the aircraft prepared for departure.

One of the nurses leaned over him. John saw a U.S. flag hanging in the cabin behind her.

"Hey, sir. We're going to get you home, alright?" she said.

Nodding in acknowledgment, John finally got a good look at his hands curled around the teddy bears and the rose. His hands were swollen. *Wow, Michelin Man hands?* He didn't remember injuring his hands. Later, he would learn it was swelling because of the massive trauma, an inflammatory response called 'third spacing'.

The nurse went to gently pull the rose and teddy bears from his hands and put them in the bag containing his personal items for safe-keeping.

"No!" John snapped, gripping them tightly. The nurse removed her hands in parley.

"Okay, no problem!" she told him, looking at the heart-rate monitor with concern.

John glared at her. *Gotta get these to Shelley and the girls.*

They covered him with a big green military-issued blanket and laid straps down over his wool cocoon again. God, he hated those ugly, scratchy things. But he looked up and saw the flag again. The Stars and Stripes. It comforted him. He tried not to think about what it normally symbolized. En route, the CCAT team adjusted their care to keep John stable throughout the flight. It was touch and go at times. They needed the monitoring and equipment that the Panama-based team had not been prepared to provide. The CCAT physician eventually put it in writing: *In light of the patient's condition at the time, arrangements were made. I told him (Joe) that involving the CCAT team seemed entirely appropriate.*

The flag was also there to drape John's body if he did not survive the flight.

In that moment, instead, it was a reminder of where John was headed. *Home. Finally, finally...*

John's hands clenched at the teddy bears for Lisette and Nicole and the rose for Shelley. He looked at the nurses (*just like my sweet Shelley*) in familiar green aircrew flight suits. John felt the sense, once again, that his brothers and sisters had him. His life was in their capable hands.

His eyes found the USA flag again. He had faith in his country and his fellow service members. And they were keeping the faith with one of their own.

I'm going home. Home!

PART III

The cave you fear to enter, holds the treasure you seek.
– Joseph Campbell

The obstacle is the way.
– Marcus Aurelius

7

REUNION

21 SEP 1996 // SAN ANTONIO INTERNATIONAL AIRPORT, TEXAS // 1500L

Shelley struggled with her own mental chaos in the days after her husband's accident. Thoughts would spin. She had no immediate focus; nothing to accomplish or solve in the moment. She would think about one thing, and then her mind would fly toward something else. She felt untethered. She just wanted to lay her hands on John, to have him alive and breathing in her arms.

The three of them—Shelley, Tevy, and Carmen—flew out in the early afternoon. They landed in San Antonio by mid-afternoon. David Gutierrez, John's college friend, and his wife Suzy met them right at the gate. She spotted their waiting party very quickly. There were not very many people waiting other than people getting on the plane.

After a moment, Shelley noticed a tall, dark-skinned man in a Navy khaki uniform at the gate. The lieutenant was stiff-backed and still, almost as if he were at attention. He did not look very comfortable about being there, nor as if he knew exactly who he was looking for.

A light went on in Shelley's head. *Len King's nephew?* It had to be. She could imagine Len barking at his nephew on the phone; *"Just be there! Her name is Shelley Alvarez, and she has dark hair and big blue eyes."*

Len, you sonofabitch. You sent him anyway.

Shelley approached him. "Are you Mike Stuart?"

The man's shoulders relaxed with relief.

They all headed first to the Fisher House on Lackland Air Force Base near the Wilford Hall Hospital. John was not expected to get in until later in the evening. They would meet his ambulance at the hospital. Tevy and Carmen went with David and his wife. Shelley decided to drive with Mike.

On the way, Shelley started to get a better understanding of Mike's personality. He seemed stoic and solid; but also someone who was not necessarily prone to emotional responses. Shelley kept saying how much she wanted to just get her hands on her husband, Mike just nodded and replied, "Yeah, you've said that a couple of times."

He, at least, seemed like someone who could help tether her whirling thoughts.

They were not sure if it was okay that a third person—Tevy—was also going to stay at the Fisher House. The group debated sneaking him in. Ultimately, the Fisher House's renowned hospitality was brought to light. They waived all charges.

While settling into the rooms, Shelley received a call from the base operator.

"Good evening. Is this Mrs. Alvarez?"

"Yes."

"Ma'am, you have a call from Naval Air Station Keflavik, Iceland. Lieutenant Varner is on the line. Patching you through now. Standby."

Don Varner was another Naval flight officer colleague of John's while at NPS and a close friend. Shelley was again amazed at how quickly the word got out everywhere and how those same people paid attention. Don, bless his heart, was close to losing his cool. He was clearly anxious and stressed about John's well-being.

"Shelley, what's going on?"

Shelley caught the concern in his voice and immediately went into nurse mode. She told Don what she knew, including the amputation.

"They tried what they could to save it," she said, "but they had to take his leg yesterday."

"How much of the leg?" Don asked, his voice tense.

"Well," Shelley replied, remembering what Joe had told her. "I think it was about mid-calf."

"So, about a foot?"

Maybe it was the lack of sleep. Maybe it was the perverse sense of medical humor nurses turned to during a crisis. Either way, Shelley let out a short guffaw and replied, "Yeah, that too."

She was met with an embarrassing silence on the other end of the line. She discovered that her sense of humor regarding her husband's leg amputation was not universal.

Too soon for medical humor? Shelley thought as she waited long hours for her husband's plane. *Sorry, Don!*

21-22 SEP 1996 // WILFORD HALL, LACKLAND AFB, SAN ANTONIO, TEXAS // 1900-0400L

At around seven in the evening, David showed up at the Fisher House to take the three of them to Wilford Hall. Mike met up with them at the hospital as well. Shelley was surprised—she thought that Mike would have considered his job done. She appreciated his calming presence, though, and thanked him again for accompanying their family.

One of the doctors met them at the door. When Shelley asked him a few questions, she could see he was ready for her to freak out when he did not have all the answers. He informed her that John's flight would land at Kelly Air Force Base, about three miles from the hospital. John would be transported to Wilford Hall via ambulance from there. Shelley could meet the ambulance outside the ER.

"Why can't we meet him at the airfield?" she replied.

"The transfer of your husband needs to take place rapidly," the doctor told her. "We're not sure how stable he's going to be."

The family waited in the emergency room for about half an hour before Shelley and Mike went to the nurse's station for an update on the flight landing. They were told they would be notified as soon as the plane landed at Kelly. Another half an hour passed; there was not much conversation while they waited. Mike was on his phone occasionally, seemingly distracted. After a moment, he went up near a door by the nurse's station again. She thought it was a little odd; it was in a staff-only area.

But Mike returned without incident or explanation. Maybe he had just gone to the bathroom?

A few seconds later, the doc approached to tell them the plane had landed at Kelly and the ambulance should arrive momentarily.

Finally! Shelley thought, her heart in her throat.

Shelley, Carmen and Tevy were escorted outside, eyes adjusting to the darkness to meet the arrival of the ambulance. Shelley's breath abated as she made out the lights of the ambulance.

The ambulance pulled into the bay, and when they unloaded John, the first thing Shelley saw was that her husband was completely cocooned in blankets. She rushed forward. She could see the faces of two teddy bears peeking out from under the blankets across John's chest.

He also had a rose in his swollen hand. Shelley reached out, and she finally got her hands on him. John was alive. He was home. She placed her right hand on his face as he handed her the rose he had clung to since Quito.

"I love you," was the first thing John said to Shelley, groggy through the haze of drugs. "When this is all over, let's have another baby." Shelley laughed through her tears. *She* had been the one pushing for a third kid, even a fourth.

"I knew you'd wise up," she murmured, holding him as close as she could.

They did not have time to linger, however. The medical team whisked John into the emergency room. It was the definition of organized chaos. Shelley tried to stay out of the way, while at the same time did not want to give up her spot at John's gurney. The team refused to let her see the amputation. The amputation surgery in Ecuador was only preliminary. They removed the non-viable part of John's mangled leg and below. It was called a guillotine cut; the wound was left open to allow the orthopedic surgeons to debride it again and determine the best option to eventually close the wound and later prep it for a prosthesis.

Shelley, Carmen, and Tevy were escorted to a family waiting room, leaving John in an ER operating room full of doctors and nurses. Dr. Joe Basinger placed a hand on Shelley's shoulder. He looked exhausted.

"Good to see you, Shelley."

Shelley gave him a hug. "Thank you for bringing him home."

The lead surgeon, Dr. Keith Bolyard, came in to talk to her at around 11:00pm, while they were just about prepared for surgery. Joe had sung praises about this guy to her, so she was confident about his skills. The first thing Shelley noticed, however, was how wired the surgeon was. Dr. Bolyard described the intention to do an initial debridement of the amputation and then work on his right femur and knee. But while he explained, he was so hyped up on caffeine that he would get caught on a word, and Shelley would have to fill it in. She kept her comments to herself.

This is the guy who is going to be working on my husband?

Joe went in with the surgeons. They were told surgery would go until 2:00am, and then John would be taken into the ICU. One of the ICU nurses, Maria Melendez, was an Air Force Captain and showed up just after the surgery to escort Shelley into the ICU to see John. It was 3:00am, and Shelley was tired, but her heart kept her up with the thought of getting her hands on John again and not letting go.

She knew, to some people, that the intensive care unit could be a distressing experience. But for her, the ICU was her home. She spent so much of her time in ICUs. The room, the layout, the monitors—everything was familiar. It was comforting.

One of the surgical interns kept the tension from taking over before they rolled John into the operating room. The intern took a military coin out of his wallet and coin-checked John by tapping it on the bed's guardrail. The intern was a former 20th SOS flight surgeon and recognized a brother in need. He said that his wife was also a highly decorated Army flight surgeon who had been a POW during the first Gulf War. Before leaving the room to let the rest of the team work on John, the intern told them he would make sure John would be looked after.

The team started drawing a blood sample from the triple lumen catheter that the OR team in Quito had placed in John's internal jugular vein on the left side of his neck. Shelley stood beside Joe.

Joe spoke, watching the process. "It's nice to see it red."

Shelley nearly choked. *Do military doctors not know what color blood is?!* "As opposed to...?"

Joe turned to look at her, deadly serious. "Shelley, his blood had been so diluted it was like Kool-Aid. It was barely *pink*." John had in fact received a total of 12 units of packed red blood cells (PRBCs), 10 units of plasma (FFP), and 8 6-packs of platelets. A massive amount of blood was infused to counter a massive loss of blood.

Shelley knew Joe had fought to keep her husband alive, but for whatever reason it had not hit her how close John had come to death. Her respect for Joe grew and solidified with every further bit of information he gave her about the accident.

After they had finished taking blood, Shelley went to John's bedside.

"Shelley," John croaked, half-conscious. "It really hurts. Can they give me something else?"

She asked the team what they were giving him for pain. They

explained he was receiving morphine and Versed, an amnesiac agent. The amnestic heightened the effects of the opioid by causing short-term memory loss/amnesia; you literally forget the pain. She asked Joe about getting John more Versed. Joe agreed and wrote the prescription for the amnesiac.

Unbeknownst to either of them, however, his ICU doctor was already increasing John's morphine. You never want to increase both morphine and an amnesic at the same time.

John, for a few heart-stopping moments, stopped breathing.

Thankfully, sternum rubs hurt like hell and are as effective as hell to force someone back to consciousness. It was also precisely what Shelley did with John.

"John, take a deep breath for me, okay?" she urged calmly as she watched his O2 levels drop.

Shelley never actually succeeded in killing him.

With her heart firmly in her throat, Shelley knew she needed to take a step back. She realized she was not a cook in this kitchen. She was not a nurse in *this* ICU, despite her experience and her concern for John and his survival.

Joe was also encouraged to take a step back.

"I'm the attending physician, Joe," the other doctor said. "You saved his life. You got him home. Let us take it from here."

THERE WAS a pressure on his chest, like he was holding his breath. He paddled through the muddy water. His hands moved sluggishly through the muck, pushing against it as if it were quicksand. It was night, and there were no stars. No moon. The air was dank with rotten leaves and something else. Fear.

There was something in the muck with him.

There, against his leg. A bump. Another. He tried to swim, his lungs heaving. He felt a sharp pain. Teeth scraping against his legs. Tugging. He tried to kick, and it would leave him, but then a black shape rose from the muddy water. He could see its angry eyes: black, wet, and cruel. It lunged, sucking him down into the river.

He woke up in pain. The past days were a repetitive torture of pain, sleep, and then pain again. His sleep did not abate the torture. If it was not river monsters, it was the mud and blood-soaked body of Javier that tried to pull John down with him into the muck. It was Javier's mangled and lifeless body laid out on a sandy beach. Or Matt's body. Sometimes both.

The nightmares dragged him down again.

~

22 SEP 1996 // WILFORD HALL, LACKLAND AFB, SAN ANTONIO, TEXAS // 0654L

The Texas morning dawned bright and restless through the large plate-glass window in the second-floor room John was assigned to. Shelley got little sleep that night. She knew John was in excellent hands, but she also couldn't stand the moments when unconsciousness took him away from her again. She made do with hospital coffee, girding herself for the day.

The medical team let her know they were moving John from the ICU to get some imaging done en route to his new room on one of the regular nursing floors. The hallways were quieter than the organized chaos of the ICU. She, Carmen, and Tevy headed to John's assigned room and walked in.

Shelley did not know what she expected, but it certainly was not four beds crammed into a room separated by curtains. One roommate would have been fine, but three? She could not conceive of trying to help, comfort, and heal her husband in a crowded hospital room.

No. Nope. "Absolutely not!" she cried. She no longer cared if her fellow nurses saw her lose it. This was too much. She rushed towards the hospital phone and dialed Joe.

"Hey," Joe answered. He could probably hear the tears in her voice. "What's wrong?"

"Joe, I'm sorry. I don't want to make this a big deal, but they have him in a room with *three other beds.* John's just been through a massive trauma. He needs privacy. We need privacy!"

"You're right. The administrator probably just saw another patient and assigned him to the first available bed. Don't worry, Shelley," Joe told her. "We'll take care of it."

They quickly switched the rooms into a semi-private room with two beds. The other bed was, thankfully, empty.

Finally, John was rolled into the room. The nurses told them he would wake up soon, but he was heavily sedated and would likely be a little disoriented. Shelley didn't care. She could put her hands on him again.

When he woke up, John's eyes found Shelley's. A dopey smile spread across his face as he reached out to her.

"Shelley," he murmured. "My sweet *Stella Meringue...*" Shelley smiled at his use of her childhood nickname.

"Hey Johnny A," she replied, squeezing his hands. "How are you feeling? Any pain?"

"Sleepy. Can you come here, please...closer?" He motioned for her to come close to him. "I just want to smell your hair."

"As you wish," she teasingly replied. She gingerly nestled into him, sliding all the wires and tubing out of harm's way, and placed her neck against his face and lips. He wrapped his left arm as best he could around her and closed his eyes. They breathed in each other's familiar smell. They kissed gently. John let the strands of Shelley's hair slide through his fingers as she stood up again and smiled.

"So, what's the news?"

Shelley tried explaining the x-rays and the initial surgery, but his attention would drift.

"What's wrong with my hands?" he muttered. "Shit, they look like Michelin Man hands... my fingers look like sausages."

"They're swollen." Shelley said. "Fluid escapes after trauma." She explained a little more, but John had a hard time keeping up. Then, a knock on the door. A woman came into the room.

John's nurse from the ICU! Shelley remembered her.

"Hi again! I'm Maria," she said to John. "I was part of the ICU team taking care of you when you arrived. Good to see you graduated out of there." She smiled. "I was told you know Frank."

"Frank?" John's eyes widened. "From the 6th?"

"Yeah, we 'Boricuas' stick together," Maria laughed. "When I heard you were also assigned at Hurlburt, I called him to see if he knew what was going on with you here. I made sure to swap patient assignments to take care of you. He's a good friend of mine. If you need anything, or if the nurses on this ward are not taking care of you, you tell me. Okay?"

Maria looked at Shelley this time. *We nurses understand each other.* Shelley smiled and nodded, acknowledging and grateful to Maria for her expert care of her Johnny A.

"Thanks, will do. Yeah, I worked together with the tech sergeant for a bit," John said. "Wow. Small world."

"Eres de Puerto Rico ¿no ves?" Carmen asked.

"Sí, Señora," Maria replied.

"Hay, gracias. ¡Qué bella eres!" Excited to connect with another Spanish-speaker, Maria responded in kind as Carmen pulled her into her warm embrace.

Carmen and Maria continued chatting in Spanish, then embraced again.

"Que Dios te bendiga mija," Carmen said before Maria departed to return to her work. *God bless you, my daughter.*

Shelley smiled, remembering her mother-in-law's insistence on keeping faith in miracles. Maria had told them that Frank had asked her to be there for whatever they needed. Her ethnicity, being Latina, would have connected them just as much as her connection to the Special Ops brotherhood.

"God puts people in the right places at the right time," Carmen told her son and her daughter-in-law after Maria left. Shelley hoped she was right. For now, she would stay in her place—by John's side.

Those first few days were nearly unbearable. By the end of his stay at Wilford Hall, John would receive three operations. Both legs were still a mess. Three four-inch-long titanium screws with washers at the heads were drilled and inserted through his condyles at the end of his right femur where it joined his knee. They would not fit him for a prosthetic until his right leg and knee healed enough for him to bear weight. Aside from the procedures, of course, was the pain. Although he received immense amounts of morphine, it quickly became apparent that John had an extraordinary tolerance to the painkiller.

John was not just suffering physical pain. His vivid nightmares continued. Morphine side-effects kicked in soon after he gained more and more consciousness. He often woke up in cold sweats, drenched. He was convinced he had brought parasites back with him. John would tell Shelley he could feel little mechanical insects under his skin, that they had burrowed in from the jungle. He would scratch, panicked, and try to convince Shelley of what he felt, what he was sure he could see.

"No, Shelley, there are bugs here," John insisted. "Right here. Look! *Look*."

Shelley recognized he was suffering from 'morphine itch' but inspected John's arms and torso closely and tried to reassure him.

"I'm looking, there is nothing there," she tried to tell him.

She was mostly unfazed by his morphine hallucinations—it was the pain that hurt her heart. The IV was providing John with a constant dose, but it barely seemed to take the edge off. On top of it, a button would give him a boost of morphine. The process was computerized on the machine. John was allowed a certain extra dose per hour. If he hit the button, he would get the boost only once every ten minutes. After he used up his allotted boost for the hour, he would have to wait for it to roll over. Of course, this process was to ensure John did not overdose.

Morphine's greatest danger lies in its ability to slow down breathing. The machine made sure John was awake enough to breathe. But, of course, as soon as he was pain-free enough to fall asleep, the morphine would wear off. The pain woke him up in a continuous, tortured cycle. The machine kept patients alive, but it was ineffective on John's pain curve.

"Shel, can't you just hit the booster while I'm asleep?" John asked, his eyes red with pain and exhaustion.

Shelley desperately wanted to give him relief, but she remembered the whole morphine/Versed incident when he had first arrived.

"I already nearly killed you," she told him, and herself. "I will not do it again."

8

MIRACLES

The ceiling tiles were the color of old bone. John lay awake beneath them, listening to the distant rattle of what sounded like a gurney in the hallway and the steady Texas hum of air-conditioning that never quite cooled his room. Shelley was talking quietly to Carmen, updating her on what Pat was saying about how the girls were doing. He let himself drift.

San Antonio sunlight leaked around the edges of the blinds. He kept his eyes up and away from his body. He still didn't enjoy looking down.

The door opened softly. Dr. Gary Benedetti stepped in. He had calm, clinical eyes, and a clipboard tucked under his arm. John straightened as much as he could in the bed, despite the haze of morphine.

John nodded. "Sir."

"How are you holding up?"

John considered that. The nightmares were draining him as

surely as if a vampire came in the night, but the doc didn't need to know that. His wife and his mother didn't need to know that either.

"I'm here, Doc. Good to go," he said, not as convincingly as he wanted to be.

The doctor pulled a chair close to the bed and sat.

"I want to talk to you about next steps," he said. "The surgeons in Ecuador preserved as much tibial length as possible. The surgical margins look good. No sign of spreading infection."

"That'll help later?"

"Yes. Below-knee amputees typically have better mobility outcomes than above-knee amputees. You'll have more control with a prosthesis. That said, we're scheduling you immediately for a revision surgery in a couple of days; on the 27th. We need to close that guillotine cut. We need to essentially sculpt what is left of the leg so it can withstand the pressure of a prosthetic socket and support the full weight of your body."

John exhaled. He had been dreading this conversation, but he had to know. "Give it to me straight, Doc. What is recovery going to look like? I mean physically? When can I walk, what about running, when will I be unprocessed from the Navy?"

"First, given aviation medical standards, a permanent lower-limb amputation, even your right knee and fracture disqualifies you from ever flying—military or civilian." If John's face betrayed the emotion he was feeling, the doc did not react. Instead, Dr. Benedetti spoke slowly, knowing how heavily his words were going to land. "But you won't be discharged immediately either, L.T., if that eases one of your concerns a bit. After all possible medical treatment is completed here, then and only then, you will have to go before a Medical Review Board to assess your fitness to stay on active duty. I have heard about a few amputees staying on active duty, but only in limited roles. I expect they'll recommend medical retirement."

Retirement? Permanently grounded? The sky, stolen. John let out a slow breath.

"How long until I'm upright?" John asked. *At least give me that, Doc.*

"You'll be in a wheelchair for several months," the doctor replied. "The residual limb has to heal fully. We'll monitor swelling and watch for complications. You may need revision surgery if bone edges or bone spurs cause problems. Your right leg also complicates matters."

"And after that?"

"If everything progresses normally, we'll begin prosthetic fitting. However, the VA will probably have taken over your care by then. Let's just plan on at least six months."

John absorbed that silently. *The VA? Maybe I'll get a civilian engineering job by then...*

"So I can start walking around then?"

"You'll need intensive physical therapy for that," Dr. Benedetti said. "With your right leg and knee too... you're going to be in a wheelchair for at least six months, L.T. Start getting used to that. With PT, they'll get you to gradual weight-bearing. As for walking...well, the prosthetics available now are primarily mechanical systems. Some carbon fiber energy-storing feet exist, but they're designed for general mobility, not high-performance demands."

John gave a faint huff. "So I'm not running marathons."

"Short distances, maybe, in time. But you'll likely rely on a cane for balance long term."

"A cane," John repeated, testing the word.

"You'll be able to walk, climb stairs, but not without a limp."

John's fingers flexed against the blanket. The outlook was bleak: a minimum of six months in a wheelchair, watching his strength ebb away.

"Will I at least walk into my house on my own?"

"Yes."

"Stand at my daughters' graduations?"

"Yes."

"Dance with my wife?"

The doctor allowed him the smallest smile. "With practice."

John swallowed hard at that. The heart monitor ticked steadily beside him. He knew the deal he had made with God. He should be grateful. *Right?* Again, the image he conjured in the river came to him. *A sad, wilted veteran in a wheelchair.*

"It will take time to adjust." The doctor paused, then continued. "Your service record is exceptional. The Navy will take care of you. They can walk you through retirement benefits, medical coverage, rehabilitation support, that kind of thing."

John looked at him then. Really looked, absorbing the timeline like coordinates on a map.

Wheelchair.

Prosthetic.

Cane.

John felt another punch in the chest. *God. That sucks.*

"Doc, what about...?" He barely started his question when the vibration ramped up, subtle at first, like someone rolling something heavy down the hallway.

"I keep hearing helicopters," John admitted. As the windows rattled and ceiling tiles vibrated above them from the inbound rescue helicopter outside.

"Local MEDEVAC flights," the doctor said. "You're not imagining it. We're a level-one trauma center. We see them fly in everyday."

John's throat tightened. John slid his hand beneath the blanket and rested it against the bandaged end of his left thigh. The deep rhythmic *thup-thup-thup-thup* continued to resonate through his bones then subsided to a high-pitched hum as the helicopter landed on the pad and began to shut down.

John's heart sank. *Maybe I can go back to being an engineer.*

Dr. Benedetti left the room after finishing his check-up. As soon as the door closed, John's mom came in and rushed to his bedside. Carmen had a tiny bottle in her hands. John recognized it as the water from the holy well in Lourdes, France.

"Come on, Mom," John muttered. "Not again, not now. Please."

"No," she told him, sprinkling the holy water onto his forehead and face. "You have to pray! Pray for a miracle! There's going to be another miracle! You surviving was the first one! You have to ask. Again and again. Ask God for what you need." She struggled to pull his blankets and sheets aside just enough to sprinkle the holy water on his legs. "You're going to walk again, you're going to run again. You will be an inspiration." She flicked more water over his heavily bandaged and wrapped-up legs. "You watch! Pray, son."

That night, John wholeheartedly gave in. He prayed.

23 SEP 1996 // WILFORD HALL - LACKLAND AFB, SAN ANTONIO, TEXAS // 1707L

John's commanding officer took out his wallet and threw his coin onto the floor to *coin-check* him. Tommy then promptly tapped it on his bed guardrails so John could understand.

John stared incredulously at Tommy Hull. Here he was, literally buck-naked under the sheets, hooked up to a morphine pump, with his wife and his mother in the room.

"Hey dude!"

"Hey sir," John joked. "If I'm buying, all I have to offer you is a hit from my morphine drip."

The tension surrounding the situation broke instantly. Everyone laughed. After the niceties, John eventually looked up and asked Shelley and his mom to leave the room to speak with Tommy in private.

"Sir," he started, "I've got a question for ya."

Tommy shrugged. "Anything, Johnny."

"When do I get processed out?"

The commander huffed. "You mean, 'when am I gonna kick you out'? No chance."

Is he blind? John pushed down his annoyance. "I've lost my leg, I'm never gonna fly again. The doc told me I'd never walk again normally or run, let alone fly. I'm looking at a med board when this is all done." It was the first time he had said it out loud, and it hurt to think about it. But it was reality, wasn't it?

Tommy Hull, already a legend in AFSOC, was always known for

his positive attitude and gregariousness...and his iron will. He was frequently compared to Hannibal, the character from the 70s television show *The A-Team*. Nothing got in his way. *We will find a way or make one.*

Clearly nothing could faze the man, as proven by the next thing that came out of Hull's mouth.

"Johnny. Dude. You're going to recover. You're gonna stay on active duty, and you're going to fly again," Tommy told John. "Oh, and then we'll inter-service transfer you to the Air Force. If you like."

John sputtered, heat rising to his face. Going back to service was impossible. *Walking? Running? Flying?* Not after this kind of injury. Incredulity turned to rage.

"Of course I'm going to get *better, sir!*" John said. "But the hell..." He held off what he was thinking: *You've been taking a hit off of my morphine is what you've been doing.*

"Johnny, we've invested millions in you and sent you through Pave-Low qualification; you're a national asset." Tommy said, nonplussed. "Pave-Low is a three to four-year payback commitment —you're gonna fly Pave-Lows. You've only fulfilled one of those years." He pointed a demanding finger at John. "You still owe me *at least two more years.* So we're gonna get you back in the cockpit. You're gonna fly, and you're gonna finish those two years."

John would blame it on the drugs, but he could just barely keep the tears in. *W.T.F.*

Tommy then changed the subject and described the classified details and challenging flying he was missing out on in the West Coast J.R.X. work-up deployment he just departed from.

John then asked, "Would you do me another favor?"

"Sure, anything."

"Can you get my mom and my wife out of here? They need a break."

Tommy smiled. "Dude, tell you what. Why don't I take them to dinner? That way you can get some rest without us bugging the hell out of you."

Tommy took Shelley and Carmen to a local Olive Garden, where they apparently drank two bottles of wine and took one to go.

When they arrived in the hospital room, John was sleeping, out cold. As quietly as he could, Tommy taped the empty wine bottle to John's IV stand. However, John woke up to three slightly tipsy and mischievous faces. He looked at his IV. There, of course, was an empty bottle of Chianti which looked like it was being emptied into his IV.

John shook his head at Tommy. "God, it's really good to see you, sir."

Tommy beamed. "Good to see you too, brother. Get some rest, 'cause we got work to do."

Tommy Hull's determination could not be swayed. John still couldn't help but feel as though the commander was patronizing him. John had never heard of a pilot going back to flying status with an amputation. In fact, he had heard of only one amputee who continued serving a bit longer after his amputation—a famous Army soldier who suffered a double amputation just two years prior, parachuting as a member of the acclaimed Army Golden Knights demonstration team.

Could I really fly again, even in the civilian world? Not only would he have to fight his own body to get back into the cockpit, but he would also have to go up against the risk-averse military bureaucracy. *Shit, I can't even walk yet.*

The boss is probably flying by the seat of his pants, John decided, *and writing checks he isn't sure he can cash.*

THE AIR STANK of sweat and beer and sex. The lights were a sickly yellow, highlighting the vision of the crumbling, decaying hut of a brothel around him. Wicked men were in corners, their figures hunched and drunken. Evil women, scantily clad and hollow-eyed, reached for and pawed at John as he passed. He didn't know why he was there; he wanted to leave so badly. But

something made him move forward. He had to keep going. He had to know. He had to make it right.

One woman snatched him hard, almost taking him down onto the dirt floor.

"Let's have fun," she moaned as John's skin crawled. Another was sliding her hands under his shirt, but he pushed her away.

He had to keep going.

He had to know.

He had to make it right.

He scrambled to his feet and pushed through the throng of bodies. He shoved off hands grabbing at him; whether they wanted to snare him, hurt him, or take his soul—he didn't know.

He had to keep going.

He had to know.

He had to make it right.

He needed to push through the darkness; he had to get back to Shelley, to the girls. To fresh air. To the sky. To the light.

Finally, the horde pulled away and one figure remained. The surrounding glow burned John's eyes and radiated into his soul.

The face was unmistakable and hard like marble. His gaze cut through John's soul.

The Archangel Michael, sword in hand and standing between him and what looked like an almost translucent curtain, stared down at John with the fire of the heavens. John was pinned under it, almost forced to his knees. The moment stretched into an eternity as the divine weighed John's heart.

He doubted whether he was worthy of leaving this place. He prayed to God that he was.

Slowly, Michael stretched his wings, the silent movement imbued with the kind of power a lion uses to stalk its prey. John's breath caught as the angel turned to the side, his sword beckoning John to see who he was protecting. The veil was now clear.

Mary, Mother of God.

Now he was outside, clear of the dungeon behind him. Everything–the darkness, the rot, the demons, the shadow of death–all melted away except for her. John began to weep. Love, like waves, washed over him. Compas-

sion and mercy washed through him. Its warmth radiated through him like sunshine.

She did not say a word. She just smiled.

It was going to be okay.

She led him forward, through the third veil, and brought John to see her Son.

You are going to be alright.

24 SEP 1996 // WILFORD HALL, LACKLAND AFB, SAN ANTONIO, TEXAS // 0900L

John violently popped up in bed with a gasp, startling Shelley. She too had dozed off, sitting on one side of the bed. His mother sat on the other side, deep in prayer for her son.

His eyes were bugged out, staring past the foot of his bed at some unseen vision.

"Shelley, we have to change everything. We have to dedicate our lives to Him! To service!"

Shelley, bewildered and more than a little taken aback, tried to calm him. "Okay, honey, okay."

John tried to describe what he had just seen, but was still too shaken to get it all out. "Shelley..."

Once he could describe what had just happened to him, John's mom said fervently, "It was a vision, my son. It was real. Thanks be to God!"

THE NIGHTMARES ABATED. John prayed more often, especially as he dozed off. He had been moved by what he saw, despite his own doubts that it could have been drug-induced. He started to experience different dreams.

He was running towards a large, looming 30-foot wall. Wearing his tan t-shirt and combat fatigue trousers and boots. He was scaling a cargo net obstacle at a beachside obstacle O-course in the sand. Wet with sweat dripping off him, dirty and encrusted with sand, with only another eight feet to go to get to the top. With his God-given legs. Arms aching, straining and groaning, but not in pain. He was about to scale the tricky cargo net in Coronado, where Navy SEALs go through their brutal gauntlet. He grasped the top of the net, panting, trying to heave himself up and over. A group of rowdy SEALs crowded below his feet.

C'mon, man, you can do it! *They shouted up at him.* Get it, Alvarez! Get it, L.T.!

And then his eyes cracked open, squinting. He could make out the metal guardrails on either side of his bed, raised to stop him from rolling off the bed in the middle of the night. The bloodied bandage wrapped around the end of his stump and the blood-stained sheet. The uncomfortable, almost claustrophobic, sensation of his right knee feeling locked up, immobilized in the rigid, soft-sided cast.

He would wake up and he would look at his legs again, and his heart would sink right back into despair. He would immediately start praying. Then he worked on his breath control, mindfulness, scanning his body, and envisioned being enveloped in light, urging it to heal him. He would methodically visualize again.

He saw himself running, jumping, climbing, but this time...with a robotic, tactical-looking, bad-ass leg.

Mind over matter. Son, focus on what you can control and create your future.

John smiled as his father's reassuring voice rang in his head. Then he'd chuckle at the thought of another voice in his head. His old drill instructor, Gunnery Sergeant Holtry, United States Marine Corps.

I don't mind...and you don't matter. Maggot!

Despite projecting a strong and positive front to the staff and his family, behind that facade John was still filled with pain and guilt. A week into his stay at Wilford Hall, John's father finally arrived from Tibet.

John knew that his parents, Juan and Carmen Alvarez, were not the kind of people who shied away from the mystical. Their Miami-based bookstore, *The Fairy's Ring*, was founded upon decades of deep spiritual experience and practice. Carmen had told John she had a headache the day of his accident, and she shared the vision she received while on a healing massage table. As she was drifting into a meditative state, her husband's Tibetan guide, a Buddhist monk, appeared before her. The man was wrapped in shining orange and gold robes. His expression was deeply solemn. The monk said nothing, but Carmen suddenly knew something terrible had happened. She then rushed home and found Shelley's phone message.

When Juan Alvarez arrived from Tibet, he shared a similar vision with Carmen, then John and Shelley. Around the same hour of John's accident, a nightmare of an explosion off the western horizon had startled Juan awake in the middle of the night. He painfully knew it was his Johnny, that something terrible had happened to his son. Juan had told the Buddhist monks about the dream, and they immediately went to the temple to conduct a ritual of cleansing and protection for his son. Juan the elder would soon desperately begin his trek back halfway across the globe.

Juan engrained self discipline, mindfulness, self control and the philosophy of the stoics in John and his brother Jorge as long as John could remember, starting with quarter-dollar bets that they could not sit still and just breathe for a minute. The bounty increased gradually, and the lessons became more profound. Juan also embraced spirituality and the power of prayer openly with his children.

The relief of having his family surrounding him was enough to make John accept the intensity of what had happened.

However, he was still conflicted. He was angry with Javier. He was also angry at himself, guilt-ridden while thinking about Javier's death and thinking about what had happened to Matt. Joe had told him that Matt was planning to finish the tour out in Ecuador with the SEAL team. He had been okay enough for that, but something in Matt's spine was still messed up.

Over and over, John told himself that he should have taken over.

He could have intervened sooner. He should have monitored the pilots better. He should not have been on that flight. If only he had listened to his 'gut.' The only consolation, other than returning Shelley and the girls, was that he had taken Mike's flight and that it could have been Mike Hargis in his place.

Could have, should have, would have...

9

EAT THE PAIN

24 SEP 1996 // WILFORD HALL, SAN ANTONIO, TEXAS //

S helley felt that the pain was the worst part. Pain was John's constant companion. It refused to let him sleep, let him even rest or nap. And with consciousness came irritation. John was good at maintaining a positive demeanor despite everything, but he was still short-fused and regularly snapped at family and medical personnel alike.

About a week into the hospital stay, they had switched him to a private room, and Shelley asked about getting him an epidural. The attending thought it would be great, especially since he would still have to undergo surgery to close his stump. An early epidural would solve two problems at once. The process was going to be difficult, however, because his legs were fixed straight out. In order for the anesthesiologist to get the needle between the disks in his spine, he had to curve forward. Curving forward when you have broken ribs, your legs are completely horizontal, and your entire body is in pain makes such flexibility extremely uncomfortable.

Shelley sat in front of John, holding him in place. The anesthesiologist was totally silent, prepping his tray. Shelley knew all anesthe-siologists were *de facto* "anal retentive". Everything has to be in place; one wrong dosage during surgery and you're dead. The whole time, John was squawking.

The doctor, of course, could hear him. "What's taking so long, Doc?" John barked. "It shouldn't take forever to stick some goddamn needle in my back." He muttered to Shelley. "He's taking his sweet time..."

Shelley tried not to smile at his complaining. It was the only way he could have control over his situation, which was honestly miser-able. The whole time John was talking, the doctor gave no sign that he cared. Then, of course, he stood up to start the procedure. Both Shelley and John could see he was wearing a pair of very colorful running shoes. They were a mash of yellow and blue. Gaudy, to some people. Of course, John could not resist.

"He even has stupid-looking shoes," John said.

Oh my god, Shelley thought, trying not to let John see her nearly burst out laughing. He was ready to rip someone's head off anyway. *This guy's putting a needle in your back and you're insulting his shoes!*

"What's taking so long?" John repeated. Shelley tried to convey covert sympathy to the doc with her eyes.

Not a minute later, the doctor stepped back. "Okay, it's done."

"Well, it's not even *working!*"

It was hilarious how quickly it changed him. John went from furi-ous, and then he took a breath. Immediately, almost all the tension released from his body. His eyes cleared. Shelley was amazed. He was her *Johnny* again. For the first time in a week, he was pain-free. Shelley could compare it to being in labor. You're in excruciating pain, and as soon as you get the epidural, your mood switches instan-taneously. This time, it was less *Woo-hoo, I'm having a baby, and it doesn't hurt anymore!* and more *Woo-hoo I'm* alive, *and it doesn't hurt anymore!*

～

25 SEP 1996 // WILFORD HALL, LACKLAND AFB, SAN ANTONIO, TEXAS //

"Hey L.T.," one of the doctors asked him after one particularly rough night. It had been almost a week since the crash. "You know, if you want to see someone, like a psychologist or a chaplain, we can make that happen for you."

John immediately knew his preference. "Chaplain, Sir!"

The Air Force chaplain who visited didn't look like what John expected. He was a Catholic priest, a Latino like John, but instead of softness, there was something steady and battle-worn in his face. His eyes were dark, observant—eyes that had seen men at their worst and had not turned away.

He introduced himself to John, offering his hand. "I hear you've been carrying something heavy."

John gave a brief nod. "Yes, sir."

"I was a prison chaplain before the Air Force," the chaplain said. "Men there had stories they couldn't outrun. Stories that followed them into their sleep." He held John's gaze. "Is that what's happening to you?"

John swallowed. "I've been having nightmares. They're better now; I've been praying, but I can't shake this feeling of guilt."

The chaplain leaned forward slightly. "Would you like to pray with me?"

John hesitated only a second before nodding. They bowed their heads. When they finished, the chaplain didn't move away. John's stomach knotted; he knew what was going to be asked next.

"Tell me about the crash," he said.

John stared at the wall for a long moment. Then he began. The morning decision to swap with Mike. The command to pull up. The sound of the impact. The shock of cold water that swallowed everything. The bargain he made with God, and his miraculous rescue. The pain of knowing Javier might have drowned because John could not get him his HEEDs bottle. The fact that Javier was dead.

"What thought comes back the most?" the chaplain asked.

"That I should have done more. That it was my fault." John's voice cracked. "That maybe I could've—"

"Saved Javier?"

John nodded.

The chaplain let the silence stretch.

"John," he said at last, "I want you to tell the story again."

John couldn't believe what he was hearing. His head was pounding. His heart felt raw. "Again?"

"Yes," the priest said, his face calm but insistent. "But this time, imagine you're sitting in a movie theater. You're watching it on a screen, and you are several rows back from it. It's not happening now. It already happened. Yes, it is unpleasant. Do not ignore its gravity. You're not in it, though. You're in a chair, not the cockpit, not in the canoe."

John winced, shook his head, and huffed. He could already feel his body seizing up, defending itself from the wash of fear and dread of reliving that day yet again. *Breathe!*

"I know..." the chaplain acknowledged. "But you're creating distance. You are not in the river right now. You're here. In this room. With me."

He waited.

Slowly, John began again.

"This is a film," he reminded him when John's breathing quickened. "You're watching it. What do you see?"

"I see... the aircraft going down," John said, voice unsteady. "I see the water coming up."

"And what do you feel in your body right now?" Check your breath. Breathe. "Notice your heart beating, scan your body, unclench your jaw, exhale, and center yourself."

"My leg hurts."

"Stay here," the priest said firmly but gently. "Feel the chair beneath you. Feel your breath. The crash is out away from you on your mental screen. You are *here*."

John would retell it again and again over the following days. Sometimes John would stop halfway through, overcome with guilt and dread. Sometimes he would grit his teeth and finish. Each time, the chaplain guided him back to the present.

Sometimes the story did not bother him, but his present physical and phantom pain did. The priest would pray with him to ask God to relieve the compounded burden. It reminded John of his dad's lessons in breath control and mindfulness.

"You will tell this story," the chaplain said one afternoon, "until it becomes a memory, not a wound that reopens every time you touch it. I promise you. Soon you will tell it without reliving it."

26 SEP 1996 // WILFORD HALL, LACKLAND AFB, TEXAS //

The priest organized a Mass for Javier Perez. John rolled his wheelchair into the small hospital chapel. He had insisted on wearing his Navy khaki uniform shirt with lieutenant bars that Mike Stuart had lent him. A soft white blanket was draped around his waist and legs. *Military honors.* When John heard Javier's name spoken aloud during the prayers of the faithful, something inside him finally lifted.

The mass for Javier helped, but the reality of the hospital continued. Wilford Hall was the Air Force's premiere teaching hospital. Not only was John's sleep interrupted by pain, but he would also get woken up at dawn by small groups of residents walking in and doing their patient rounds. John was the hospital's most interesting current case, but that did not make him feel any less cranky about it.

Finally, one early, groggy morning, John snapped.

"Can you cut it out? I can't get sleep as it is, and you guys are strolling in and out of here like you're out of fucking *ER!*"

Jorge "Georgie" Alvarez flew in around that time. The second Alvarez child and his nefariously gregarious attitude lightened the mood. Jorge was also annoyed at the residents on behalf of his big brother. Laptop computers were just becoming more common in 1996, and Jorge had brought his into John's hospital room one morning before shift change. The entire entourage of residents, once again, arrived at John's hospital room. This time, the lead doctor asked if it was okay for them to enter. John said yes.

And as soon as they started trickling into the room, Jorge played the *ER* theme from his laptop. *ER* was a hugely popular medical emergency room drama set in Chicago. Its urgent instrumental theme music was instantly recognizable. He managed not only to instigate laughs but also to make a point. The senior resident, Dr. Gary Benedetti, stepped in a little later and assured them only he or the attending—Dr. Keith Bolyard—would be the ones coming in and checking up on him from then on. It was little comfort. John had gotten to the point where he just wanted to sleep and forget everything else around him.

Carmen upheld a familiar Catholic spiritual conviction for John's sake. She anointed John with holy water from the holy pilgrimage site in Lourdes, France whenever she could. When she noticed the full moon up, she went out at night and prayed for John's healing. His mother could see the darkness surrounding her son. She felt as if the spirit of Javier Perez was still clinging to John.

Jorge had protested when, on their way back to the Fisher house one night, Carmen stopped in the middle of the street to pray under the moon. John's brother was clearly uncomfortable with the spiritual spectacle on a military installation.

"What if someone sees her, John?" Jorge said. "She's outside praying and muttering to herself...Dude, it might get our mother arrested!"

John laughed; his ribs hurt.

"Look, try to see Mom's side of things," John replied. "This is her way of coping; she doesn't have much control over the situation. I mean, how would you feel if it was one of your kids?"

Jorge started comically chanting in response.

～

27 SEP 1996 // WILFORD HALL, LACKLAND AFB, SAN ANTONIO, TEXAS //

Shelley hated call bells, and she knew why other nurses hated them. People would abuse them. Patients would hit that bell when they sneezed, or at the slightest discomfort or inconvenience. It was often used to gain control over what felt like an uncontrollable situation. She always felt bad using the call bell, so she tried to head to the nurses' station instead to ask for something John needed. Most of the nurses knew from very early on that Shelley was also a nurse. She got used to expecting professional courtesy.

Except for this one nurse. Once, Shelley went to the nurses' station to ask for something for John. It had been the first time in the day she had gone up to the station, but as soon as Shelley got into view of this one particular nurse, the woman rolled her eyes. Shelley realized immediately she would not like this nurse.

Early in the second week of his stay at Wilford Hall, John was scheduled for a revision and closure of the stump of his left leg.

The doctors had explained to Shelley and John that John's left stump had been open-packed with gauze. The revision surgery would address a number of issues. They would need to debride and slice away the raw, granulated tissue left from the old guillotine cut. A rasp scraper would be used to manually grind down the tibia's sharp edges to a smooth, rounded bevel. Each major nerve would then be clamped, stretched tight under tension, and then snipped so the nerve endings snapped back deep into the muscle to be protected from future pressure. The surgeon would then insert a tube deep into the muscle to collect and suction any blood pooling in the area. This vacuum, for the following forty-eight hours, would draw out blood and fluid to keep the stump from swelling.

It would be a long and difficult procedure—and likely one that would need to be repeated throughout his life due to common bone spurs—but, in the end, it would allow John to more quickly adapt to a prosthetic.

The family was told to wait in the family waiting area. Hours later,

Shelley received a call during surgery to tell them he was doing fine. They were told John would be in surgery for another half hour, and then he would be in post-op for another half-hour. Afterwards, the family could come with him back to his room.

THE EPIDURAL WAS SUPPOSED to be pumping drugs into his system to block the pain the entire time while they were operating. It had slipped out of position. So, when John woke up in pain and with a crew of masked doctors staring down at him with confusion, it was a bit of a shock.

He could almost hear their wide eyes asking, *What the hell are you doing awake?*

"Doc," John said, "it's starting to hurt." *Damn, this hurts.*

The pain ramped up very quickly. John started to say the Lord's Prayer and Hail Mary over and over again as the doctors tried to quickly put him back under.

He could hear someone screaming over on the other side of the room through an almost translucent curtain separating them. Maybe it was the adjacent bay area. It was kind of horrible.

Man, he thought, *that poor guy must be in a lot of pain. Pray for him.*

John did not realize that he was the only patient in the room as he went back under.

SHELLEY MONITORED THE CLOCK. Time clicked by. Forty minutes after post-op. Then an hour. Did the doctors take him upstairs and not tell them?

Shelley went up to the room to check. No John. She went back to the nurses' station. The nurse, the rude one, was at the station.

"Hi, I'm Shelley Alvarez." She tried her best to be polite. "My husband is Juan Alvarez. He was in surgery; they said he'd be out no later than thirty minutes ago. It's been an hour. Do you know what's going on?"

Initially, the nurse seemed cordial enough. "Let me check. Give me a second," she told her, heading to the phone.

Maybe she's not so bad, Shelley thought as the nurse spoke on the phone.

"Yeah okay. Okay. Okay, thanks. Bye." The nurse came back to the front. "Yeah, he's still in post-op. They're having some problems with pain control." Her next words were delivered with the flippant air of someone without an ounce of empathy. "At least that's what I could tell because I could hear him screaming in the background."

Shelley inhaled, her skin prickling with a chill and an urge to punch the nurse in the face. "Okay, thanks." She turned and went back to the family waiting room. *How can you say that to someone? You do not say that someone's husband is screaming in pain!*

It was, thankfully and coincidentally, the last time Shelley laid eyes on that nurse.

They did not try to insert the epidural again. The post-op pain was brutal, and John went back to being the frustrated—and frustrating—version of her husband. She had that emotion again—helplessness. She hated that feeling. She was helpless in taking the pain away. She could provide some emotional comfort, but she had no control over her loved one's physical pain. It did not help that they were now in a second week into a hospital stay.

28 SEP 1996 // WILFORD HALL, LACKLAND AFB, SAN ANTONIO, TEXAS //

Shelley and John asked his attending doctor about physical therapy. He agreed that light PT would be a good thing. John was determined to get out of bed, as it was his prison. He just wanted to stand to pee and go to the bathroom, and be able to clean himself.

Jorge jokingly would challenge John to do pull-ups on the bar overhead meant to assist the patient in sitting up. John instinctively accepted the challenge from his little brother. John would attempt curls just to pass the time. His ribs protested and creaked. His stump tingled, and involuntary tremors pulsed through him with what felt like electrical shocks. Phantom pain. He'd try to smile back at his brother with a strained look. *Eat the pain!*

Physical therapy turned out to be the turning point in his demeanor. John's PT lead was an Air Force Lieutenant; a big kid who played college football.

John's progress was swift; with simple rubber exercise bands attached to his bed rails, he was almost immediately able to transfer from his bed to a wheelchair. He'd wheel himself down to the PT clinic if the techs were not early enough to get him. He'd try to ride wheelies. The PT tech smiled but kept a close eye on him. John wanted to stay in PT rather than get back into bed.

He was being fitted for a custom wheelchair that had been ordered for him because they had already decided he needed one for at least six months. The local company that supplied the wheelchair was owned by a former Navy SEAL. When he found out John was a Naval Aviator, flew Pave-Lows, *and* had been deployed with SEALs, he showed up with a top of the line wheelchair instead of the standard rental. John now had a chariot to escape the confines of his bed. His wheelies would get better, much to the chagrin of Shelley.

"Don't worry about it, L.T.," the former SEAL told John when he asked about the price. "I'm taking care of a brother. All I want is for you to be walking when you get rid of this chair."

Later, a second Air Force chaplain showed up in John's room in uniform during rounds. John saw he was wearing Navy wings. Naval Flight Officer wings, in fact.

NFO wings? On an Air Force uniform? On a chaplain? How many chaplains out there have warfighter wings? John thought as the chaplain introduced himself. The chaplain told him he had been a Vietnam-era Marine Corps back-seater in F-4 Phantom jets.

"Hey, I don't know if this means anything to you," the chaplain said, "but when I was in pre-flight training in Pensacola in the early sixties, I saw the damndest thing. There was a Navy lieutenant on the obstacle course, working out near us. And he had two wooden legs."

John sat up straighter. "Really?"

"All we knew was that this Navy pilot was trying to get back to flight status." The chaplain/NFO shrugged apologetically. "I don't know his name or whatever happened to the guy. I just thought maybe you might be interested." That revelation changed something for John. It was a spark of hope.

John's assigned chaplain also had just given him a book to read: *One Tough Marine*. It detailed the legendary story of First Sergeant Donald N. Hamblen, a Reconnaissance Marine who lost his leg in a 1962 parachute accident. The memoir recounted his recovery and return to duty as a Special Operations advisor behind enemy lines during the Vietnam War. The book also briefly mentioned an unnamed Navy pilot who returned to the cockpit after having a leg amputated. Nothing else about him.

John re-read those fleeting few sentences over and over. He recalled what Colonel Hull had said to him. He thought about what the chaplain said to him.

He's out there! There's someone out there who's done this before!

It would take a miracle for him to fly again. He decided right there. He was determined that he would be free. Free of his wheelchair and free again to reach for the sky. Free to dance with Shelley and their girls.

The spark, now a red-hot ember, seared into John.

29 SEP 1996 // WILFORD HALL, LACKLAND AFB, TEXAS //

When the pain receded, however, other concerns lingered. Shelley saw that the emotional trauma was still taking its toll. John refused to let people sit in the space underneath his left knee. Dr. Ockey, an Air Force major and podiatrist who oversaw the prosthetics and orthotics shop, visited. He was very nice, a Mormon and a family man. He was also the first person to sit in the space where John's foot used to be.

"Doc, look," John said, his voice tight. Shelley felt for him. "Do you mind? That's where my leg was. Can you not sit there?"

Dr. Ockey carefully stood. "Okay, yeah, we'll honor that."

Aside from the reality of his body, Shelley could see that her husband had to face the vast, uncertain future in front of him. He was drinking a lot of Metamucil, and since his catheter had been removed, he was using a plastic urinal and bedpan. He had to pull himself up by the trapeze/metal triangle suspended from a bar installed across his bed to go on and off the bedpan. Shelley and his brother, Jorge, had to help clean him up. It was degrading on top of being painful. But Shelley was grateful she wasn't the only one trying to relieve John's pain–physical or emotional.

Shelley would catch John blowing into his spirometer and would encourage him. To John, it was not just a game. He would tell her it reminded him of his heroes from the movie *'The Right Stuff'*, which was about the original Mercury astronauts who underwent a lung capacity test that quickly devolved into intense competition.

Whatever works, my Johnny A, whatever works.

Shelley, meanwhile, had settled into her own routine. She would stay overnight at the hospital in a reclining chair, wake up in the morning, and go shower at the Fisher house when Carmen and Juan arrived in the hospital room. It helped catch her breath and be outside.

In the fall of 1996, San Antonio saw an unusual influx of beautiful little yellow butterflies, known as cloudless sulphur butterflies. Besides monarch butterflies, these bright yellow butterflies' normal migration patterns peak in September and October. Carmen called them a "good omen". Whether or not they were, Shelley loved how they would be a surprise for her every day. When she would go out in the morning, the bushes and trees were literally covered in butterflies.

One afternoon, Carmen met Shelley outside the hospital room.

She asked to talk for a moment. John's mother looked anxious, which in turn made Shelley a little anxious.

"I'm worried about John."

"What? Why?" Shelley asked. With PT and more movement, he seemed to be much happier.

"John is upset," Carmen told her. "He doesn't think you will see him as a man anymore."

Shelley's jaw nearly fell through the linoleum. "*What?*"

John had given no sign that he was worried about their marriage, or about her attraction to him. To think he was hiding his feelings from her... well, she was pissed. *Are you kidding me? He's gone through all this and he's gonna come up with this crap?*

She did not wait for Carmen's answer; she stormed into the room ready to chew him out for daring to even *think*—

As she walked through the door, however, she looked at the room. The white walls, the hospital smell, the machines. *He has got to get out of this room and outside,* she realized. His wheelchair sat beside his bed.

John lit up and smiled as Shelley walked into the room. It did not necessarily change her mood.

"That's it," she barked. "We're going outside."

John's smile faltered. "Okay?"

The nursing staff okayed his outing. Soaking in the September Texas sun was a blessing for John. He hated when they had to go back inside, so John and Shelley made it a practice to take time to get some sun for at least an hour a day for the rest of his hospital stay. Soon he and Shelley would not only eat lunch outside, they'd spend as much time out in the courtyard together as they could.

Later, when Shelley talked to John about what his mother told her, she learned Carmen had lied about *John* being worried. It was Carmen's way of voicing her own fear. Shelley understood, but did not feel the need to confront her about it. Shelley knew—and John knew—she wasn't going anywhere. She loved John deeply. He was her soulmate and the love of her life. She had made a vow, and she was more than happy sticking to it.

She even arranged some private time to make him *feel like a man* again.

30 SEP 1996 // WILFORD HALL, LACKLAND AFB, SAN ANTONIO, TEXAS //

Shelley was tired of being snapped at by her husband. He was irritable and ornery. For example, John would want a drink of water. Someone would take it from the table to give the cup to him, and when he handed it back, they would be yelled at because they did not replace it exactly where it had been before.

She overheard John's brother talking to his wife on the phone after one such incident.

"Shelley's a friggin' saint for putting up with him," Jorge said to her.

Not everyone thought about it like that. She could feel the eyes on her, people judging whether she would be the kind of wife who would abandon her husband after such a trauma. Whether she was considering a life of caretaking another dependent along with her young girls. On the better days, she could shrug off the insinuations. She was confident in her relationship with John, and his confidence in her. No one else could take that from them.

But on the bad days? She felt alone.

Even if Shelley knew, intellectually, why John was so nasty, she would still steam over it. She was his wife, and he could *not* talk to her like that. It also did not help that Carmen was watching their petty arguments. This was her baby boy, who has gone through a huge trauma, and his wife is getting annoyed with him. It made for many uncomfortable moments.

Around this time, they were preparing for John's return home. A social worker visited to help make a list of physical things they would need to take home with them: a wheelchair, commode chair, and things of that nature. John was cranky and dazed from pain medication; he was zoning in and out of the conversation. Shelley knew she could do the list. She was a nurse, of course. She knew what they had at home and what they would need.

So when she told him, "Don't worry, honey, I got this," she meant it from a place of professional capacity. John, however, took it as patronizing.

"I want you to be a *wife*," John hissed, "not a *nurse*."

Shelley shut down. "Alright, you want me to be a wife and not a nurse?" she replied, sickly sweet. "You got it. Fine. I'm a wife now." She picked up a magazine. "Don't ask me any medical questions. I'm a *wife*."

Shelley read and sulked through the rest of the day. Working in the hospital was where her control was. As a nurse, she could understand the medical side of things. It was her comfort zone after his accident. Nursing John was primarily the way she could feel useful to him. When he tore that away—trying to maintain his own control after *his* trauma—she was left hurt, and her feeling of powerlessness was overwhelming. So yes, she was angry as well, but mostly she was wounded.

A nurse came in later in the evening. She was doing something with John's morphine pump. Shelley, still suffering from bruised feelings, was not really listening. The nurse asked John about how much morphine he was getting.

John turned to Shelley, "How much am I getting an hour?"

She looked up, stony-faced. "I don't know, I'm not a nurse!" Shelley went back to her book.

Later that evening, it was time to set hurt feelings aside and reconnect. One of the strengths of their marriage was that they could rarely stay angry at each other for more than a few hours.

John asked Shelley to lie in bed beside him. She curled up against his left side with her head on his chest. He fell back asleep as she listened to his heartbeat and felt his chest gently rise and fall.

She thought of how close it had come to his heart stopping and his breathing ceasing. A few years later, Faith Hill's song "Breathe" would bring Shelley back to that moment and reduce her to tears.

~

01 OCT 1996 // WILFORD HALL, LACKLAND AFB, SAN ANTONIO, TEXAS //

In the middle of his stay at Wilford Hall, a few of the SEALs from NSWU 8 and Golf Platoon had presented him with a plaque, anointing him with a new callsign: "LT AHAB". John's dreams were riddled with both promise and despair, but he sensed that being a pilot was something he couldn't simply walk (ha!) away from.

John's priest, whom John was now calling Padre, came by one afternoon for their usual chats.

"So, what are your goals, son?" the priest asked.

"I have a few, Padre," John said. "I don't want to be in a wheelchair for the next six months. I want to dance, dance with Shelley and my girls again."

"Okay, then," the priest said. "I suggest you tie some of those goals to personally meaningful dates."

John decided he needed to talk to Shelley about his future. *Their* future. John had already talked to her about Colonel Hull's insistence on bringing him back to flying Pave Lows. She also knew about the chaplain who came by and Hamblen's mention of an unnamed Navy pilot.

"So you want to fly again." Shelley confirmed, her face calm. John could only imagine the worry she was keeping in for his sake. "What do you need to do to make that happen?"

"Being DNIF'd, it's pretty straightforward," John explained. "I have a year to fly again."

In the Air Force, the acronym DNIF stands for Duties Not Including Flying. In Naval Aviation, the term is Not Physically Qualified (NPQ). Both require formal medical documentation. In the Air Force, it's referred to as a DNIF (dee-nif) form, and in the Navy, it's informally called a 'Down' Chit. The physical paper document is placed in an officer's medical and flight records, stating the reason for grounding, restrictions, and expected review date. Only a flight surgeon can take you 'off DNIF' status (Air Force) or declare you 'Up' (Navy). That same form is again dated and signed by the appropriate authority to return you to flight status; in this case, a flight surgeon. They are interchangeable in both services.

John was considered DNIF'd or "down" the day of his crash and injury on September 19th, 1996.

Normally, DNIF is a temporary status for flyers when they are deemed medically unfit to fly. It can be as simple as a cold or excessive congestion, a broken finger, or more severe like an amputation. This status means the airman cannot perform their flying duties, but they are still usually able to report for other non-flying military duties.

The catch is if you are DNIF for *over* 365 consecutive days. This triggers several implications. The first is financial; you lose your flight pay. Second, your aviation career is at risk, and you face separation from the military. Your designation as a Naval Aviator, which you fought so hard to become, is now gone. Your identity is stripped away from you.

If LT "Ahab" Alvarez wanted to fly again, he had just one year to do so.

That day, with Shelley by his side, John proclaimed his three simple goals:

1. Walk into his aunt's house for that Thanksgiving. November 28, 1996.
2. Run on Lisette's birthday. February 22nd, 1997.
3. Fly within a year of the accident. September 19th, 1997.

02 OCT 1996 // WILFORD HALL, SAN ANTONIO, TEXAS //

Shelley hoped she was seeing the end coming. John's progress was enough that he was being considered for temporary discharge to go home to Florida and home to the girls; with the caveat of returning to Wilford Hall for further treatment a couple of weeks later. Shelley and John also had to figure out how they were going to tell the girls about the amputation. Shelley's mom, Pat, was still with the girls in Navarre.

As part of his departure protocol, John and Shelley had a consultation with a social worker. The advice was clear and laid out in plain terms.

"They're gonna deal with it depending on how well you two deal with it."

As a team, the two phrased their response carefully to their girls. They would not even imply the doctors *took* or *had to remove* the leg, rather that the doctors tried to save it.

"And now the cool part," John said over the phone to Nicole and Lisette, "the doctors are going to make me a robot leg! Won't that be awesome? We can dance and sing the Cheeseburger song together!"

Honestly, they did not seem to understand. They were more concerned about when their parents were coming home.

With departure well within their grasp, Shelley's sensation of helplessness still lingered, and was brought to a head when John developed a fever in the evening.

"I don't know what to do. I'm going to lose him," Shelley sobbed to her mother over the phone. "I can't do this. After everything, I'm going to lose him to an *infection*."

They had been trying to get John processed out of the hospital for days. Things had become easier. John was healing; his pain was better managed. They could even bring him out to a restaurant. The doctors agreed to begin homecoming preparations, with John needing to return to Wilford Hall in two weeks.

However, John kept popping a low fever at night, just around 99 or 100 degrees. The doctors had done a blood culture, looking for some kind of infection that would raise John's body temperature. They were afraid to discharge him in case it was an infection. To Shelley, it was the straw that broke the camel's back. She was tired; she wanted to go home to their sanctuary where she could heal him, where she could heal as well. Going through everything only to be stopped or stalled by the possibility of infection was too much.

After she calmed down, Shelley remembered something. John was *always* a furnace at night. He was her own personal bed warmer; he radiated heat at night. When nothing came in on the blood culture, Shelley mentioned this to one of the doctors. It was the same intern from the 20th SOS, in fact, who had coin-checked John when he first arrived.

"You know," he told her, "they can't take his temperature if he's not there during their rounds."

Yeah, well, Shelley thought, *they'll track you down. Eventually.*

But she had another idea to beat the system. She knew the nurse came in at around 8:30 pm. She would get John to drink water, not ice water, right before the nurse came in. The goal would be to make the temperature in his mouth slightly cooler than it actually was, tricking the thermometer when placed into his mouth.

It worked.

Home. Soon, I'll be taking my Johnny A home!

19 SEP 1996 // Wreckage of the Gazelle helicopter recovered a couple days after the crash.
Courtesy of LT Rick Ledbury, US Navy

28 MAY 1987 // First salute with Gunnery Sergeant Holtry, USMC.

1988 // T-34B Navy primary flight trainer (Naval Air Station Corpus Christi, Texas)

1988 // Shelley and I met on February 29th (a leap year) in a country western bar on rock night. I asked her to dance and that was it - whirlwind romance.

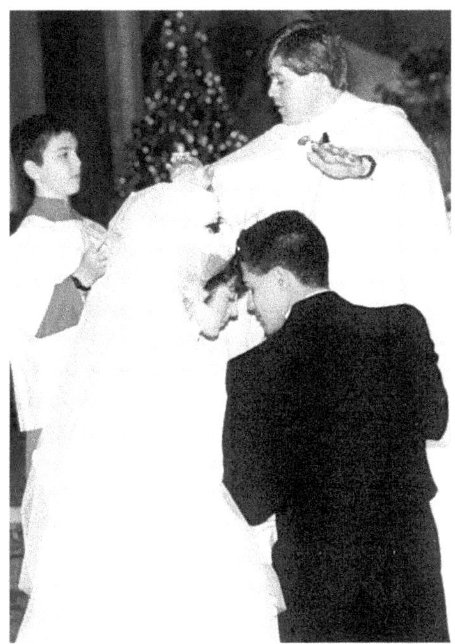

JAN 1989 // Shelley and I were married in front of God and our families in a Catholic church near her hometown. For six months before our wedding, we kept a secret - we had gotten legally hitched in a courthouse less than four months after meeting.

MAR 1989 // One of my proudest moments was having my grandfather, Antonio Mori, slam my Navy Wings of Gold onto my chest. (Naval Air Station Milton, Florida)

1990 // Landing the mighty MH-53E Sea Dragon on a Navy Amphibious ship in the Pacific Ocean. (Courtesy of LT Mark Augustave, US Navy)

1989-1992 // Assigned to my first operational unit: Helicopter Mine Countermeasures Squadron Fifteen (HM-15) - pictured with my first boss and mentor LCDR Len King.

SEP 1991 // The most important assignment, and one of the hardest tasks I had to carry out, was being the Casualty Affairs Coordination Officer (CACO) for a friend and fellow Blackhawk - LTJg Craig Valentine. He was lost along with seven other crew members in the Persian Gulf on 14 SEP.

1991-1994 // Cuddling with my girls

22 JUN 1994 // My Lil' Parrot Heads in Hawaii.

26 SEP 1994 // My future aerospace engineer.

27 JUL 1996 // Last family picture before deployment to Ecuador - at the wishing well in the Magic Kingdom, Florida.

1990-1998 // Pictures of Shelley and the girls I carried on deployments.

SEP 1996 // Selva (jungle) survival course meant eating lemon ants and pirañas. (front row from left: Lt Col Rick Newton, LT John Alvarez, Capt Mike Hargis)

SEP 1996 // Formation flying in the Ecuadorian Army Aérospatiale SA 342L Gazelle helicopters.

SEP 1996 // 'Strapping in' the cockpit with Ecuadoran Army pilot Lt Javier Perez. The HEEDS steel pony scuba tank & LPU pouch are under my left armpit. As a leftie, my holster was on my right side of my vest or strapped to my left thigh. (Courtesy of Capt. Joe "Doc B" Basinger)

SEP 1996 // Cayuca (canoe) ride to village. (from left: Capt Joe "Doc B" Basinger, Combat Controller, LT Alvarez)

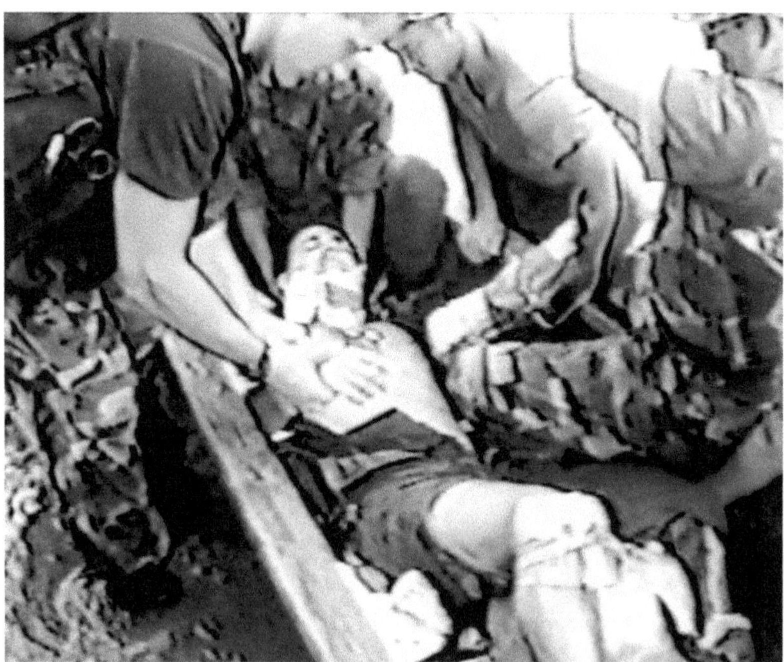

19 SEP 1996 // Doc B and HTFN Jeremy Trump initiating critical care to me in the cayuca just within the "golden hour" after the crash. (Video still by Petty Officer David Scott, US Navy)

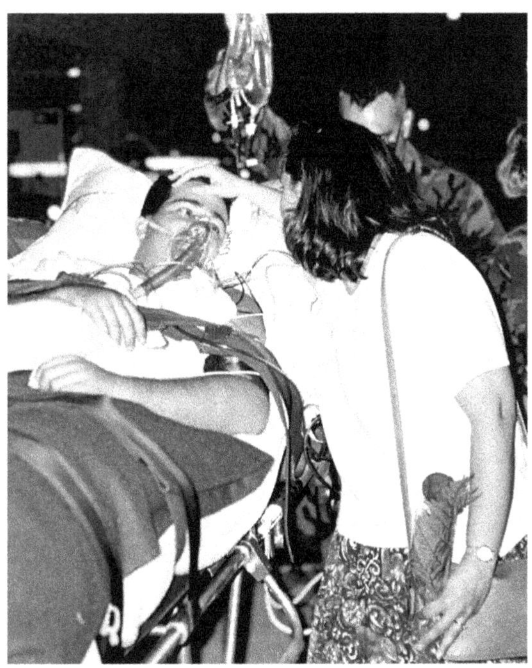

21 SEP 1996 // After a 2,433 mile flight in a C-141B Starlifter, Shelley finally got her hand(s) on me. I also delivered my precious cargo - two wrapped teddy bears for the girls and a rose for her (Wilford Hall Medical Center Texas).

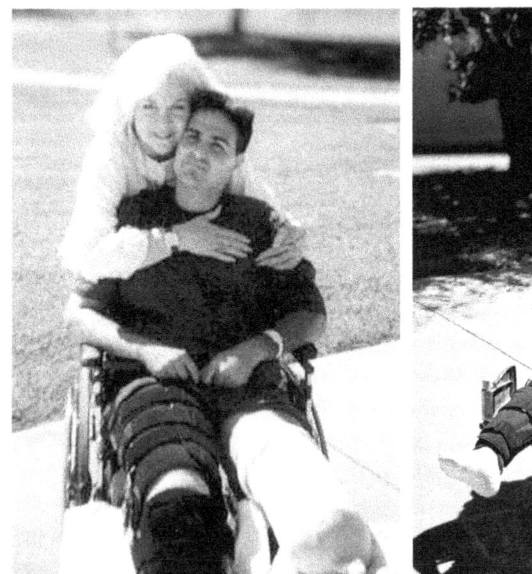

SEP 1996 // A week later with my mom, Carmen, and dad, Juan.

29 SEP 1996 // Much needed visit by Doc B and my brother, Jorge.
Jorge would challenge me to do pull-ups with the trapeze handle over
the bed.

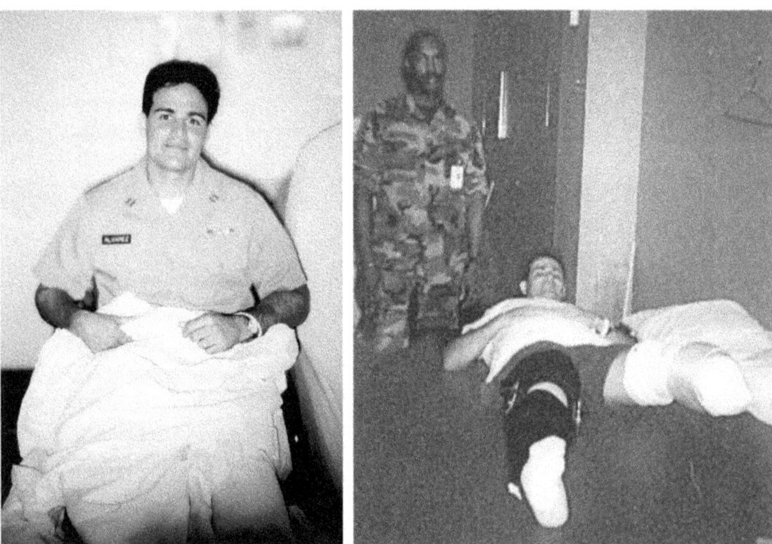

OCT 1996 // Projecting a motivated and positive attitude.
Haircut, uniform, and PT.

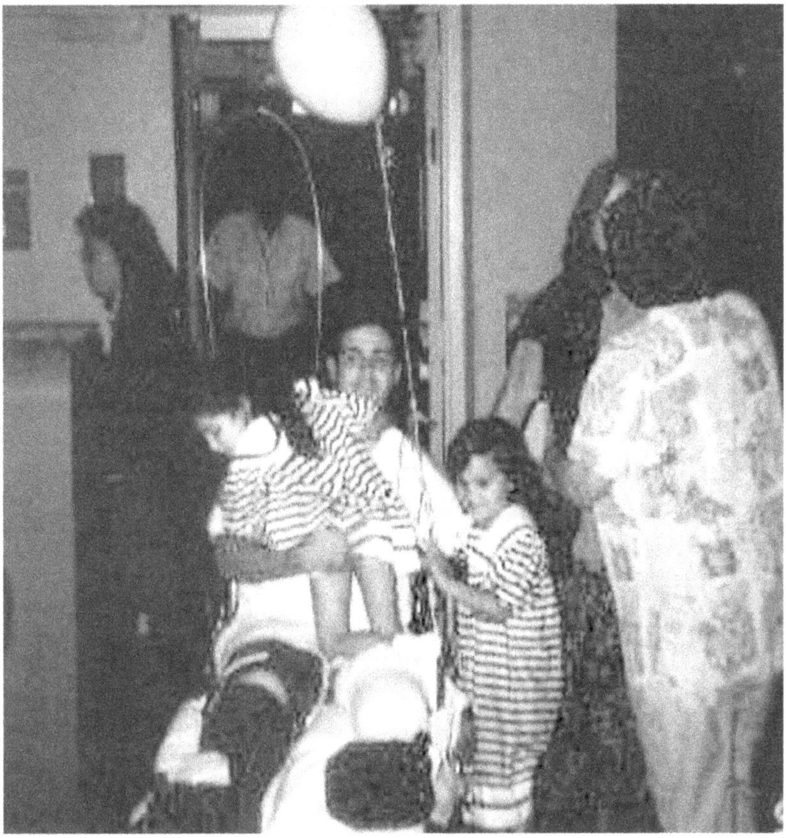

5 OCT 1996 // Returning home to my girls - four year old Nicole (left) and five year old Lisette (right) at the gate at Pensacola Airport. Shelley and I were overwhelmed by the welcome from our Air Force family. My wheelchair quickly became a toy to push or ride on for the girls.

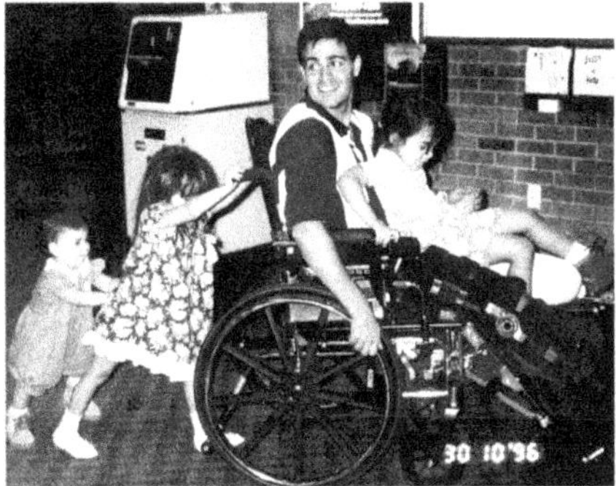

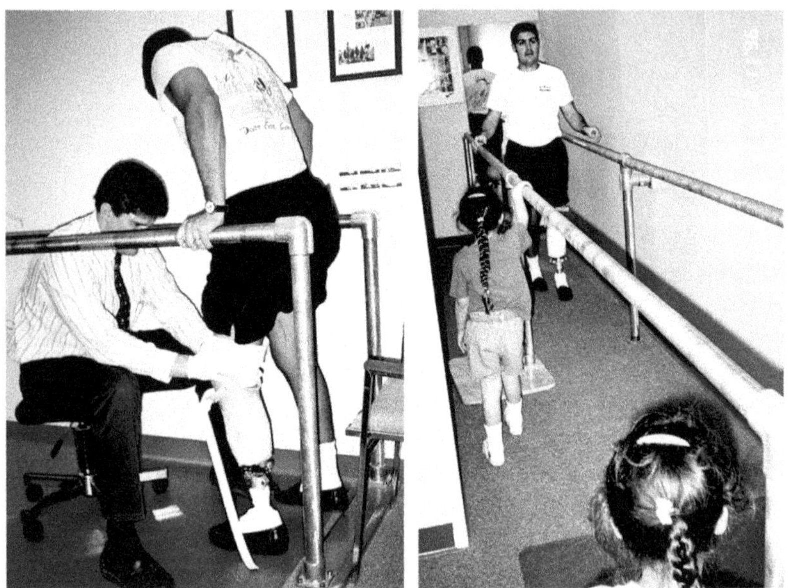

15 NOV 1996 // Final fitting for my prosthetic leg and taking my first steps at Love Prosthetics and Orthotics in San Antonio, Texas.

22 NOV 1996 // First Dance with my girls and Shelley at a Cuban restaurant in San Antonio, Texas (Dance Floor for adults ONLY).

WALK AGAIN

28 NOV 1996 //
Thanksgiving with my grandparents, Antonio "Pipo" and Carmen "Lela" Mori.

1997 // First meeting with Navy pilot LCDR Frank Ellis in Ocala, Florida.

RUN AGAIN

28 JAN 1997 // First run
outside of Tidewater
Prosthetics parking lot
in Norfolk, Virginia.

MAY 1997 // "The Jungle" TACP Obstacle Course Hurlburt Field, Florida.

FLY AGAIN

5 SEP 1997 // Lt Col Tommy Hull hosing me down with champagne after my first flight back in the cockpit - exactly 2 weeks before the 1 year anniversary of my crash. Our Group Commander Col Donny Wurster, Wing Commander Col Rich Comer, Major John Groves (retired Pave Low legend), and my 20th SOS brothers there to celebrate this victory.

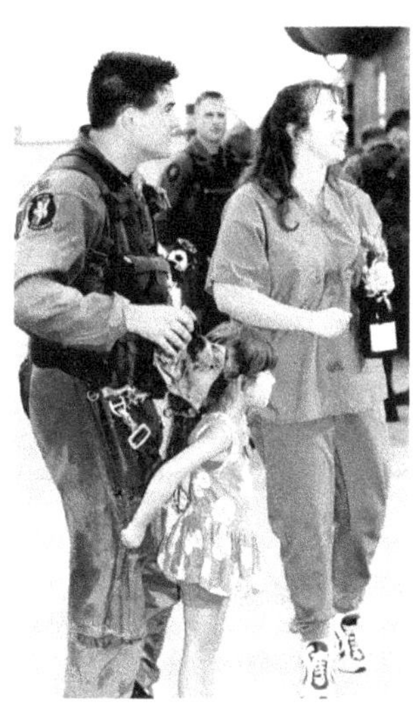

5 SEP 1997 // Post flight celebration with Shelley and Nicole.

5 SEP 1997 // Lt Col Tommy Hull and I after the flight. (USAF photograph by MSgt Dave Nolan)

MAR 1998 // Promoted to LCDR U.S. Navy with Shelley and the girls.

OCT 1998 // McGuires 5K in Destin, Florida.

MAY 1998 // Sworn into the U.S. Air Force as a Major by Lt Col Tommy Hull. As always, Shelley is by my side (holding the US Flag). This took place at the Soundside Family Picnic Area on Hurlburt Field AFB, right before the Pave Low Beer and Taco Run.

1998 // Dancing to "Stars fell over Alabama" outside Hemingways Island Grill at Pensacola Beach, Florida.

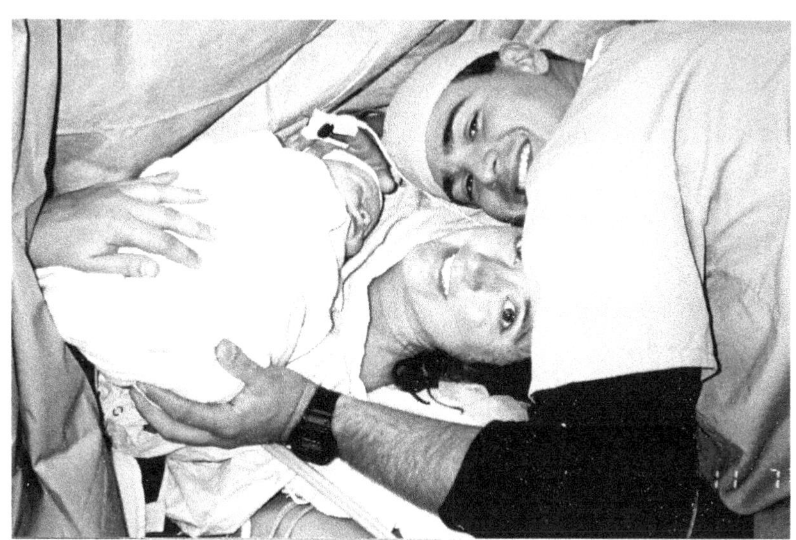

1998 // Our Miracle Child John "Jakey" is born.

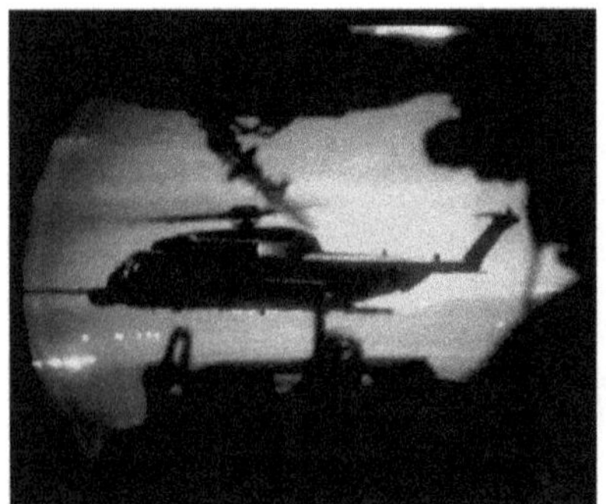

1997 // Back in the Pave Low. (USAF photograph by Tech. Sgt. Manuel Trejo)

1999 // Hovering over IX-514 after fast rope infill of Sr Chief Rat. (third from left)

1999 // Operation ALLIED FORCE - Kosovo // A-Flight ADO at the 20th SOS and first combat deployment after amputation.

2000 // Back to the 6th SOS as SOUTHCOM A-Flight ADO. Pictured here with Capt AJ Gaston in Colombia.

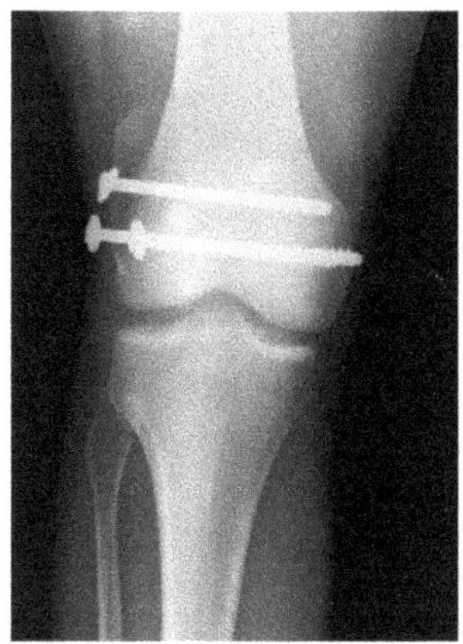

SEP 1996 // X-ray of my right leg with screws holding the end of my femur together.

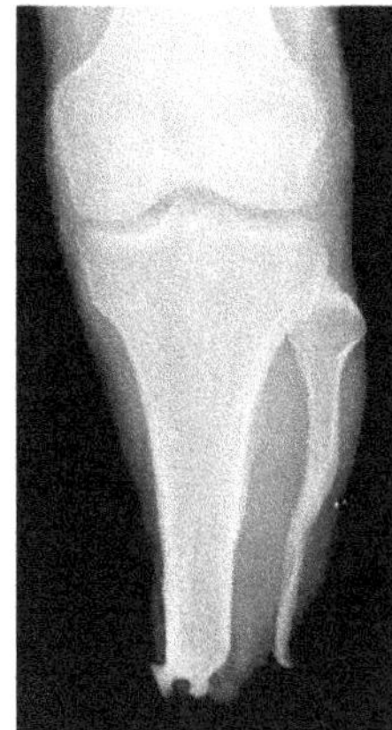

JUL 2001 // X-ray of left amputation with fibula growth and bone spurs that grew over 5 years. Drawing depicts the experimental Ertl revision and reconstruction plan.

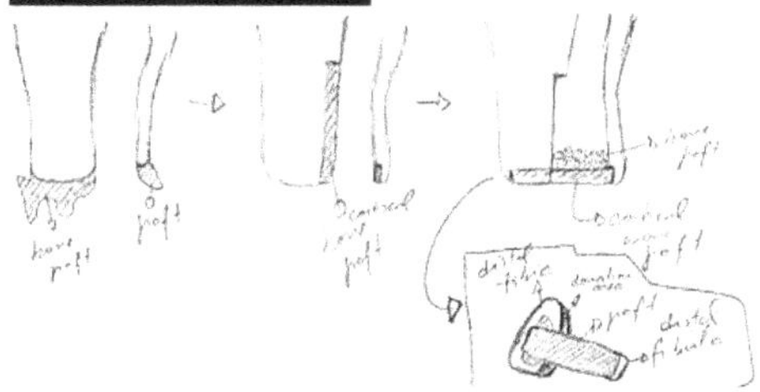

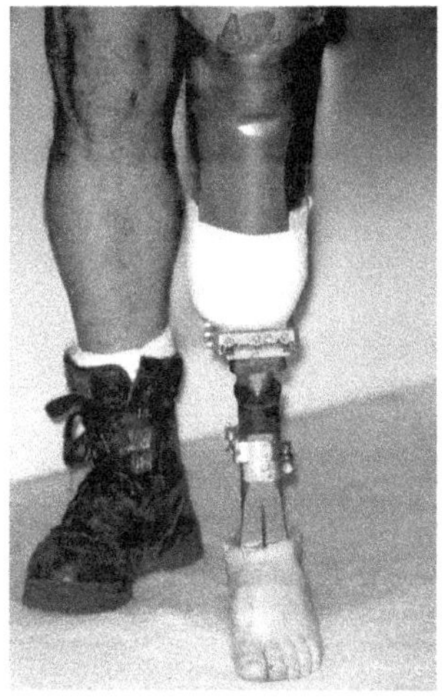

1997 // Initial 'check socket' testing of high-tech flight gear. The operational leg was later tested in an altitude chamber.

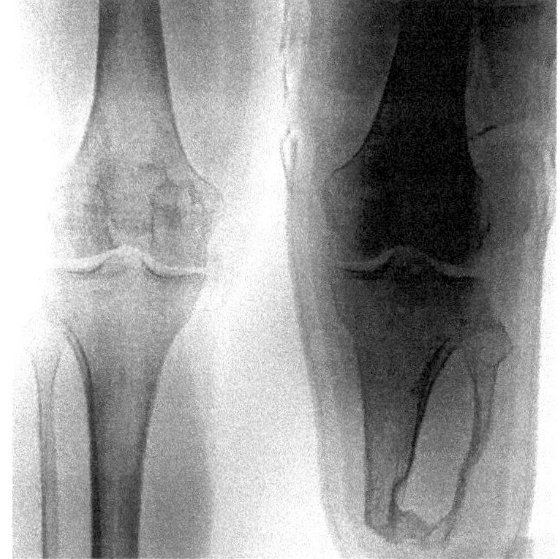

2006 // X-ray after the Ertl revision of left leg and screw removal from right knee (screws were holding the end of my femur together).

2002 // NATO AIRSOUTH - Working with French Special Forces

2002 // With LCDR Rico Lenway at my promotion ceremony to Lt Col.

2004 // With Ross Perot at his Eisenhower Award Reception.

2004 // 6th Special Operations Squadron command photo with my squadron and 'non-standard' aircraft fleet. (USAF photograph by Airman 1st Class Ali Flisek)

2003-2006 // 6th SOS Mi-17 Hip in formation with a UH-1N Huey and BT-67 Basler, a modified C-47 Dakota (picture taken from the BT-67).

2003-2006 // My 6th SOS teams deployed world-wide for the Global War on Terror. MSgt John Dubisson and I are pictured here with the Colombian Air Force AB-212 Rapaz crew we flew with.

2005 // Operation IRAQI FREEDOM - Balad Air Base, Iraq // On the flight line with Major William Brian "Downer" Downs (1965-2005).

2006 // Last flight as a CAA.

2010 // Last flight in uniform in a HH-60G Pave Hawk with Combat Rescue Warriors.

2010 // Retirement ceremony from the Air Force with CAA instructor cadre where they 'issued' me a customized Colt 1911.

2010 // Pictures Jimmy Buffett and I exchanged for my retirement.

2019 // Combat Aviation Advisor Qualification final 'Raven Claw' excercise - Warlord Alvari with the 'extracted' team.

2025 // Happily retired and grandparents.

1997+ //
Biebere ex
Cruris

29 OCT 2006 // Marine Corps Marathon

27 OCT 2019 // Marine Corps 10K
with Jakey and Nicole.

13 OCT 2019 // Army Ten-Miler

Major Brooks "Chuckie" Gruber, USMC (1965-2000).

SMSgt Daniel "Labby" Labrador, USAF (1960-2015).

DEC 2000 // MSgt Ramon Acosta hosing me down after my fini flight at the 6th SOS.

AUG 2006 // Presenting Col Tommy Hull "The Leg" at his retirement ceremony.

MAY 2016 // With retired CAPT Rico Lenway in Tampa, Florida.

DEC 2018 // With Master Chief Jeremy Trump at his retirement.

JUL 2010 // Inside the cockpit of a Russian MI-17 with Mr. Raymond "Pops" Francis after my retirement ceremony.

OCT 2014 // With Pops at my induction into the Air Commando Hall of Fame. He ensured we had the most rugged and durable high-performance prosthetics to walk, run, swim, fly and jump out of airplanes with. He never charged me or my brothers a dime. Most importantly, he was like a father to all of us. We could not have have performed as well without him.

APR 2025 // Point Romeo Foxtrot Undisclosed location, Atlantic Ocean // Laying Mr. Francis "Pops" to rest. Flounder, Ahab, Lennie, and Rat - all brothers thanks to this great man.

DEC 2021 // The Alvari
Parrot Heads at Jimmy
Buffett's last concert in
Tampa, Florida

PART IV

Through discipline comes freedom.
– Aristotle

No man walks alone.
– Frank Ellis

10

WALK

Dr. Ockey stood at the door of John's hospital room right on time, folder in hand, glasses low on his nose. John was holding a stationary wheelie, leaning back in his wheelchair, his fingers deftly making tiny adjustments back and forth to keep the caster wheels off the ground. Shelley sat close to John's right side, clutching a legal pad already filled with notes.

"All right, Evel Knievel, let's get to it," Dr. Ockey said, looking down at both of them. "We're revising the treatment plan."

John raised an eyebrow. "Is that good or bad, Doc?"

"It means," the doctor replied evenly, "that if everything continues to heal the way it has been, we can let you go home. Temporarily. You'll return in mid-October, then again in November. Your residual limb is still healing from the revision surgery, and the swelling needs to resolve before we remove the stitches. The staples in your right knee will come out then as well."

John shifted slightly, glancing down at his immobilized right leg sticking straight out in front of the wheelchair. "Knee still feels like it belongs to someone else."

"That's because it's been through significant trauma," Dr. Ockey said. "Your right knee is fixed in that removable cast for a reason. You've got several shrapnel puncture wounds, a femoral fracture, and your knee was disarticulated. That all takes time to heal. But starting now, you can remove that cast daily. You can break up the scar tissue manually." He looked directly at John. "It won't be comfortable."

John gave a dry half-smile. "Doc, that's become my theme. I'm good to go!"

"Before we let you bear weight and walk on it, you need to get your knee flexion to at least one hundred and thirty degrees." Dr. Ockey continued.

"Great, Doc!" John said. "Just enough to kick some ass?"

Shelley rolled her eyes. Dr. Ockey didn't, but the amusement was muted.

"And you need to rebuild your quadriceps and calf muscles. They've atrophied significantly."

John nodded. *Building up muscle is easy.* It was the next part he was concerned about. "How long before I can try a prosthesis?"

Dr. Ockey was direct. "You won't be fitted for your left leg until you build enough leg strength and regain range of motion in your left knee as well. And even then, I need that left residual limb stable. It may require another revision surgery by the new year."

Shelley's fingers tightened around John's. "Another surgery?"

"Yes, likely," he said gently. "The muscle and soft tissue need to settle. You will most likely have at least another surgery on your right knee—maybe two. The screws holding your condyles together for now will most likely have to come out. Immediately, if they start to back out on their own, in order to avoid damaging your ligaments. We want the best long-term result, not a rushed one."

John nodded once. "Copy that, doc."

Dr. Ockey walked to the counter and picked up a strange, cup-shaped plaster cast. "This," he said, holding it up, "is a protective plaster shell or 'socket'. They are custom-fitted; made just like a cast that is wrapped around a broken limb. It will go over your bandaged residual limb."

"My stump?" John blurted out.

"The appropriate term is 'residual limb,' Lieutenant," Dr. Ockey corrected. "The plaster socket will protect your residual limb: the stitches, the redirected blood vessels, and muscle tissue if you fall. It will protect all the hard work that went into reconfiguring the end of your residual limb."

Shelley's head snapped toward him. "Fall?"

John was still thinking, *Why can't I just call it a stump?*

"It happens more than you'd think," Dr. Ockey said. "New amputees wake up, swing their legs over the bed, and forget there's nothing there. They stand...and they go down."

John grimaced and shared a concerned look with his wife.

"So," the doctor continued, "you move slowly and deliberately. You sit upright first. You think before you shift your weight and reach for your crutches. We expect you may be up on crutches with your right leg before the stitches have healed on your residual limb. With a knee brace at first."

"Crawl, walk, run..." John chuckled.

Dr. Ockey nodded. "Exactly. You need to retrain your body and your brain. For now, before we fit you for a prosthesis, force your left knee straight as often as possible. Don't let it stay bent."

"It wants to stay bent when I relax," John muttered, now catching on.

"I know. The muscle and sinew were cut. As they heal, they contract and atrophy. There's a natural tendency for the knee to stay in that contracted position. Your body will think it's your 'new normal.' We see it all the time with new amputees. It stiffens in a bent position, and then it's a real struggle to fight that later, when it's time to walk. Your gait will be affected significantly. That's why most new amputees have a considerable limp. Most times, it takes years to overcome, and many never do."

John exhaled slowly. "So straighten it. Keep it straight, especially when relaxing. Like watching TV. Even if it hurts."

"Especially when it hurts," Dr. Ockey replied.

Eat the Pain! Echoed through John's skull.

Shelley flipped a page on her notepad. "And the current wrapping?"

"You'll change the bandages daily," the doctor said. "Tight compression wrapping reduces swelling and shapes the limb for a prosthetic socket. You'll also be doing desensitization exercises. Apply gentle pressure, tap the bottom of the limb. You need that tissue to be durable before you can put your weight on it, right?"

There was a knock at the open door.

"Right on time," Dr. Ockey said.

A man stepped in carrying casting materials. "Hey there, L.T.," he said with a friendly smile. "I'm the prosthetist Dr. Ockey recommended. I'm based here in San Antonio."

John studied him. "You're the guy building my new leg."

"That's the plan," the prosthetist said. "Today I'm just taking measurements and making a mold. First to make the plaster cast, the cup. When you come back, we'll do it again without the bandages— making a perfect copy of your residual limb. That becomes the foundation for the socket that will fit snugly over your wool socks, the part that interfaces directly with your limb."

"Interface," John repeated. "Like docking a spacecraft."

The prosthetist grinned. "Like docking a spacecraft. The wool socks come in different ply thicknesses and can be changed or even worn with one over the other to make up for volume changes. They also provide some cushioning for your limb and skin against the hard fiberglass and eventually carbon fiber socket. The socket fit determines comfort, control, and whether the suspension system keeps the leg securely attached."

John looked between the two medical professionals. "Suspension system? Like a shock absorber?"

"No, L.T., that's how the prosthesis stays on you. The prosthetic is suspended underneath you," Dr. Ockey explained. "There are different mechanisms—suction, locking pins, even outdated suspension straps—just like suspenders. Read up and learn as much as you can. Know the proper terminology, Lieutenant. You're an engineer; you're a pilot. Consider this your ground school before you can fly—I mean, walk again."

He handed Shelley a thick packet of material.

She laughed weakly. "Homework."

John was squirming in his wheelchair, squeezing the push rims on his wheels, ready to devour it. "Good to go, Doc!"

They explained that upon John's return in November, the prosthetist would then fit him with a 'check socket,' (the cup which his wool covered limb would snugly fit in), then a definitive fiberglass socket, leg and prosthetic foot. John was told to expect a new socket every three to six months until the *residual limb* shrinkage stabilized.

One of the last requirements before departing was to meet with an occupational therapist. The therapist was young—in her mid-twenties. She was a recently commissioned Air Force Second Lieutenant, much junior to his Navy Lieutenant rank. She walked them through a makeshift kitchen with his wheelchair and provided them with some tools wheelchair users could use. John's favorite was a grabber-reacher tool with a claw; a tool with which he planned to pinch Shelley's rear end with.

"Okay, sir," the therapist told him. "We need goals. Have you given any thought to what you want to accomplish?"

"Yes," John said, prepared for the question. "I'm planning to walk into my aunt's house for Thanksgiving, run by my daughter's birthday at the end of February, and get back to flying within a year."

"Whoa!" the LT chuckled nervously. "Take it back a notch, sir. You need to accept that you could be in a wheelchair for the next six months at least. Let's be realistic, you'll probably not walk normally again or even run."

John ground his teeth. *She does not get it.* He took a deep breath. *Breath.* Shelley gripped his hand.

Control. He leaned forward. *Who the hell are* you *to tell me what I can and can't do*?

John recognized her well-meaning, but he wanted to make a point of her lack of experience. He smiled.

"Thank you, *Lieutenant.*"

That was the end of the meeting.

04 OCT 1996 // WILFORD HALL, SAN ANTONIO, TEXAS //

The day before they left Wilford Hall, John received a call from a Navy SEAL officer who had served with Colonel Tommy Hull at JSOC. Tommy had immediately called him after hearing about John's crash and amputation. The SEAL, LCDR Pete Van Hooser, introduced himself and said he was also an amputee, assigned to Naval Special Warfare Development Group (NSWDG), often referred to as DEVGRU.

"I'd like to welcome you to our exclusive club," Pete said solemnly.

John was confused. "Oh, really?"

"Yeah. It literally costs an arm or a leg to join."

After some more ribbing, and a bit on his background and injury, and how Tommy Hull asked if he could get his support, and that of DEVGRU behind him, the SEAL cut to the chase.

"I'd like to help a brother navigate this situation," he told John. "You want to get back to flying, right?"

"Yes, sir."

"Listen, I don't know who you've been talking about so far regarding prosthetists," Pete said, "but I want you to come out to Virginia and check into Portsmouth Naval Hospital. Raymond Francis takes care of me and other SEALs both at DEVGRU and Little Creek NAB, as well as being a well-known Navy diver. He's also an experienced Civil Air Patrol pilot with thousands of hours. He knows exactly what it will take to keep you on active duty and get you back to the cockpit. I'm backed up by the DEVGRU commander also to guide you."

"Thanks, sir," John said. "You know, I'm getting ready to go home and have to return to San Antonio for my prosthetic care in a couple of weeks. And I have additional surgery for my right knee…"

"Hey, I get it. But the doc who took care of me and our DEVGRU operators is also the chief orthopedic surgeon at Naval Portsmouth and will take care of you."

John was torn. His experience at Wilford Hall was extraordinary; the staff had ownership and pride in taking care of him. Shelley and John trusted them and Joe, who was a product of Wilford Hall and had saved his life. The prosthetic practice here was even called Love Prosthetics and Orthotics. However, he also needed to reach his goals on *his* timeline, and he had met quite a few in San Antonio who were already critical of his plans.

"Thanks for the advice, sir. I need to discuss it with my wife. Can I call you when I get home?"

"Lieutenant Alvarez…"

"Yes, sir?"

"Well…I just have one request in return, now that you are in our club," Pete said. "If it all works out for you, you need to promise me you will take care of the next guy who goes down. You understand?"

John

"Yes sir, absolutely!"

"Tag," the SEAL commanded. "You're it. Hooyah!"

John agreed wholeheartedly, "Hooyah! Sir. Good to go!"

05 OCT 1996 // SAN ANTONIO AIRPORT, TEXAS // 6:50PM

John braced himself after he settled in the seat, the whirr of the idling plane surrounding him. Shelley and his mom were seated in the row across from him on the right. The plane was small, with single-seat rows on the left and two-seat rows on the right. He was seated on a single seat, right up front.

It was not the fear of flying, especially not in a plane that was taking him home. It was not pain; his pain management was under control at that point. No, he was braced for the flow of regular passengers boarding the flight after him. They would pass by, one by one, and here he was—on display like some zoo animal.

Look at the legless man; I feel so sorry for him! John imagined as he made awkward eye contact with some of them as they walked by.

Finally, the plane door closed, but he could still feel the burn of eyes at the back of his head. He looked over at Shelley, who gave him a sympathetic smile. At least she understood what he was feeling.

Once they were at cruising altitude, a flight attendant unbuckled and sidled up next to him.

"Good afternoon, sir," she said, placing one hand on the back of his seat. She leaned forward, a little closer than John thought was polite. "Can I get you anything?"

"Orange juice would be great, thank you," John said.

"*Anything* you want, sugar," she responded, letting her Texan drawl linger as she winked and turned back down the aisle.

John's eyes widened and flickered over to Shelley. His wife had been observing the interaction with a smirk. Slowly, pointedly, Shelley made a show of picking up her book and opening it. She was obviously fine with this harmless ego boost.

05 OCT 1996 // PENSACOLA AIRPORT, PENSACOLA, FL // 9:00PM

John was nervous. He imagined the girls impatiently waiting for him at the gate when they arrived. How would they react? His heart lurched. He, Shelley, and Pat had tried to prepare them best they knew how, but no one could really know how his daughters would see their father now that he was down half a leg in a wheelchair.

They were the last to disembark once the plane had landed. His mom went out ahead of them while Shelley stayed back to set up the wheelchair for him to transfer into at the jet bridge. Once he transferred from the aisle chair, Shelley took control of his wheelchair and pushed him out to the gate. Gripping the padded handles in anticipation, John sat himself up as straight as he could.

The sound hit him first.

Maybe it was the painkillers, too, but John was stunned by the number of people cheering as he entered the terminal. Led by his wing commander, Colonel Norton "Norty" Schwarz, Squadron mates and spouses from the 20th and 6th filled the space in front of the gate.

The next thing John knew, two tiny bodies in sailor-striped white and blue dresses rushed to his wheelchair. Lisette and Nicole were grinning and screeching their delight. Lisette was dancing and bouncing by his wheels with a handful of balloons, and Nicole immediately reached for him to ride on his lap. He instinctively raised her onto his lap. Lisette leaned on him. Both girls looked at his leg with a little confusion, but the sound of cheers and the fact that their daddy was back immediately distracted them. The balloons floated towards the ceiling, forgotten.

He revelled in their warm embrace. *Home. My girls... Thank you, God!*

Captain Brett Hauenstein, a fellow 20th SOS pilot with whom John flew hair-raising missions in Croatia, pushed his way through the throng. He arrived at John's wheelchair with a determination to wheel him towards his family. Col. Schwartz parted the sea of people. The next few minutes were a blur of people coming in and out of his personal space, with hugs and tears. Welcoming him home.

Eventually, the crowd let John go home with his family. His mom and dad, his mother-in-law, Pat, and aunt Elvira would stay for the initial days. His squadron mates from the 20th and the 6th had widened the master bedroom door for his wheelchair and would later come over to build a ramp to the front door.

The girls chattered about their school while John was set up in the living room. Jimmy Buffett playing in the background. He was tired, but he would never be too tired not to drink in the relief of being with his babies once more. He was back. He was alive.

He was truly home. *Sanctuary!*

17 OCT 1996 // NAVARRE, FLORIDA // 6:30 PM

Shelley finished cleaning off the remnants of chocolate frosting and loaded the dishwasher. Chocolate normally did not last long in the house. After John's birthday, they were not only stocked with chocolate cake but also John's favorite chocolate-covered donuts. He saw it as a treat after self-monitored PT to tear up his knee's scar tissue. Frank Rivera and his teammates had come to the house with gloves for John to use with his wheelchair, as well as another very important set of items—John's wedding ring and his dog tags. In the chaos, John and Shelley had simply assumed someone had taken care of them but, apparently, it caused quite a frenzy in the 6th when the team tried to track down where they went. Ramon "Lobo" Acosta, of course, had kept the ring and tags safely in his possession from the moment Doc Joe handed them to him.

In the early days, being home, Shelley just wanted to let John sleep. Their bedroom and bed were their sanctuary. Mornings were especially difficult; he would still have to work out the scar tissue in his right knee before getting into his wheelchair. But he was already tired of being in his wheelchair.

"I just want to stand up to pee, dammit," John joked with her.

She would encourage it—perhaps to the detriment of her in-laws seeing her push her husband into doing things for himself. John had not been set up with any additional training aside from the initial physical therapy and what he did on his own. He would sit in his wheelchair while watching cartoons with Lisette and Nicole, doing resistance training with the elastic bands tied to his handles. He'd place his right foot against the windowsill and roll the wheelchair forward, forcing his knee to bend. At least three times a day: morning, noon, and night without fail.

Shelley was worried about his single-minded obsession, but she began to quickly realize if anyone was going to get back to flying, John was not waiting for someone else to do it for him.

His birthday had been a calm affair. The girls got him a round, yellow smiley-face pillow to rest his 'baby leg', as they named it. John and Shelley had agreed not to show the girls the still-bleeding and unwrapped stump.

Drying her hands on the kitchen towel, Shelley went to see what the rest of her family was up to. The living and dining rooms were quiet. Too quiet. As she walked down the hallway, she heard little voices and John's sweet responses coming from the primary bedroom. Shelley was smiling as she got to the end of the hallway, but the expression froze on her face when she saw Nicole was helping John wrap his 'baby leg' in clean bandages. Lisette hovered near the bedroom door.

"Seriously?" she muttered at a sheepish John; their mutual agreement was in shambles.

"Nicole insisted!" he responded, blaming their morbidly curious four-year-old. "She wanted to see and help Daddy with his baby leg. Besides, she's a tough little girl. Lions don't scare her either. Right, Coley-coconut?" Nicole giggled and roared at him. He roared back.

Shelley shook her head at him. Blaming their admittedly curious and brave little child was a low blow. John's sister, Cuqui, had visited a little after John's birthday. She had brought her baby, Kinzie, and the family took a trip to the local zoo. John had been packed into the wheelchair, and Nicole and Kinzie were in a double stroller. The Gulf Breeze Zoo was small, but they had giraffes and, of course, lions. At first, the lionesses and the lion pacing the cage did not seem to notice the small family. And then the lion had caught sight of John—a man with what was basically a fresh wound and stuck in a wheelchair. Cuqui and Shelley had screamed when the lion lunged at the cage, rattling it and the air with a deafening roar. Tiny, fearless, four-year-old Nicole had roared back. The terrified mothers had grabbed the girls, *accidentally* leaving John behind in front of the cage. John, after the initial shock, had rammed the fence with his wheelchair to further egg on the lions. Thankfully, Shelley's husband did not end up as lunch.

"I don't like it," Lisette was whispering to her. The five-year-old pointed at the stitches. "It looks like a frowny face." She pointed at the y-shaped, uneven scar at the end of the 'baby leg'. It did, in fact, look like a frown.

That evening, when they were getting ready for bed, John brought up another tender subject. His parents had called him after his birthday with more news. Through their connections at the University of Miami, his Alma Mater, they had gotten in touch with Dr. John W. Uribe—the orthopedic surgeon for the Miami Dolphins, and at U.M. He also had previously treated Army elite special operations forces.

John had been invited for an appointment with Dr. Uribe in Miami. He could squeeze John into his schedule a day before Halloween.

Shelley was already stressed, worrying about money and the future in general. Everyone had taken up necessary roles to help cocoon John through his recovery. Carmen, Juan, and John's aunt Elvira had stayed another week in Navarre. Her mom, Pat, was helping to take care of the kids through November. Shelley had her role, too; she did everything. She managed her daughters' childcare, carried the wheelchair, made sure they were stable financially, and handled so many question marks about John's future—*their* future. It was barely a month after the accident. Every day, she had wild impulses to lay hands on John, just to assure herself he was alive and okay.

And now he wants to get in an airplane, still in a wheelchair, alone, and fly away from me? NO!

"Send him your x-rays, he doesn't have to see you in person!" Shelley protested. Her anger hid her shaking fear. Helplessness, like an echo from before the crash, threatened to overwhelm her again.

"Dr. Uribe is a world-class doctor," John told her. "I need to take this chance. When will I ever have another opportunity like this?"

She pointed violently at her husband. "I need to have you *here*. I can't do this. We can't afford for me to fly down either. Can't you just send him your medical file?" The argument went nowhere, and John refused to reconsider. He made plans to fly to Miami, coordinating with his parents.

There was nobody who understood Shelley's turmoil, simply put. There was nobody around them who had gone through anything like this. There was nobody to whom Shelley could vent her fears and frustrations.

John had told her about his promise to the Navy SEAL about paying it forward to future amputees. Shelley, after another long day without a sympathetic ear, made her own promise. She promised herself that she would forever offer to be a compassionate ear to the military spouses who would suddenly find themselves the caregivers of their own cranky, injured heroes, so no one else would have to carry the burden alone.

~

05 NOV 1996 // WILFORD HALL, LACKLAND AFB, TEXAS //

John was devouring all he could on prosthetics and orthopedic terminology. He re-read *One Tough Marine*. He re-read books from Greek and Stoic philosophers that his father had given him. He wrote out their quotes on post-it notes: Plato, Socrates, Epicurus, Chrysippus, Seneca, Marcus Aurelius, and Augustine.

John's tattered and stained paperback copy of *Jonathan Livingston Seagull* was a regular companion when he wasn't at the gym. It was John's childhood favorite book; his parents gifted it to him as an elementary school graduation gift in sixth grade. Written by former Air Force pilot Richard Bach, the story was about a young, outcast seagull obsessed with his unconventional approach to perfecting flight. It was a fable about pushing beyond limitations.

In the first week of November, John was headed back to Wilford Hall for more therapy; with all of his girls this time. He was eager to try on his first prosthetic. Shelley had the girls' home-school assignment plan for their excused absence from school. She had already taken a leave of absence from the hospital; she prepped the house, packed all their clothes, dropped their dog Monty off with friends, prepped snacks for the trip, packed the van, wheeled the chair, loaded John and the girls, and drove to San Antonio.

After another set of conversations with his wife, John tried to show more appreciation for what Shelley was doing to support him. The four stayed in a temporary lodging facility on base. Emotions were still frayed, and chores became part of the frustration for both John and Shelley. They both hoped the trip would be worthwhile.

During John's earlier appointment in Miami, Dr. Uribe had initially offered to redo and clean up some of the scar tissue around John's knee. But after the doctor had completed his evaluation, he was honest.

"I learned my trade in the Army, son. I've seen a lot of nasty hits. Whoever did your knee was guided by the hands of God. I could not have done a better job."

On November 5th, his physical therapist allowed him to stand on his right leg while wearing a knee brace. John purposefully waited for Shelley and the girls to arrive. They saw him stand up again (at least on one leg) for the first time.

John had been working on his upper body strength, so the crutches worked like a charm. The orthopedic surgeon approved the transition, as long as it did not hurt. John lied about the pain and pressed on with the crutches, determined not to return to his wheelchair. His knee was constantly braced, and the brace allowed for 90 degrees of flexion. However, he could only bend it about 10 degrees because of the scar tissue and immobility for almost six weeks.

Two days after getting his crutches, Lisette accompanied John to physical therapy. Shelley had dropped them off and went with Nicole to have their new van repaired at a local dealer. John's quads were still shaking from their intense workout as he and his eldest child went down the elevator to the basement of the hospital to have lunch in the cafeteria.

The highly polished and waxed terracotta tiles were wet in front of the freshly washed trays stacked near the entrance. Lisette chatted about life in kindergarten as John tried to focus on moving them through the line.

"Oh, ummm, Miss Cameron says that we're going to the um, the plane museum soon! And then...then my friend Jade, well, Jade said that there's a place where you can see planes from a long time ago—"

Just as John handed Lisette a tray, John's left crutch slipped out from underneath him. Lisette was hovering right beneath him. Struggling to avoid falling on his little girl, John's black high-top on his right foot was firmly stuck to the floor, and down he went. His left stump, encased in a plaster cast adorned with cheerful faces and sunbeams drawn by the girls upon his return, was protected.

John fell back, landing on his rear end. The only problem was that his right knee bent to the 90 degrees the brace allowed for. And he could hear a ripping sound coming from it, and the pain made him woozy. Stunned, he lay next to his now crying and scared little girl.

Lisette was terrified for her father, frozen in place and her breathing coming in rapid puffs. "Daddy?"

"Hey darlin', I'm okay," John grimaced. "Look at me. baby girl, I'm okay..." He wrapped her up in his arms as she sobbed. Thankfully, this had all happened in a cafeteria full of medical professionals. Wilford Hall's lunch crowd was ready and scrambled to the scene. After initial triage, John was lifted onto a wheelchair. Before he could be rushed to the orthopedic clinic, John insisted on having his baby girl with him in his lap for the ride.

Shelley and Nicole were immediately ushered back to the casting and examination room. His wife, red-eyed and wild, rushed to touch John. He still had Lisette wrapped in his arms, both waiting for some pain relief. Once Shelley confirmed they were both okay, she told John about her experience at the car repair shop. While she had been negotiating with the service rep regarding the car repairs, a call from the hospital interrupted her, informing her that her husband had fallen and might go into surgery. She had burst into tears as she tried to explain to the service rep why she needed to leave immediately. The man was very sweet and had simply told her, "Ma'am, don't worry. The repair is on the house. Drive safe, please."

After new X-rays and a nervous half hour, the orthopedic surgeons emerged back into the casting room.

"Son, you must have some guardian angel looking after you," the department chair said, smiling. "The fall ripped the scar tissue with your knee perfectly aligned. Amazingly, there is no damage to the bones or cartilage. This basically amounts to one giant physical therapy session!"

Dr. Bolyard, who originally put John's knee back together along with Dr. Benedetti, injected John's knee with some pain meds for alleviation and continued to manipulate the joint. Dr. Bolyard, taking advantage of the now numbed knee, bent John's knee forcefully to break up some more scar tissue. He was relieved that his work was not in vain.

Nicole whispered in awe: "Bend it, bend it, bend it!"

Dr. Bolyard smiled and invited both the girls over to help him bend their daddy's knee. Lisette stayed clinging to Shelley, not wanting to hurt him. Nicole—on the other hand—rushed gleefully over, shrieking, "Bend it! Bend it! Bend it!" as she said, pushing with all the might a four-year-old could muster. All the adults laughed; a nervous sigh of relief.

John, however, was confined back to his wheelchair for another two days before he would be allowed back up on his crutches to stand on his right leg again.

The cafeteria updated its policy on washing and drying trays.

15 NOV 1996 // LOVE PROSTHETICS & ORTHOTICS, SAN ANTONIO, TX //10:00AM

John's heart raced at the thought of walking again. Doc Ockey had fought for the hospital to pay for more than a basic foot. This case was an anomaly, as military hospitals were not equipped or budgeted to provide for active-duty amputees. There were only a handful of amputees serving in the U.S. military, after all, and none of them were in the Air Force. The Department of Veterans Affairs was expected to take care of prosthetics after medical discharge or retirement.

The podiatrist's explanation to his department head was very direct: *How much would your son's foot be worth to you?* And when the hospital commander, Brigadier General Carlton, caught wind of the argument...he ended it. *Just do it!*

Needless to say, John's first foot would end up being a higher-end carbon-fiber prosthetic from the local civilian prosthetist with an appropriate name: *Love Prosthetics & Orthotics.*

At the prosthetic clinic in a strip mall, John was taught how to put on wool liner socks over the stump as a cushion between his skin and the socket. The surgical scar was still not fully closed. He was instructed to be patient; the scars and skin of his stump would have to heal, toughen up, and be calloused before he could truly bear weight on it. The next day, the prosthetist had adjustments made to a test socket made of clear plastic. Days later, John would have a new flesh-colored, fiberglass socket fitted with a carbon-fiber foot.

His knee was already protesting at the thought of unsupported body weight, but John did not care. He was finally going to stand again and walk on two legs. Well, if only Shelley would hurry and bring the girls into the room. The crew encouraged him to wait for Lisette and Nicole. He impatiently agreed to keep off his feet until they showed up.

It was worth it. The girls and Shelley finally arrived, and John took his place at the handrails. He gingerly placed his weight on his right leg. When it hurt, he applied weight to his left side. The prosthesis remained steady. He took a step. Another. He walked—awkwardly, and applied a little more support on the handrails than he would have liked—but he made it across the room to the cheers of his girls.

He pulled Shelley close in a tight embrace and kissed her. He buried his head in her hair and neck, pressing up against her tightly and breathing her in. The girls hugged both of them around their legs. He continued to walk, assisted by crutches again. Their family celebrated at the ice cream shop in the same strip mall before driving back to base.

He spent a few more days at the hospital, going through several rounds of physical therapy with the prosthetic leg, navigating obstacles, steps, ramps, and staircases, all while assisted by crutches.

In follow-up appointments with the podiatrist and surgeon, John informed them about the SEAL from DEVGRU who offered to get him connected to his prosthetist and the orthopedic surgeon at the Naval Hospital in Portsmouth, Virginia. He was still torn, and wanted his current team's opinion.

They recommended that John go home and think about it, and that they would be there for him regardless of his decision. In the meantime, John would continue PT at Corry Station and keep his right knee in the now-adjustable brace.

Before the family returned to Florida, they went out to a Latino restaurant for dinner in San Antonio with Dr. Ockey and his family of six. The restaurant was filled with salsa music and the smell of garlic and onions. It served Puerto Rican and Cuban cuisine and had a dance floor in the back.

John, for the first time since the accident, danced with Shelley. They reveled in the embrace, lingering in relief and love like a cocoon.

A sign hung on the wall by the dance floor.

No children allowed on the dance floor, it declared.

Lisette and Nicole could not help themselves. Signs could not stop a father from dancing with his daughters again, either. Besides, the owner did not complain.

He, too, was an amputee—the elderly Cuban had lost his arm when he was younger.

28 NOV 1996 // HOLLYWOOD, FLORIDA // 4:32PM // THANKSGIVING DAY

John worked on his gait while wearing the athletic leg. His walk was still stiff—his right knee remained in a brace, and he used crutches for brief periods of walking. He pushed through the pain of his still-bloody stump. He had to be ready to walk through his aunt's doorway for Thanksgiving. When the third week of November rolled around, the Alvarez family packed up their van and drove down to Hollywood in South Florida.

Tia Elvira lived near John's grandparents. John was most eager for his grandfather to see him. Antonio Mori—Pipo, as he was affectionately called—had supported and encouraged John throughout his life and military career. Every one of John's uncles but one served in the US Army and Air Force before earning their citizenship. Pipo would lecture his children and grandchildren about the greatness of the United States. He would tell stories of the Spanish-American War, about Teddy Roosevelt and the US helping Cuba gain its independence from Spain. He told them how the US saved the world in WWII from tyrants. He repeatedly expressed his appreciation and love for the United States and how his family was accepted with open arms after being exiled from Cuba.

He told his grandchildren how the family came to the US. After initially supporting the revolution to free Cuba from the dictatorship of Fulgencio Batista, Antonio Mori criticized the similarly tyrannical excesses within the new Castro government and was summarily imprisoned, tortured, and then exiled. He got his family to Miami before he could leave himself, hoping they would never again have to face the horrors of political violence. He expressed his belief that, through hard work and education, the United States of America was the best place on the planet where one could succeed. Pipo shared a deep-seated appreciation for his adopted country; a sense of patriotism and duty to protect this fragile privilege. One of Pipo's proudest moments—John had the privilege to witness as a boy—was when he took his oath of citizenship. Later, one of John's proudest moments was to have his grandfather pin on his Navy wings of gold.

John needed to show his grandfather he would continue to make him proud—with two legs or fewer.

It hurt. *God, it still hurts to walk.* But he sucked it up and waited outside Tevy and Elvira's house. He heard everyone moving inside, talking and laughing. Shelley smiled at him and gave his hand a squeeze. John inhaled and handed her his crutches. *Eat the pain.*

He stepped through the doorway of his own accord.

The room hushed. And then, as Latinos are wont to do, pretty much everyone burst into tears. He spent the rest of the evening being accosted by emotional family members and pretending blood was not seeping through his sock. It was worth it. Goal number one was complete.

Walk again! Check.

11

RUN

22 FEB 1987 // NAVY AVIATION OFFICER CANDIDATE SCHOOL // 0500L

"Come and water my rose garden, maggots!" Gunnery Sergeant Holtry, United States Marine Corps, ordered.

He had nicknamed John "Godzilla". The other Latino from Miami was "Mothra". They were sparring partners and the two even fought each other during battalion boxing matches. They were not fighting today, though. After the first week—Hell Week—the 15-87 class of the Naval Aviation Officer Candidate School had dropped from 64 down to 21 people. The surviving students would name their class "Holtry's Angels of Death". Holtry had purposefully whittled his class down by the first week. He'd repeatedly run the remaining class through the obstacle course in the deep Pensacola sand. The instructor timed their runs and used them to evaluate the class's opportunity to earn a physical fitness steamer (or award). This meant all candidates in that class needed the highest fitness ratings. In their limited free time, John and two others dedicated themselves to practicing the O course obstacles, aiming to shave off precious seconds for top times.

"It's all mind over matter," Gunnery Sergeant Holtry, United States Marine Corps (God help you if you did not address him with his full title) would roar over the shaking, panting men. "I don't mind...and you don't matter."

John Couch wrote about Navy Aviation Officer Candidate School (AOCS) in *The Pressure Cooker: Forging Naval Officers Through Marine Leadership*. In his opinion, AOCS was considered the most intense officer commissioning program in the world; even more intense than Marine boot camp. According to John, Gunnery Sergeant Holtry, United States Marine Corps, was "the voice I shall never forget". Civilians might be familiar with the hard-assed, foul-mouthed, rage machine of a drill instructor in the film *An Officer and a Gentleman*. They would not be far off to compare the fictionalized OCS with the real deal.

Holtry had them running towards the side of the building. It was muddy and stunk in the Pensacola humidity. A little scraggly rose lay in the mud. This was the entirety of what remained of the rose garden, and the AOCS candidates were tasked with watering it.

With their sweat, of course.

John could no longer think. The days had passed in a rush of pain and exhaustion. He stood at attention as the drill sergeant walked down the line.

"Diamonds, girls!" Holtry barked. "Get 'em!"

"Yes, sir!" the students chorused.

The candidates all dropped in unison into the mud and counted out Holtry's diamond pushups; where the pointer fingers and thumbs would touch to resemble the shape of a diamond.

4-7 DEC 1996 // PORTSMOUTH NAVAL HOSPITAL, VIRGINIA //

"I'm convinced it's the right thing to do, Shel," John told her. "This knee surgery can give me a head start, they've seen real results. I need to give it a shot."

John had been on several calls with the SEAL from DEVGRU, and with a Mr. Raymond Francis out of Virginia. Eventually, they shared enough information with the Wilford Hall medical team's to give the agreement to go.

Shelley had given her blessing reluctantly. She trusted the doctors and surgeons at Wilford Hall. They had been nothing but amazing to John. Besides, she knew that her husband was still feeling torn about changing doctors. In the end, though, it was John's decision and she knew that when he made up his mind—he was going to go through with it.

In early December, John and Shelley flew up to Norfolk for his knee surgery.

At the security checkpoint at the Fort Walton Beach airport to fly to Norfolk, Virginia, Shelley teased John for hobbling through the metal detector with his prosthetics and then turning around to take stuff out of his pockets when the detector went off.

"A little pointless," she said as he scowled at the noise. "You know, considering the big metal pole under your left leg."

On the day of the surgery, Shelley waited in the family waiting room. She was only one of two people in the room. She was distracting herself with a book when two men walked up to her. One was a Navy SEAL officer in uniform, and the other was an older man in civilian clothes. The Navy SEAL, Pete, reintroduced himself and introduced Shelley to Mr. Raymond Francis.

"I own Tidewater Prosthetics in Norfolk," Mr. Francis told Shelley. Shelley shook Mr. Francis's hand. She decided not to mention that John already had a prosthetist. She was not comfortable talking specifics with this stranger. She was feeling protective of John.

"Do you know when John will be out of surgery?" Mr. Francis asked.

"It shouldn't be much longer. Maybe about an hour? They will still have to move him into recovery."

"Understood, we can come back later. When he's in post-op."

Shelley nodded as they took their leave. Neither man was particularly forthcoming or friendly. They seemed focused on business. As for the SEAL, Shelley could understand him not being warm. But she wondered why Pete brought the prosthetist to meet her while John was still in surgery. She thought about the doctors in Texas, and their kinder bedside manner.

She was not impressed. *These are the guys who are telling me to just trust them with my husband?*

The doctors notified Shelley that she could accompany them to post-op with John. Mr. Francis also came by, as promised.

Shelley introduced Mr. Francis to a still groggy John. The man spoke with John, asking him questions about his prosthetic and his plans. He asked about the bloody wool socks and John's military future. He said he could fit John with a real state-of-the-art running leg. Shelley noticed that the prosthetist was very direct and did not coddle her husband.

After John dozed off again, Francis looked at Shelley. The look he gave her shocked her. His eyes softened, and his face looked both stricken and filled with absolute conviction.

"Let me help him," Raymond Francis said quietly and urgently.

Francis then told Shelley his life story. He talked about his piloting experience. He knew exactly what John needed in order to walk normally, to run, and to fly again. Not only in fixed-wing airplanes but also in military combat helicopters.

The short man, balding in hair and straightforward in temperament, had been in the prosthetics industry since the Vietnam War. He had enlisted in the Army and become a helicopter mechanic.

After he got out of the military, Raymond finished college and trained in the prosthetics program at New York University Medical School School, and had gotten his feet wet at the VA hospital in New York.

After World War II, the VA was frustrated with the prosthetics they had to deal with for their patients. A veteran would step out into the rain, the foot would get wet and squeak, he would go to the VA hospital where they would take it apart and lubricate, send the man on his way, and the man would turn up again the next week for the same problem.

The VA eventually brought in innovative solutions and funded private practices like Raymond's, changing the prosthetic industry. One thing they explored was the early fittings of new amputees. Even through the 90s, most hospitals were conservative. The standard attitude was *'Go home and heal up, afterwards we'll worry about fitting you with a leg'*. Very few hospitals would allow an amputee to receive a prosthetic fitting the day after surgery.

"I learned about John through Pete," Raymond explained. "I have a network of Navy SEALs I have worked with and helped keep back on duty, not only with prosthetics but with braces and orthotics."

Raymond Francis had moved to Norfolk, Virginia, and opened up his own practice in 1968. The Naval hospital in Portsmouth was the second largest in the nation. He experienced the aftermath of the Vietnam War and the overflowing hallways of injured soldiers. He built relationships with the younger doctors working in the hospital, and together they implemented newer standards for amputees.

"I took one look at John and I knew," Raymond told her. *"I could do wonders for this guy."*

Shelley could tell Raymond was not naturally an emotional person. For this kind of man to be so open with his desire to connect with John, to make his goals a reality...it had to come from a deep and authentic place. He respected Shelley's role in John's life, her duty to protect her soulmate, and wanted her to understand that he would do everything in his power to help John. Raymond had let Shelley see his heart.

Trust your gut.

Surprising even herself, Shelley immediately let go of every hesitation and metaphorically placed John in Mr. Francis's hands.

THAT AFTERNOON AFTER SURGERY, John was on a stationary bicycle to keep the right knee from locking up. Mr. Francis went to him and asked him if he had read about the state-of-the-art "FlexFoot" prosthetic. John immediately had flashes of running on it.

"Yes. But I was told I would not be ready or strong enough for one for at least a year."

"Son, that's B.S.," Raymond said. "Let me take your current leg overnight and see what I can do with it." John spent the night in the hospital with a contraption strapped to his right leg that would bend and straighten his knee so it would not lock up.

The following morning, Shelley and another SEAL showed up after breakfast. Chief Tom "Rat" Rothrauff was an enlisted Navy SEAL also assigned to DEVGRU. Rat was built like a WWE wrestler and sounded like one, too. He was wearing chaps, having just gotten off his Harley.

"You'll be okay, brother. Just a bump in the road," Rat declared shortly after introducing himself. He told John and Shelley how he lost his left leg in a motorcycle accident. He then dropped his pants to show them his carbon-fiber socket leg and state-of-the-art FlexFoot.

"Okay, I'll leave you two for your male bonding," Shelley commented as she promptly left the room.

Rat talked about embracing the prosthetic as a piece of operational equipment, a tactical asset. "It is an advantage to a meat leg," the SEAL told him. Rat gave him some tips for leg squats to build up posture and strength in both legs. "You have to build up your quads. Even if it hurts, make them all believe the shock absorber in this bad boy helps for jumping and running. Shit, it will even take a five-five-six round. I personally tested one out on the range."

John had to admit, he was quite impressed.

"Trust me, if I can jump, dive, and run around ships," Rat said, "we'll get you back in your helo and fly, sir."

Overnight, Francis took the socket of John's prosthetic and attached the FlexFoot with a carbon fiber spring—used for high activity and running. He also brought a gel liner to replace the bloodied and archaic wool socks. A Mt. Sterling, Ohio company had launched the groundbreaking gel liner sock a few months earlier. Its mineral oil content was a revolutionary departure from the traditional wool socks used for nearly a hundred years, as it nourished and protected the skin. It would prove transformative for thousands of amputees worldwide. Amputees could walk sooner and heal faster. Eventually, some right out of surgery could bear weight.

Everyone told John it would be months before he could walk, even after his latest knee surgery. Raymond Francis was about to put John on a new trajectory with his new *badass* prosthetic the day after his latest surgery.

When Raymond came to present John with the new foot and liner, a bald, burly African American also accompanied him. While John was still marveling at the FlexFoot and fiberglass socket, Raymond introduced Carl.

"Carl, tell the Lieutenant here what you did in the Navy."

'Carl' was Master Chief Carl Brashear, the Navy's first African American diver. He was also the first sailor returned to duty as a Navy diver with a leg amputation, and had a movie in the works to tell his story starring Cuba Gooding Jr. Raymond Francis had made some of Master Chief Carl Brashear's legs.

"L.T. If I could run with a wooden leg and swim under ships," Brashear said, "you can get your fat ass back in a helicopter." He placed his hand on John's shoulder and smiled at Raymond. "Especially with all this newfangled gear Mr. Francis here's fitting you with."

Raymond smiled at John like a Cheshire cat. "Remember: just shut up and walk, son."

8 DEC 1996 // CORRY STATION, PENSACOLA, FLORIDA // 0800L

With dawn peeking through the curtains of his sanctuary, he was woken up by a nudge, then another by the cold nose of their loyal but insistent yellow lab, Monty.

"Okay, boy, let's go potty."

He begrudgingly sat up and groggily inspected the deep scab on his still-healing stump as he leaned over the edge of the bed.

Don't stand up yet, John.

He rolled the cold gel liner over the stump. The gel liner had proven its weight in gold. John no longer bled as often from the thin wool socks that would repeatedly open his scars time after time. His stump was healing at a faster rate. John still had to apply bandages after the gym—he couldn't let himself off the hook that easily.

He then deliberately inserted his stump, nerves now buzzing with electricity, into the socket. He'd lead Monty outside, then he'd lead himself to another grueling round of PT.

Upon returning from Portsmouth, John was still relegated to crutches. John had started physical therapy at Corry Station near the Naval Air Station in Pensacola, Florida. Shelley would drive John to the Naval Air Medical Institute (NAMI) at the Naval Air Station. As a Navy exchange pilot operationally assigned at Hurlburt Field, his administrative records were kept in Pensacola and his admin chain of command were still there.

Two Navy-enlisted PT techs were assigned to his case. They were the perfect fit—they were almost as motivated to get John back to flight status as he was. One afternoon, the techs brought John to one of the leg exercise machines to surprise the pilot with a machine fitted with helicopter pedals from an old Huey helicopter so he could leg press when he got his prosthetic. PT at home was progressing well, but he still needed another surgery for his right knee.

Despite his tough talk, John was still unsatisfied with his progress. He wasn't shaving. He would suffer occasional bouts of depression and then immediately take it out in the gym.

The reps would tear at the edge of his willpower. The smell of sweat and the iron tang of pain in his mouth overwhelmed him. His bed beckoned; his quiet sanctuary with Shelley. The seductive idea of letting the next set wait for another day.

John would simply crank up the volume in his CD headset.

The pain of giving up will be far worse than the pain I'm feeling right now, he told himself.

John's arms screamed at him. John mentally screamed back.

Come on, John, let's go, right here, right now!

Van Halen blared through his skull as he upped the weights on the bar in front of him. *One more set!*

10 DEC 1996 // NAVARRE, FLORIDA //

"If I got through AOCS, I can get through anything," John had told Shelley after peeling off another bloody bandage and gel liner. "If I can survive Gunny Holtry, I can survive anything."

Shelley had been thinking about Holtry for weeks.

John was doing PT on his own and at Corry Station, building his strength and aiming for his next goal. Shelley, meanwhile, was on her own mission. She was given an extended leave of absence from the hospital. Her director was incredibly supportive and told Shelley she could return whenever she was ready.

In the brief lulls in her schedule, Shelley contacted all of John's positive influences, aiming to fortify him. Len King tapped in, and even shared that his nephew had been more invested in helping her back when she was waiting for John to land in Texas—more than Shelley initially suspected. Len retold the moment when Shelley had thought it was strange that Mike went into the restricted area by the nurse's station. Well, Mike had not just gone to the bathroom. He had spoken to the doctors who had been in contact with the flightline. Mike had found out that even though they knew John had landed, they had not come out to notify Shelley. Len King's seemingly calm, stoic nephew had gone into the back office and *reamed* the hospital staff for making the family wait. It was that kind of brotherhood and support that Shelley knew John needed at that moment.

She knew that this goal of John's, going back to flying, was a monumental task. She had confidence that her husband had the guts and grit to get there. But surely it would be easier if he were hearing the voices of people who cared about him rooting him on? Some of his friends and colleagues, scattered around the country, could get in touch and talk with him. Some could visit, but not everyone. It helped, but she realized there was one voice that could maximize the effect.

After a particularly rough week, Shelley called NAS Pensacola and tracked down Holtry's phone number. John had told her that Holtry was now a Master Gunnery Sergeant and had returned to Pensacola as the chief drill instructor of the reinstated Navy OCS. Shelley was patched through to the drill sergeant's secretary, who patched Shelley through to Holtry's office.

Shelley immediately recognized Holtry's tone. He was a big, bad Marine and sounded like it. She quickly explained who she was and what had happened to John.

"He's been saying if he were able to survive AOCS, and especially you, he can get through anything. I even hear him imitating your voice to himself," she told him. "It would be really neat if you could meet with him."

"Does he need a pick-me-up? Motivation?" Holtry asked.

"Oh no, he's doing fine motivating himself and is very disciplined," Shelley said. "I just think it would be a great connection. A reminder that he's doing right by you." Holtry agreed to meet the Alvarez couple at a local Mexican restaurant in Pensacola. Shelley decided to make it a surprise.

The day of the meeting, Shelley casually dropped a suggestion before John's PT session.

"Why don't you get a haircut? You look so handsome with your high and tight." John agreed, totally oblivious and eager to please his wife, and got cleaned up.

After PT, Shelley picked him up. "Hey, let's go on a lunch date and get Mexican food."

"Sure," John said. It took a little finagling since John hated having his back to a door, but Shelley got him to sit in the chair with the back to the entrance.

John did not know why Shelley was acting weird, but he was too tired to debate. He was eating chips and answering Shelley's questions when someone spoke behind him. The voice was low, gruff, and chillingly familiar.

"What's this I hear about a fallen angel?" Master Guns Holtry growled.

The hairs on the back of John's neck stood up. His spine involuntarily straightened to attention.

Holtry laughed when he entered John's periphery. John stood up as quickly as he could. The Master Gunnery Sergeant shook his hand and gave John a tight hug. Holtry was in his Class-Charlies; his business uniform. He had an OCS candidate with him. The kid had red tape on either side of his nametag, meaning he was in the holding battalion. John recognized it as a sign that the cadet was probably injured or sick.

As they chatted, Holtry eventually addressed the kid. "See, candidate, here this Lieutenant has gone through all this special ops shit and he's fighting to stay on active duty and get back into the fight. And here you are whining and complaining about your little *Achilles tendon* injury! C'mon, L.T., tell him!"

The candidate swallowed. John chuckled to himself. *Master Guns, always motivating.*

John told him about the missions he'd been on and Holtry described the counter-drug and riverine missions he also deployed to in Latin America. Just before they left the restaurant, Holtry pulled a T-shirt out of a bag. It was the 15-87 class shirt. John's class shirt. It had a rose and diamond on the sleeve, with "*GET 'EM*" written underneath the image. It had the Angels of Death insignia. He handed the shirt to John.

"I want you to wear this at PT," Holtry told him, "and I want you to bring it back to me with your sweat on it."

God help anyone who defied a command from Master Gunnery Sergeant Holtry, United States Marine Corps.

11 DEC 1996 // HURLBURT FIELD AFB, FLORIDA //

"Your job is to get better," Tommy Hull told him. "Your duty location is Corry Station."

"Sir, I gotta come back to work," John protested. "I have to say thank you to everybody. They built me a ramp for my wheelchair. They brought all those meals when I was recovering. They deserve recognition for taking care of me and my family. They really proved that we're a brotherhood." Tommy eventually agreed to let John show his face. It was going to be at his squadron's end-of-year commander's call, also known as an all-hands.

John was adamant. "I'm part of the squadron. I'll be there, sir."

Tommy instructed him to stay outside of the auditorium and wait in the secured special missions planning room known as the vault. John was still on crutches. He was hurting. He was only just outside of his last surgery, and his bloody stump wound was not fully healed. John took a big breath, exhaled, and put the crutches down. *Eat the pain.*

"We have someone special here who wants to say hello to everybody," Tommy was saying to the entire squadron.

LT John "Ahab" Alvarez, SOF aviator, in his flight suit with a new call sign on his name patch, walked through the door and toward the stage. The squadron was in shock to watch him walk across the stage in his flight suit. The room erupted with cheers and applause; some guys had tears in their eyes. Tommy beamed as he finished his call to inspire his squadron of gruff, unconventional warriors. Hannibal's plan was finally coming together.

"Hey guys," John said. "I wanted to come here and say thank you. I know I haven't kept in touch, but heck, I've been busier than a one-legged man in an ass-kicking contest."

Tommy immediately assigned John as Chief of Special Missions.

~

20 DEC 1996 // PORTSMOUTH, VIRGINIA //

The prosthetist—quickly becoming a close family friend—worked on touching up the socket and foot. Mr. Francis got John climbing stairs, jumping on the leg, and other ways to test what John could do with the new leg. He made tweaks to benefit John's specific needs as a helicopter pilot. Since most cockpits, especially in combat aircraft, were crowded with not a lot of extra space, his team balanced security of fit with John's needed ability to be agile. He needed to run, to operate the pedals, and to climb out of various aircraft.

They structured the socket so John could bend his knee more easily. Raymond applied his own unique and unconventional approach to aggressively align the leg and add resistance to the toe so John would have to work his quads and hamstrings harder than normal to control his gait. The ordinarily accepted practice was to get the foot under the ordinary patient so it was easier to stride across from heel strike to toe and walk.

However, Raymond was no ordinary prosthetist and his 'boys' were no ordinary patients, but warrior athletes. He took John into the back shop where he and his technicians trained John to build, disassemble and work on his own prosthetics—something unheard of in any standard practice. But if John were to return to combat status, he would have to make adjustments and maintain his equipment out in the field or remote locations just like any other piece of operational gear. Chief Rat was also there, mentoring John and providing practical advice from the experience he had with his 'gear'.

John was rapidly gaining a sincere affection for Raymond. He was a gruff, no-nonsense, salt-of-the-earth kind of guy. He also loved to fly, and there is something about a fellow pilot's logic-free love for the sky. Later that month, the Alvarezes drove to Canada for Christmas. This time, John was driving. They made the long, three-day trip by minivan, stopping in Norfolk for John to meet up with Mr. Francis again.

As a Christmas gift, Raymond embedded a pair of gold Naval

Aviator wings into the next high-tech carbon-fiber socket of John's prosthetic. *Even more badass!*

Raymond also showed Shelley and the girls his sweet and gregarious side. The girls introduced their Labrador Retriever, Monty, to him, and he let them play with his German Shepherd, Orf. Orf's name was the three-letter identifier for the Norfolk airport (ORF) where Raymond hangared his aircraft and flew with his trusty, furry copilot. He had an incredible love for dogs; all his canine companions had aviation monikers.

Before the Alvarezes left, Raymond instructed the girls to kick their dad if he was not weight bearing or standing on his new "robot leg."

Nicole quickly replaced the command of "bend it!" with "kick it!". Lisette would also chime in, but also made sure not to hurt her Daddio. John and Shelley had to adjust the tightly packed van with all the gear and extra parts Raymond provided, among all the other Christmas presents. More gear would be shipped to Florida over the holidays.

Raymond never charged John or his 'brothers' a dime for any of it.

01 JAN 1997 // HAMILTON, ONTARIO, CANADA // 8:30PM

On New Year's Day, John relaxed at the dining room table, watching the girls pretend to be ice skaters on the tile. Christmas and New Year's were spent with Shelley's parents. Pat had knitted slippers for Nicole and Lisette. They spent most of the trip twirling around on the tile floor in their new slippers. His prosthetic was off, resting at his side while he snacked on Dennis Hammond's chocolate ice cream. Dennis, Pat, and Shelley were chatting in the other room.

Then he heard a loud *THUD* and a heart-stopping wail. Nicole had fallen while dancing in her knit slippers and popped her tooth out. John's prosthetic leg was off and he could not reach his daughter.

He panicked, screaming for Shelley over Nicole's cries and Lisette's frightened hovering. Shelley came in and checked on Nicole, who had blood coming out of her mouth. For a few blood-chilling moments, Shelley inspected the four-year-old's mouth. She finally determined Nicole was fine. They found the little baby tooth on the tile.

"We can save it!" John insisted as he scrambled to put on his leg. "Put it in milk! You have the number of a dentist, right?" *Shit, we have to save it. God, please, not her. She's too little to lose anything!*

"It's just a baby tooth, John. For God's sake, breathe!" Shelley protested. John was determined and hellbent on saving the tooth, so she let him find and call an emergency dental line.

"Press one if you've lost a tooth playing hockey," the recorded voice on the other line told him. The message was so stereotypically Canadian, John was momentarily forced out of his frantic insistence to save the tooth. He laughed so hard in relief that he almost cried.

∾

06 JAN 1997 // NAVARRE, FLORIDA // 10:00AM

If I can drive stick, he thought, *I can sure as shit fly a helicopter.*

Upon their return to Florida, John continued his steadfast and obsessive routine of getting stronger and more capable. One day, he decided he wanted to drive his Honda CRX.

After starting up the car, he cranked up the tunes. Boston's *More Than a Feeling* vibrated and resonated through the car and through John. He thought back to his 'death runs'—running on the beach in Key Biscayne with his high school and college soccer teams, and again at Corpus Christi during flight school. He shook his head back to reality. *Soon, John. Soon. Focus.*

He adjusted the driver's seat and quickly figured out which part of his carbon fiber foot to find and rest on the correct part of the clutch pedal without catching his foot in the footwell under the dashboard.

Again. Again. This time without looking down, John. He continued, trying to figure out how much pressure was needed to manipulate the clutch with controlled and minute movements from his knee. He then methodically practiced a few times without looking to retrain his limb and ingrain this new habit.

Muscle memory. Mind over matter!

Shelley was not as easily convinced. She stepped outside when she heard John starting up the CRX.

"What are you doing?" she yelled over Bon Jovi's *Wanted Dead or Alive.*

"Going to see if I can drive it," he told her, grinning as he turned down the radio. "Want to come?"

"Ahh no way, *cowboy*," Shelley replied, bringing up the 20th SOS callsign. "Besides, if you get in a car accident, who would rescue you from the burning wreckage?"

"Well," he considered, "if my left leg is pinned, I can always take it off and hop out. Or maybe the Rangers will come to the rescue this time, babe." He pulled her near, and they kissed. "See ya, Stella."

John waved off her skeptical but amused look and pulled out of the driveway. He practiced around the empty cul-de-sac for a bit. Once he got comfortable driving without looking down at his foot or clutch, John drove out to Highway 399. He brought it up to speed, windows and sunroof open, savoring the freedom, music, and rush. *Just like riding a bike.*

That is, until John realized he did not have his wallet or license on him. Florida cops were no joke. John turned the music down, turned around and carefully drove home...at the speed limit, this time.

John convinced the techs at Corry Station to let him use the physical therapy facility as his gym. He would lift for his upper body and core while they focused on his legs and gait. He had upper body days where he was lead, called Push-Pull days. Alternating large muscle groups that pulled on one day, followed by working push muscles the next. Wednesday would be a rest day.

Well, as far as the techs are concerned.

He plugged away at the stationary bicycle as the required warmup instructed by the PT techs, then the treadmill, and worked quads, knees, and calves. Then he would work single-leg balance drills for both legs. Raymond had given John a challenge back in Virginia.

"My 'profession' has accepted that the vast majority of amputees can barely balance on their prosthetic side for a few seconds at best. Let's prove them wrong, son."

To prevent his prosthetic leg from dislodging while curling heavier weights, John employed modified techniques on the quad and knee machines, focusing the effort on his left leg. On the knee machine, he'd work his legs individually. He learned to position the hinged pads of the weight machine just over the carbon fiber socket so he could lift heavier weights.

He would usually finish his therapy portion of his sessions with brutal Russian current electrical stimulation sessions on his quad muscles and thighs, especially on his right side to make up for the atrophy as quickly as possible and to protect the instability in his knee. Russian current-stimulation was adopted in the U.S. starting in the 1980s. It was a high-intensity neuromuscular electrical stimulation protocol that used a 2,500 Hz medium-frequency current delivered in 50 Hz bursts. It contracted muscle fibers much more strongly and generated much more torque than a human can voluntarily produce.

It was uncomfortable, to say the least. John convinced his PT tech to turn it up so high once that he involuntarily kicked the tech hard in a sensitive spot. *Eat the pain!*

He was sent home immediately after icing the knee down and was told to take a day off.

His therapists also set up a mirror and would videotape him as he was on the treadmill for feedback on his gait training.

During one session, a tech critiqued his gait.

"Ease up, you're swaying," the tech said. "You're walking like John Wayne, sir. We're not trying to swagger."

"What's wrong with that?" John pretended to protest. "John friggin' Wayne!"

"Hell yeah, pardner!" another tech called out in his Southern twang.

He continued to stay at PT far longer than scheduled. John was their favorite patient. He spent a lot of time on the squat station and on his upper body, lifting heavy weights again. For him, PT and working out were also part of his emotional therapy.

Ever since John was a kid, distance running had been his go-to for getting over frustration and stress. He still dreamed of experiencing that runner's high again, of being in the zone. He was working out hard and continued his mindfulness and visualization exercises. The exercises helped keep the emotional, mental, and physical turmoil at bay and dissipated thoughts that tempted him into depression. Corry Station was his battlefield, and he would win this war.

God willing.

～

08 JAN 1997 // NAVARRE, FLORIDA // 10:00AM

His physical therapist walked over to him. "You got a call. It's your wife, sir."

John frowned. It was a strict policy not to take calls during PT sessions, but he guessed it must be urgent.

"Hey, Shell, what's up?" he said when he got hold of the phone.

"Guess who just called?!" Shelley squealed.

"Uh..." John paused, confused. "I dunno."

Shelley was unabated in her enthusiasm. "You voted for him!"

John furrowed his brow. *What kind of politician would... Oh.*

"...Ross Perot?"

"Yes!" his wife chirped. "Ross Perot just called, and he wants you to call him back!"

John broke into a wide grin. "Ross Perot? Okay!"

Ross Perot, through a convoluted chain of communication that was the "Special Ops network", had been notified of John's situation by the Navy Seal Team commander whose platoon had deployed with John in Ecuador. John had written a formal letter to Commander Bo Basilivack and praised his platoon for saving his life. John and Shelley had also visited SEAL Team Four while he was still in his wheelchair after his knee surgery in December.

Like so many other SOF unit commanders, Bo had met Mr. Perot earlier and was given his number. Perot directed Bo to call only when a SOF warrior really needed his help. After seeing John, Bo gave Mr. Perot John's squadron information.

Mr. Perot had called the 20th Special Operations Squadron. Captain AJ Gaston had picked up.

"Sir, I can't give you his number," AJ told Mr. Perot after the former presidential candidate identified himself. "But I can get him to call you."

"Do you know who I am?"

"Yes, sir. Sorry," AJ apologized. "But I'm not allowed to give out his personal number. I can, however, take your number and pass it on."

AJ had remained calm and matter of fact throughout the process, but apparently was frazzled when he called Shelley.

John got Perot's information from Shelley and called him from the clinic.

"Well, I understand you have an engineering degree," Ross Perot told John after a few pleasantries. "Your future is secure if you need a job."

"Thank you, sir. I truly appreciate your help. I'll keep that in mind," John said.

"I'd like to get you out here to Dallas," he continued. "I also have the name of a prosthetist, one of the best in the world."

"No, sir, thank you. I already have one who I think is one of the best."

"What's his name?" Perot pressed.

"Mr. Raymond Francis. He is a Civil Air Patrol pilot," he told him. "He's worked on Navy SEALs, and some are already back to combat duty."

"Okay, well, I'll check him out," Perot mused. "So, what are your goals?"

"Sir, I want to stay on active duty and I want to get back to flying."

There was a brief pause on the other line. "Well, I can't tell you what you can or can't do, son, but if there is anything I can do to help you heal, if you need any equipment for your PT, I will buy it as long as someone else can use it."

John put Ross Perot on the phone with the Corry Station PT director. While they initially wanted a pool, Ross Perot ended up buying equipment for John to use and for the clinic to keep after he was finished. On the phone, Perot reiterated his desire to make sure John had a secure future should he leave the military. John thanked him for his concern and promised to stay in touch with his progress. Mr. Perot was clearly not done yet—and he had Mr. Francis and Tidewater Prosthetics checked out.

15 JAN 1997 // NAVARRE, FLORIDA // 10:00AM

While at PT, John met an elderly gentleman. A retired Navy officer going through cardiac rehab. Jorgen Fog would exercise on the bike next to him, and they would strike up a conversation. He told John that he was a veteran of WWII and later served in Vietnam. Fog told John that he had met Sir Douglas Bader after WWII. Bader was the first British pilot to go back to combat flying after losing both his legs. Fog gave John his copy of the book: *Douglas Bader, a biography of the legendary WWII fighter pilot.* Fog signed it *Courage, faith, love, and charity.* John read it along with *One Tough Marine* again. John still wondered about the mysterious Navy pilot who tried to get back to flight status in the 60s.

There's precedent with Bader. Who is this unnamed Naval Aviator?

This unnamed pilot was mentioned only in passing in the book, but John also remembered the NFO who visited him in Wilford Hall and his story about the grounded Navy pilot with two wooden legs on the obstacle course in Pensacola.

He stopped at NAMI again to ask about the pilot in Pensacola. He was told that such a pilot did not exist. They had no information about any officer, Naval or otherwise, who was an amputee and tried to return to flight status. They even let him search through the microfiche archives. Nothing.

In early January 1997, Mr. Francis fitted John with another carbon fiber socket for the prosthesis and a sleek, high-tech knee brace. In late January, John again returned to Norfolk alone on several trips to have adjustments made to his prosthesis. His flexibility in his right knee finally reached 135 degrees. He got rid of his cane. He hung out in the 20th SOS break room behind the bar. John worked his way up to a run on the treadmill. He had nearly a month until Lisette's birthday.

28 JAN 1997 // TIDEWATER PROSTHETICS, NORFOLK, VIRGINIA // 11:11 AM

John started work at the squadron again. He kept up his running practice. When folks checked in on his progress, he would say, "Easy, piece of cake," while cleaning blood out of his prosthetic's socket. Eventually, he was sent to Virginia Beach as a Special Mission Planner, supporting the Navy SEALs at DEVGRU. On January 26, John drove to nearby Norfolk again to get more tweaking and adjustments with Mr. Francis.

"We still gotta get more reinforcement," the technician told John as he strapped the transparent socket and leg to John's stump. "This socket is just so I can see how your leg moves within the mold we have."

"Alright, what do you want to see me do?" John asked, levering himself to both feet. He leaned to his left gingerly, testing his weight in the socket.

"Just walk on it, there and back." John obeyed, taking some initial strides down the hallway. The extra length of strap tapped against the socket and he had the urge to grab it and hold it in place. But what was stronger was the urge to pick up the pace.

"Now, hold on, sir. I'm not sure…"

It was slow. It was ugly. But on that day, John ran down the hallway of Raymond Francis's office. The technician was nervous—the socket wasn't meant to withstand a beating. But John insisted. The technician started recording, and John took a few more jogging steps along the hallway. The strap was annoying, flopping around as he ran.

John wanted to go outside and run, despite the cold and wet, overcast day.

"Can I take it outside?" he asked. "There's more space to run."

"I don't know, sir, it's cold. I don't know how well that socket will hold up." The technician chuckled nervously. "Man, I didn't expect you to lay into it this hard…"

In the parking lot, John pushed harder. He found he could take longer strides. It did not feel great and there was none of the runner's high he missed.

But a win is a win, John told himself. *And it's on tape.*

He could now stroll over to Shelley with his swagger, embrace her, twirl her, and even kiss her in mid-dip. Chores that he no longer had an excuse for not doing awaited him. He still had to take out the garbage. Walk and clean up after the dog. Clean the pool. Cut the half-acre lawn.

But when John got back home to Navarre, he took Shelley and the girls outside to run and play with them again. Three full weeks before Lisette's sixth birthday.

Goal Two: Run again. Check!

12

FLY AGAIN

2 APR 1997 // NAVAL AIR MUSEUM, NAS PENSACOLA, FLORIDA // 1400L

John loved the Naval Air Museum. He was happy to volunteer on Lisette's school field trip to the museum on the Navy base in Pensacola. He had visited plenty of times before, but he never really got sick of looking at planes and helicopters from every era. While the class was drawn to one plane, a man approached him.

"I apologize, sir, but are you a pilot?" he asked, gesturing to the Navy wings in John's prosthesis. John told him the story of his accident. The man introduced himself. He was a museum volunteer, and a retired Marine Aviator.

"Have you ever heard of Lieutenant Commander Frank King Ellis?" the Marine asked. "Frankie Ellis was a Navy pilot who tried to get back to flight status here back in the sixties."

The breath rushed out of John's body. His heart pounded as he responded, "Sir, I've been trying to find this guy for *a long while now*. The staff at NAMI told me he doesn't exist!"

"I'll tell you what, son," the Marine told him. "We're about to do a story on Frank Ellis in our Naval Aviation journal. I'm going to take you back to our historian's office."

John checked in with Lisette's teacher to explain his brief absence and then followed the man to the historian's office. John told his story again, and they gave him the draft of the article they were going to publish on Frank Ellis.

My god, he exists, John thought in wonder as he read the article. He learned the Navy pilot lost both his legs in an ejection. In 1962—the year John was born—Lt. Frank Ellis was injured in a Cougar fighter after deciding to delay his ejection when something went wrong with the flight controls. He refused to eject in order to direct the plane away from base housing at Point Mugu Naval Air Station in California. His skill saved the lives of countless Navy family members. However, it cost him—multiple burns, a broken back, and both legs. After years of fighting the Navy to return to flight status, and despite all his trials and tribulations "as a guinea pig for their curiosity", the pilot was offered limited flight Medical Service Group 3 waiver status in 1963. Frank could not fly alone and had to be accompanied by another aviator. He was even a short-lived candidate for the Gemini Space Program. Bureaucracy, pre-conceived notions, and downright prejudice were all in his way.

There was a single, simple sentence at the end of the article.

Frank Ellis is retired, married, and lives in Ocala, Florida.

John finished up the field trip with Lisette's class. As soon as he returned home, he and Shelley booted up their computer and looked for a local Ocala number for Frank Ellis.

Shelley found it. The search returned two names and two numbers.

John dialed the first number. An elderly man's voice answered and confirmed he was the Lieutenant Commander Frank Ellis John had been looking for. John told Frank who he was and why he had called.

"—So now I'm trying to get back on flight status." John waited for a response, but the air was silent on the other end. "...Hello? Mr. Ellis?"

Frank finally spoke. "Sorry, I'm trying to regain my composure." His voice cracked, and John realized the older man had started to cry.

"It's alright, sir. I can call back another time—"

"No, son," Frank Ellis told John. "I've been waiting for this call for thirty years."

John told Frank how he'd been trying to find him after the Chaplain/NFO's story, and Hamblen's mention of an unnamed pilot, and how no one at NAMI Pensacola knew who he was until he visited the Naval Air Museum. The fire of a fighter pilot in Ellis emerged once again.

"That's bullshit; I've got all my records in my garage!" Frank declared. "I'll drive those records up to Pensacola myself!" He did. He turned all his files over to NAMI and tore into the flight surgeons he met with.

John, Shelley, and the girls drove down to Ocala and visited Frank and his wife, Christine. The girls took turns pretending to stand in Frank's two prosthetic legs, and John talked with Frank about his ultimate goal to return to unrestricted flight status.

After dinner, they both had a heart-to-heart, alone, about how blessed they were to survive their ordeals and return to their families. About what was truly important. The strength of faith, the unwavering power of love, and the grace of those around them.

"No man walks alone," Frank said. Frank gave John more sage advice and finally discussed the ultimate obstacles; ones that he himself could not overcome in his time. Bureaucracy and prejudice.

The ember was now a raging fire within John.

APRIL 1997 // OPERATIONAL LOCATIONS - GEORGIA, NORTH CAROLINA, VIRGINIA //

Colonel Tommy Hull had John back full-time as Chief of Special Projects and as the squadron's lead Special Missions planner. John continued to go on deployments to train with SEALs in Virginia, 75th

Rangers in Georgia, and an elite Army Special Forces in North Carolina. On those trips to Virginia, he would get tune-ups from Mr. Francis. It felt good to be part of the action again, even if he could not be flying helicopters.

His restrictions couldn't keep him from the cockpit entirely, however. John returned to the sky for the first time in Raymond's Cessna 152, and later his Cessna 206. He practiced and perfected using his prosthetic in the cockpit under Raymond's watchful eye.

John was given the go-ahead to be officially evaluated onboard the ship and would fly from Naval Air Station Oceania in the back of a helicopter for the first time. John prepped to fly out to the USS WASP. Before the brief, he was in the aircrew locker room with the Pave Low's tail gunner, Eric "Tater" Tate, who was also responsible to 'keep tabs on Ahab', keep him safe, and assess how well he handled himself onboard the helo.

They donned their required dry suits that would protect them from hypothermia if they had to ditch in the frigid waters of the Atlantic and prepped their flight gear. The Pave Low crew was going to conduct night landings for currency and Visit Board Search & Seizure (VBSS) maneuvers while John would disembark and be in the ship's tower for pri-fly. John would also show that he could run around the ship, climb and descend the ladder wells, and navigate other obstacles on board the ship.

After the aircrew brief, the two were reviewing additional checklist items in the aircrew locker room. Tater frowned at John. He appeared hesitant.

"Sir," he said. "I wasn't sure if I should tell you, but I had a bad dream about us being in the water."

John's good mood dried up. Their flight path was over eighty miles out over the cold ocean to the Navy amphibious helicopter assault ship. He was sure Tater was messing with him before his first ride in a helo. He didn't appreciate it.

"You son of a bitch. Shut up."

"No, sir, seriously," the gunner protested. "I'm not kidding!"

"Shut up, Tater," John ordered. "I don't wanna hear it."

Tater raised his hand in defeat. "Okay! Fine, sir."

He didn't persist when they got into the helicopter and flew out to the USS WASP. They ran through their maneuvers onboard the helo. John exited the helo to run around the stairs and the decks. John's other task was to make sure that the ship's assigned doc could get a good look at how he navigated the ladder wells with his prosthetic. He knew it was one of the unit's concerns about deploying with him.

John was doing great. He also spent time in the pri-fly control tower to observe the landings. He even got a PB&J during MIDRATS in one of the messes. He finally returned to the blacked-out flight deck, waved his chem light, and was cleared to board the chained-down Pave Low to depart the ship. As he looked out over the blank, horizonless ocean, John felt a deep sense of gratitude. He reveled in the rush of the cold sea air and the downwash of the deafening metal beast as he jumped into the helo.

As they took to the air, John leaned against his taut gunner's belt. He peered out over the open tail ramp and .50-caliber machine gun mount to watch the ship's deck disappear. He felt the grinding and then acceleration of the helo as they headed west towards the shore.

After the first thrill of being back in a helo, John soon started dozing in the back of the helicopter on the fabric troop sheets. Just as he was soaking in the dull roar of the helicopter, Tater came forward and shook John's shoulder.

"Sir, you gotta help me with the raft."

"What?"

John could also hear the pilots up front. An engine emergency indicator was flashing. Something was wrong with the left number one engine. Small metal chips in the engine's gearbox could damage it, or even the compressor blades, which would cause catastrophic damage.

They were a little more than halfway from the boat and closer to shore; about fifty miles out from the Naval Air Station on the coast. The pilots headed for land instead of returning to the ship. The flight engineer pulled the speed control lever (engine throttle) back and climbed. The pilots flew with one engine disengaged and briefed the ditching procedures over the intercom. They had to be prepared to ditch in the Atlantic if necessary. John resisted the urge to go up to the cockpit and take over.

No, he berated his panic. *These are great, experienced pilots.* He took a deep breath and went to help the gunner get the raft set up. Tater and John sat on the tail; the raft was ready for deployment.

Shit, John thought, looking between Tater and the water flashing in a dark sheet underneath them. *He wasn't kidding about that dream.*

The crew landed at Naval Air Station Oceania, rolling on a single-engine—nice and smooth. Tater, of course, did not let John live the incident down.

"See!" he exclaimed before deplaning and heading to the debrief, pointing a righteous, prophetic finger at his lieutenant. "I told you, sir!"

In late April into May, John deployed again on a joint special ops exercise as the lead aviation Special Missions planner and air liaison onboard the USS Enterprise, which had just come off its 6-month deployment.

"Hey Frito! John Alvarez!"

John was again the Special Op's "tower flower" on another training mission out on another of the Navy's amphibious ships, the USS Shreveport. "Frito" was his first callsign in the Navy. He wasn't expecting to see a familiar face other than his unit's. When John turned around, he grinned.

"Shilada! Hey brother, it's been a while," John said, laughing and smacking his old pilot buddy on the shoulder. Shilada's callsign was given to him because of his Cajun accent and a habit of saying "Shit-like-dat."

"Holy shit, it is you!" The other aviator declared. "I heard you were in a helicopter crash and a Navy SEAL had to cut your leg off to rescue you from drowning."

John snorted. "No, that's not what happened," he said. "I had to cut my *own* leg off to get out of the helicopter before I drowned." After an awkward pause, Frito-now-Ahab explained to his former squadron mate what really happened.

John flew a Navy MH-53E simulator at NAS Norfolk and received an endorsement from the evaluators for an attempt to return to flight status. John also continued flying Mr. Francis's Cessna 206 for his FAA demonstrated waiver.

~

28 APR 1997 // KIRTLAND AFB, NEW MEXICO // 1400L

At the very end of the month, he travelled to Kirtland AFB for a week-long, structured Air Force MH-53J Pave Low simulator refresher training that most crews do annually. He was sent with a pilot and an experienced flight engineer. Before heading to Kirtland, John would sit alone in the cockpit. He'd re-familiarize himself and practice in the cockpit of parked Pave Lows.

Failure is not an option, John told himself. He'd simulate ground taxiing with the stationary helicopter. Pilots needed fine motor skills to operate the toe brake pads hinged over the top of each pedal. He figured out a way to get around that problem by moving his seat forward and using his knee more to gingerly apply the left wheel brake, just like he did with the clutch of his car.

He received glowing evaluations from all the evaluators. They also cut him slack to approve his new taxiing technique.

"You can do this as well as anyone with two legs," a flight engineer told John. The flight engineer sneered at another pilot on the flight line. The captain had recently trimmed a tree with the helicopter's blades in one of the Eglin Range landing zones.

"Hey Captain, if you're having trouble," the flight engineer mocked. "I'm sure LT Alvarez could have his prosthetist make you some hands so you can fly as well as he can."

In May, John deployed again to Naval Air Station Oceana as the lead Pave Low planner for a JSOC bilateral exercise with SEALs from DEVGRU and also worked up with SEALs. He visited Rico, the Golf

Platoon leader that helped save him and had dinner at the home of the Navy SEAL who introduced him to Mr Francis.

1- 11 JUN 1997 // HURLBURT FIELD, FLORIDA //

By the summer, John was still being tested by his comrades. He accepted it as part of the process of getting his waiver package together. The special operators needed to see what he could do and needed to trust him.

Captain Brooks "Chuckie" Gruber, the Marine exchange pilot with the 20th SOS, had taken it upon himself to work out with John and get him on the obstacle course at Hurlburt. The Tactical Air Control Party (TACP) Obstacle Course was renamed "The Jungle" to pay tribute to the Vietnam-era "Jungle Jim" program that trained Air Commandos in unconventional warfare.

During their Pave Low qualification at Kirkland, John had accompanied Gruber as the other exchange pilot. Gruber had broken his back after flight school and got through his injury to continue on as a pilot. Gruber also brutalized John in the gym. The other pilot made sure he did not trip, slack off, or miss a single beat.

Later, Master Sergeant Randy Anderson—the squadron's Ops senior NCO and grizzly combat-seasoned flight engineer—joined in prepping John for including an obstacle course video to strengthen his waiver package application. Randy was tasked with videotaping John's obstacle course that would be submitted along with his waiver package. Anderson arrived in the early morning, forcing John to run through the course over and over again.

"You didn't look cool enough, *Lootenant*," the Master Sergeant barked in his Tennessee drawl as the Navy pilot panted in the dirt. Anderson reviewed every piece of obstacle course footage with John and nitpicked at everything.

"Drop down from higher on the wall this time."

"We need to see that your foot can take the shock."

"Again."

John snickered, then complied. Anderson, a combat-hardened flyer, was trying to make John look good for the waiver package. Torturing one of his favorite officers was just a perk of being a Master Sergeant. The video was punctuated with Bon Jovi's rock anthem *Wanted Dead or Alive*, edited to spotlight the pilot's coolest moves, and ended with a shot of John jogging away from the camera. It was perfect.

THE 30-FOOT CARGO net wall was the next target in front of him. John ran through the dense, white silica sand, determined to conquer it. Wearing a black 20th SOS T-shirt, fatigue pants, and boots, John was straining, nearing the top. Gruber and a CCT combat controller were out with him that morning.

John jumped and started climbing, using both his feet and legs to propel himself up the undulating net.

Brooks yelled at him. "Keep going Johnny! You know how…"

The CCT jeered after him. "The Navy loves those nets! Get right up into that boat! On that net!"

Brooks let out a Marine Corp grunt: "Aaaooahah!" And then a Navy "Hooyaah!"

John cleared the top and rolled to the other side of the obstacle, 30 feet above the ground.

"All right, roll! Okay, keep your feet… there you go!"

He jumped the last several feet to the ground.

"You were made for climbing nets!"

"Net monster!"

Reveling in the heat and exhaustion—and still running, visualizing his attack to the next obstacle—John had a flashback of his time on the O-course in Pensacola during AOCS, where he had one of the fastest times recorded in his class. He thought about the dream he had in Wilford Hall, when he was on the SEAL O-course.

And this time it was for real—with his badass robot leg.

"IF WE CRASH," AJ said, "and we have to go running around in the jungle or brush, are we going to have to carry you?"

John laughed. "No, I can keep up with you."

AJ, better known as Angry Man, was like a brother to John. However, he was also the squadron's tactics officer and one of the unit's best and most demanding pilots. He was a PT animal. AJ wanted proof that John could keep up. So John threw on a backpack, and the two went out on the range in Eglin. It was the middle of summer in the Florida Panhandle. Hot and the kind of humid that made you feel you were drowning on dry land.

AJ was keeping a relentless pace. The other pilot leapt over a log, then darted around the heavy brush. After the third or fourth log jump and continuous crashing through nettles, John could tell that AJ was doing it on purpose. He wanted to see if John would trip over the obstacles. John managed to keep up, but he was huffing.

After running both of them ragged, AJ had satisfied his curiosity.

"Okay, yeah," he said as John gulped down water. "I'm going to recommend you. I know they're testing your flying, but I wanted to make sure we can trust you on the ground and you wouldn't be a liability to us."

"So you're on board?" John asked, wiping away sweat from the Florida heat.

"Hell yeah, I'm on board, brother!"

John spent a full week undergoing the medical evaluations at the hospital in Pensacola and at NAMI. He was chased on the Eglin range through heavy brush to show he would not trip on the "slow-me-down" vines. Well, he did; he just didn't tell anyone.

In the helicopters, John ran through one emergency escape scenario after another. The observers made him tax his left leg and right knee in emergency situations. He had to jump out of the pilot's window onto a mattress, fireman-carry Dr. Joe Basinger out the right door, and then off the ramp.

John passed their demands flawlessly—with one exception.

"Hey John, think you can carry me farther?" Joe prodded him while still draped over the pilot's shoulder.

"Seriously?" John huffed. The doctor was not a small man after all.

"Just curious if you even can," the doc teased. That did it.

John carried him out to the edge of the flight line and, with little ceremony, body-slammed Joe onto the grass.

"Is that far enough, Doc?" John smiled as Joe rolled over with a pained 'oof'.

Joe B laughed breathlessly. "Check."

John also completed both the Navy and Air Force annual physical fitness tests: pushups, sit-ups, and timed distance runs. His performance on both was deemed 'outstanding,' the top rating achievable. He maxed out the required pushups and sit-ups and scored in the top 90th percentile in the run.

He completed Air Force water survival refresher at the Special Tactics pool at Hurlburt Field.

~

20 JUN 1997 // NAMI Code 42, NAS PENSACOLA, FLORIDA // 1400L

Near the end of June, the Navy Commander who ran the physical standards section named Code 42 at NAMI asked John to come into his office. The Commander would consider John's waiver request package before a formal Special Board of Flight Surgeons convened on the final recommendation: John's fate. The recommendation would then go up the chain to the Navy Bureau of Personnel, and possibly to the Chief of Naval Operations for final adjudication.

After the Navy higher headquarters, the Air Force would also have to accept and endorse his waiver in some fashion before he could fly again. All were trying to fathom how to process this unprecedented request. His Naval Aviation assignments officer, known as 'the detailer', in the meantime was interested in keeping

John if he passed the board. John was tentatively offered the assistant air ops position on the USS Wasp. It was a career-enhancing job, being on the Navy's premier amphibious carrier.

John, however, wanted to fly. He requested to finish his exchange tour. He had a deal with Colonel Hull, after all.

"Look," the Commander at Code 42 said. "We're gonna convene a Special Board of Flight Surgeons for your flight waiver review in July. Plus, I really want to get this done before I retire. You have a month."

Shit, John thought. *Am I ready?*

"July." John repeated. He straightened. "Yessir. Good to go."

"In addition to what you have already completed, the rest will be done here at NAS Pensacola. We are putting together a draft schedule for the week of 21 July." He pulled out a paper from the folder on his desk. "You will need waiver recommendations from each of the specialties: orthopedics, internal medicine, optometry, internal medicine, psychology."

John knew he would be examined head to toe, but looking at the packed schedule still made him feel a little concerned.

The Commander continued. "We already know about some of the other items you have completed and will need those documented as enclosures to your waiver request. Shipboard assessments, the simulators, the field evasion demo on the Eglin range, the Special Tactics obstacle course, your PT scores. You will also go through a full Navy water survival refresher. We will have to get special permission from the Chief of Naval Operations for this. You'll be expected to go through the helo dunker again." At the last detail, the Commander sat back and looked at John. Clearly, he felt the dunker was going to dampen John's enthusiasm to get back to flying.

John remembered the feeling of blindness and submersion. Pain. The taste of panic. However, he also knew that water survival training and the dunker helped save his life in Ecuador.

John breathed deeply. He could do this. *Heck, I already did this for real.*

"The dunker," Ahab repeated. "Yessir, good to go!"

30 JUN 1997 // AFSOC HEADQUARTERS, HURLBURT FIELD, FLORIDA // 0800L

John's case was unique. Docs Joe Basinger and Leo Cabanilla (a fellow flight surgeon), and their team of operational flight medics at the 16th Special Ops Wing within AFSOC were leading the charge in preparing Ahab's waiver package. They all knew his case was about to set a precedent, possibly across all the services. In true Special Ops and Naval Aviation fashion, where there's a will, there's a way. John, and those around him, would press it to the limit.

The cover letter was required to be a waiver request from LT Alvarez himself:

(SUBJ: REQUEST FOR WAIVER OF PHYSICAL STANDARDS) from LT Alvarez to Chief, Bureau of Naval Personnel (PERS 43C) via the following:
(1) Flight Surgeon, 16th Operations Support Squadron
(2) Commanding Officer, 20th Special Operations Squadron
(3) Commander, 16th Operations Group
(4) Commander, 16th Special Operations Wing
(5) NAVAEROPMEDINST, CODE 42 (NAMI)

THE FIRST ENDORSEMENT would come from the 16th SOW flight surgeon at the 16th SOS. He allowed Joe to sign it.

"...GIVEN the above history and physical examination, the only diagnoses currently rendering LT Alvarez NPQ for flying as a Naval Aviator in Class

I/Service Group (SG) I in accordance with the Navy's 1997 Aeromedical Reference and Waiver Guide (ARWG97) are the amputation of the left lower leg (ICD9 897.0) and the history of right PCL disruption (ICD9 717.84; ARWG97, 13.6).

"... For these reasons, I recommend his return to military flying, with waiver for left BKA and history of right PCL disruption. This action would pose no risk to personal health, flying safety, or mission completion, and would retain an aviator who is fully trained and proven effective as a resource for the US military.

A waiver of physical standards is therefore recommended for LT Juan Alvarez, for the diagnoses of left BKA and history of right PCL disruption, for duty involving actual control of aircraft as a Naval Aviator, Class I, Service Group I, without restrictions."

THE SECOND, third, and 4th endorsements were all combined in one letter crafted by Tommy Hull himself; their Group and Wing commanders also signed it.

1. *With my strongest recommendation for approval, I request a waiver of physical standards for LT Juan Alvarez.*
2. *In order to expedite the approval process, and due to the exceptional nature of LT Alvarez's waiver request, I recommend that his case be reviewed by a Special Board of Flight Surgeons.*
3. *After reviewing and personally observing LT Alvarez's amazing recovery and achievements since his injury, I am convinced Juan is more than ready to return to flying duties. His physical condition, warrior spirit, and drive to succeed are in the top 10 percent of my 70 plus pilots. I would fly in combat with Juan Alvarez. The country needs LT Juan Alvarez to be returned to flight status.*

THE WAIVER RECOMMENDATION package had fifteen enclosures, including a VHS tape of the aircraft egress demo and obstacle course. The package was compiled, reviewed, double checked, and multiple copies were made.

The original was sealed in a manila folder to be submitted in person to the Naval Aerospace Medical Institute (NAMI) Code 42 at Naval Air Station Pensacola, Florida.

$\sim$

07 JUL 1997 // I-10 BRIDGE, PENSACOLA BAY, FLORIDA // 8:30 AM

Shelley glanced at the thick manila envelope in the passenger seat again. Understanding the weight of what that package represented. She tapped her finger against the steering wheel. John was away on another classified TDY. He had asked her to drop off his final waiver paperwork to NAMI Pensacola before the formal Board of Flight Surgeon's deadline.

Dan Labrador had tried to ease her discomfort.

"What are the chances he'll get into another crash? He's got his out of the way already!" Labby had joked. Wrong move. He had found himself with Shelley's finger in his face.

"Can you *guarantee* me?" she had demanded. He couldn't. No one could.

So, there it was. Sitting beside her. The one thing keeping John on track to fly again.

The bridge to Pensacola loomed up in front of her, and she had a thought. She felt guilty about it almost instantly but, nevertheless, she thought about it. She imagined the papers which were stuffed into the envelope fluttering through the air, drifting down, down, down to the Gulf which ran relentlessly under the bridge.

Wouldn't have to worry about him flying again, a part of her wheedled. She resisted the temptation. Telling John he should not go back to military flying would be like telling her not to be a nurse. Flying was John's heart and soul. It was his passion and calling; flying made him feel right in his own skin. Shelley knew it was wrong to impede that, no matter how afraid she was for him.

Instead, Shelley sent out a prayer to the universe and let her husband live out his dream, no matter how dangerous that dream was.

God, keep him safe.

~

21 JUL 1997 // NAS PENSACOLA, FLORIDA //

NAMI Code 42 had to request approval up the chain of command to get John into the dunker. Tommy Hull had to sign another endorsement letter to recommend approval. It took a letter of approval from the office of the Chief of Naval Operations (N889J3). The approval letter from the CNO's office was signed on 14 July, probably with some background help from AFSOC and DEVGRU.

On 21 July 1997, Navy water survival refresher at NAS Pensacola would be first gauntlet to pass in the week of his final evaluation of medical evals, finishing with the Board on that Friday. Originally, during AOCS, officers were expected to tread water for fifteen minutes in steel-toed flight boots and flight gear without flotation equipment. They would then transition to drown-proofing for another fifteen minutes. They were made to swim a mile in full flight gear and boots. The refresher course, however, was five minutes for each challenge, and they had to demonstrate the four basic strokes for the length of the Olympic-sized pool.

The refresher course still required testing in intense emergency scenarios. They would jump off the high tower and then swim—underwater—the length of the pool. Then a parachute-dragging simulation through the water and having to untangle themselves from the parachute cords. Immediately after treading and drown-proofing, they had to manually inflate their flotation lobes, link up as survivors, flip over a capsized life raft, and all climb in.

Then there was the dunker. They were expected to all go through the helicopter dunker four times. Normally, pilots who had to go through the refresher dunker portion were put in the two cockpit positions only. This time, however, the instructors rotated the order so the focus would be on John at the end of the course. The last two runs in the dunker would be conducted while blindfolded with swim goggles, which were painted black.

John was doing great through the first part of the refresher, and their key strategy was to save the best for last. John was being video-taped after all. A Navy cameraman video-recorded the entire evolution to officially document it for the board.

Then he felt it. The feeling was faint at first, but eventually John could tell his prosthetic foot was getting loose. He had worked on it the day prior, in his garage.

Dammit, John thought, *I didn't lock tight it enough.*

His group was out of the pool and waiting instruction for their treading water portion to begin, so he quickly went over to one of the instructors. The instructor was a former member of SEAL Team Four. He knew who John was and what had happened. The former SEAL was John's best shot.

"Hey Chief, I need a hex wrench," John said quietly.

The instructor frowned. "What?"

"My foot is getting loose," John hissed, trying to keep from drawing attention to himself from the other instructors. "I don't want it to slip out... I need to tighten it."

For a second, the instructor stared at John with no sign that he would help the Navy pilot. And then he said, "What size do you need?"

Relief eased through the tension. "Three millimeter Allen wrench."

"Meet me in the head."

John excused himself to the bathroom, dripping wet, with all his gear on. The SEAL entered after him with the wrench. The instructor tightened the leg himself, pulling hard on the wrench. The leg wasn't going anywhere.

"Don't let this fall off, Lieutenant," the instructor ordered. "They're all watching you. It's *all* on camera."

Lesson learned: extra lock tight on everything, every time.

The first part had John's group treading water in the pool. The five minutes were excruciating for some, and eventually someone gave up and grabbed the edge. A groan exploded through the room, but then someone shouted.

"Wait, that's not him. *There's* Alvarez!"

John was still at the center of the pool. He easily lasted through the five minutes of treading. His leg held up perfectly and did not act as an anchor. He also looked damn good outlasting the younger kid who looked a lot like him. He transitioned to a successful drown-proofing exercise where he had to float face down in the water. Ahab got cocky again. The dunker was next.

The rules were the same: if you leave early or unbuckle your harness early, you flunk. You get one shot at each of the four dunks. There were four other Navy helicopter aircrew in the dunker with him. The first ride was the easiest; no blacked-out goggles. John had initially planned to take his leg off and give it to the safety under-water diver as a point of confidence.

In the end, he kept his pride in check and kept his leg on, but he *did* wave to the underwater safety diver as he exited the dunker. In the second ride, John was placed in the co-pilot seat and was blinded. He knew where the window was and exited the dunker in time. In the third round, John was placed in the back, close to the door. Everyone was expected to go out of the same door. No problem.

The final and fourth round was set up to screw with him. They changed rotation once again, and John was placed directly opposite and farthest away from the door. In that position, many people could get kicked in the face. He would be blinded. The dunker was chaotic, and anyone in that position would have to be the last one out. He could not be totally sure when someone was already swimming ahead of him, putting his head at risk if he swam too close. John imagined the doctors were watching, eager, almost as if they were ready for him to fail.

John refused to give them the satisfaction. He belted in, counted the seats, and placed his goggles on. John reached down and gripped the seat edge with his right hand, ready to release the buckle with his left when the time was right. He took a breath before the plunge and exhaled.

The dunker dropped.

The crash was just as deafening as before. The giant machine sank and rotated. John sucked in one more big breath as the cold water violently rushed over his body, his face, and his helmet. The sound of it triggered an old, instinctive panic. Muffled, but still there.

Finally, the dunker settled. Upside-down. The water pressure surged up his nose.

Wait. Wait for all violent motion to stop.

He told himself to wait longer than the minimum count, trying to look cool and collected for the underwater safety divers evaluating him. He kept his right hand on his seat as a reference. John kept himself under control despite the mounting pressure. Normally, he would be expected to wait a minimum of five seconds after the dunker sank and flipped over underwater and settled before making his way out. He waited eight seconds instead.

One Mississippi... two Mississippi...

He knew if he left too early he would be screwed.

Three Mississippi... four Mississippi...

If he got kicked in the head, he would be screwed.

Five Mississippi...

Anything that would make him receive help from an instructor, he would be screwed.

Six Mississippi...seven Mississippi...

He waited. It was long enough for his chest to hurt.

Eight!

With his left hand, John unbuckled himself. He methodically made his way clear of the harness straps. He twisted his body into a prone, gliding position to head out of the dunker. He reached for his next handhold, counting each blind grab, hoping desperately he was going in the right direction. He could feel the thrashing of the others around him as they struggled to get out. In his mental picture of the submerged and inverted interior, he counted the chairs.

Just two more, and then the door... right? Crap.

He kicked forward and felt nothing. His heart lurched, but he kept kicking.

Finally, John broke to the surface. He was the last guy out. In fact, the cameraman had panned to the fourth survivor exiting the pool ladder, thinking it was John. Ahab was a good eight seconds behind the fourth survivor to surface and 20 seconds behind the first survivor to surface.

The pool training facility echoed with shouts and cheers as his fellow survivors, his fellow Naval aviators, congratulated him.

He had passed.

~

22-23 JUL 1997 // NAVAL HOSPITAL PENSACOLA, FLORIDA

"Do I really have to see every freakin' specialist on the planet?" John whined to an unsympathetic Shelley. "They already have my medical records."

He just hated being poked and prodded. He provided sarcastic and (what he thought were) funny responses on two of the three psychological questionnaires.

The psychiatrist's interview, though, was not as fun. John had to talk about the accident, but the shrink also asked personal questions about his childhood, his parents, his wife and kids. John quickly got fed up.

"What gets on your nerves?" the doctor asked. "You know, what annoys you about people? What sets you off?"

"It annoys me when people pry into my private life," John said with no irony. "It annoys me when doctors want to know all this crap."

The doc caught on quickly. "Well," he said with a conciliatory smile. "What's good is that I can tell you don't have a problem with your confidence—some people call it cockiness." He shifted forward in his seat, growing serious. "But here's the thing about PTSD: it could come back years later. Have you had any symptoms? Maybe a time when something unexpected happened, and your reaction surprised you?"

John rubbed his face. John realized he needed to be honest. The shrink would be smart enough to see through his 'cockiness' if he answered this question falsely.

"Yeah," he confessed. "In the first few days when I was in the wheelchair, I would have to get in the elevator, right? So for a while, when the elevator would jolt—you know, when it went up or down— I would tense up, like this..." He talked a little more about his survivor's guilt and the nightmares that plagued him when he first woke up in the hospital.

"How about the last few months?" the psychiatrist prompted. "You've been back in helicopters. Have any of these reactions come up?"

John told him about his first flight in the back of the Pave Low over the Atlantic, when he put his fear in check and told himself to trust the skills of the other pilots. The doc smiled, and John felt like he had passed the shrink's test.

"Yep," the doc said. "You're gonna be fine."

He asked if he could call Shelley and whether she would be okay to talk to him. John agreed. As the psychologist was signing off the waiver, the shrink warned John about 'devotees'—people who have a sexual interest in amputees. John held his tongue until he saw the psychologist finish his signature. As soon as he handed the form back to John, John snapped.

"That's *sick*! You're *gross*! I don't know what the hell you're talking about! Devotees... *Jesus Christ*, who even thinks like that?!"

John headed home and complained some more about being harassed by shrinks, but told Shelley she should expect a call from him. The psychiatrist called her later that afternoon. Shelley lay on her stomach, sideways across their bed, talking on the phone. John was uncomfortable, pacing back and forth behind her. Eventually, Shelley shooed him out of the room because she couldn't focus on what the guy was saying.

After the call, Shelley went out to find John. He was in the kitchen.

"What did you say?" John demanded. "What did you tell him?"

Shelley kept a straight face. "I told him I was scared to leave you alone with the children." John looked stricken, and she started cracking up. "I'm kidding, I'm just kidding!"

John grabbed her and pulled her close. "Smartass!"

She kissed him and then laughed again.

She told him the psychiatrist was mostly focused on how John was doing emotionally, and Shelley was happy to report that John was remarkably resilient. She thought the doc certainly wasn't as weird or invasive as John made him out to be.

The crusty old Navy orthopedic surgeon was only a little better than the psychiatrist. He eyed John with the kind of critical expression usually reserved for evaluating racehorses.

"Your prosthetic is fine," the doctor said. "I want to see you do single-legged squats on your right leg. Do ten of them."

The doctor knew about John's bad right knee. Still, John agreed, bending his left leg behind him and balancing on his right leg. The doctor placed his hand on John's knee as he squatted. It hurt, but John had been working on his poker face. *Eat the pain.*

"It feels a little crunchy in there," the doc mused.

"Yessir," John replied evenly. He could feel the pops and strains, too.

"Does it hurt?"

"No, sir, not at all"

"Okay, then 9 more."

"Good to go, sir!"

The surgeon smiled. The doc knew he was not admitting it at all. He stood up and walked out to the main clinic area. John overheard him speaking with a young flight surgeon waiting outside.

"We're going to help this guy get through," the doc said. "This is going to be good for the Navy."

The surgeon recommended approval for John's waiver in huge chicken-scratch handwriting on the SF Form 600 - Chronological Record of Medical Care form.

Hx + Package reviewed.
Excellent L knee stability, healthy stump.
Good R knee stability Ø
Gr I MCL + ACL "Give" Ø
good End Points AND
NO FXNL Impairment!
(Single leg. deep knee bend N)
Recommendation: Waiver, CLASS I
JM Riccardi
CAPT MC USN
22 July 97

~

25 JUL 1997 // NAMI, NAS PENSACOLA, FLORIDA // 0800L

The assembly to decide LT John Alvarez's fate was conducted by the College of Flight Surgeons at the Naval Aerospace Medical Institute or "NAMI". Every naval aviator, astronaut, and former POW has gone through NAMI. Naval aviators like to pronounce the acronym NAMI as a rhyme: "NAMI whammy" because of the fear of losing one's flight status or medical clearance to fly.

Because of the special nature of John's case, they had also gathered all the student intern flight surgeons to observe. One of them was LT

Charlie Godenas. Godenas was originally from Texas but had gone to Harvard and had picked up a strong Boston accent. His callsign was, unsurprisingly, 'Harvard'. John knew him from AOCS. He had left aviation after his first tour to become a doctor and a flight surgeon. John felt, yet again, that the universe was conspiring to work with him by placing people John knew to look out for him and fight for him.

Truthfully, John was stressed. Shelley was with him, and he appeared in his dress whites, his hair in a fresh "high and tight" cut. He knew he looked good. But no matter how good he looked, John knew his fate rested on the decision of the U.S. Navy senior flight surgeons. They could place restrictions on him, keeping him from combat or any special missions. They could deny his waiver entirely, recommending John's retirement. He really did not know what outcome he could hope for.

The formal panel was placed in front of the hall, sitting at a long table. The panel, as senior flight surgeons, consisted mostly of hospital commanders. They were all O-6s (Navy Captains), and the commander of NAMI, a one-star admiral, headed the board. Colonel Tommy Hull and Mr. Raymond Francis were also present.

John did not, however, expect one particular attendee. Before the board was scheduled to begin, Master Gunnery Sergeant Holtry—United States Marine Corps—appeared in his Class-A dress uniform. NAMI's commander approached Holtry as the drill instructor entered the hall.

"Master Gunns," the Commander said. "What are you doing here?"

"Sir," Holtry said, "Lieutenant Alvarez is one of my graduates from that day in AOCS. Class 15-87. I am supporting one of my officers. And you should know, sir, if he survived me... he can survive anything."

The Admiral nodded at Holtry, and then at John. Everyone took their seats, and the board presentation began. A flight surgeon candidate stood.

"I have the honor and the privilege to present the case of LT John Alvarez..."

The surgeons presented key aspects of John's case, and then the senior panel of flight surgeons asked John follow-up questions. The demeanor of the panel was not necessarily ominous—it appeared that everyone was clearly rooting for him—but one surgeon, a Navy Captain, shuffled his papers and would not look John straight in the eyes.

"Lieutenant, what if you're in another crash underwater?" he asked, appearing to sift through his notes. "What are you going to do?"

"Well, sir," John said. "The way I see it, if my left leg is pinned, I can always take my leg off and swim out. Someone else with a flesh leg might get stuck and drown or bleed out."

The crowd laughed. The captain, however, did not even smile. "Thank you, Lieutenant."

John was eventually asked to change into exercise gear. He jumped onto the stage in his brown t-shirt and black shorts, then jumped off it. He ran around the hall to demonstrate his prosthesis. The panel asked him to take his prosthetic off and put it back on to see how familiar he was with his leg.

Once the questioning was complete, Shelley and John were asked to leave the hall, allowing the deliberators to convene. John was expected to get dressed in his whites again, but Holtry exited the auditorium to the waiting room and chatted with them. He started cracking jokes to keep themselves occupied.

"How long do you think it'll take?" John asked. Holtry shrugged.

The administrative assistant in the room said, "Some of these things take hours to deliberate. Since this case could set precedent... who knows?"

Back in front of the board, Raymond Francis was asked to speak on John's behalf at the panel and was also questioned on the prosthetic and how well it would hold up in combat and harsh environments. The captain expressed his concerns about the prosthesis to Raymond. He stated he had two primary concerns: 1) could John perform duties and 2) if he crashed, how quickly could he get out? How strong was the prosthesis?

Mr. Francis was direct, as always. "Well, it's stronger than his regular one. His regular leg will break before this one will. Similar to a tank, it is very durable and can take a hit."

John did not have too much time to sweat and stress, however, because it barely took forty-five minutes for the panel to decide. The admiral walked into the waiting room. He appraised John, who was still in his brown tee and black shorts.

"Lieutenant, you haven't had time to change?"

John grimaced. "No, sir."

"Alright," he allowed. "Well, we're ready for you. Come in."

John looked at Shelley. She took his hand and squeezed it once.

I will follow you anywhere, her eyes told him. *No matter what happens.*

They followed the admiral into the hall.

The first thing John saw was the smiles. Everyone—all the flight surgeons in the auditorium—was smiling. That's when he knew.

Yes! he thought. *Yes! This is awesome! I don't care what restrictions I have, but at least I will get to fly again.*

John stood at attention in front of the panel. The admiral walked behind the table to sit in his chair.

"Lieutenant Alvarez," he said. "The board has come to a decision..."

Yes!

The admiral paused, as serious as the day is long. "...and you have the right to appeal it."

John's heart dropped. *No...no.* He looked at Shelley, whose heartbreak mirrored his own. *After all this? They are going to take this from me... after everything?*

John finally dragged his attention back to the admiral, whose eyes danced with a strange kind of amusement.

"It is a unanimous decision," he declared. "Class One, Service Group One. You have been approved for a full and unrestricted waiver. And Lieutenant, you're out of uniform."

The hall exploded with cheers. Shelley leapt up and hugged John.

He looked out at the crowd. He soaked it in with gratitude. Mr. Francis and Colonel Hull were both smugly smiling. He was eventually dragged into a bear hug by Master Guns Holtry. The rest of the room took turns shaking his hand, hugging him, and congratulating him. It was surreal.

Before departing, John called his parents, and they immediately burst into tears. His next call was to Ross Perot, as promised. He was directed to Perot's secretary, Sharon. "He's flying right now in his jet. I'll pass the message."

Almost immediately, Perot called John from his jet to congratulate him.

Finally, John called Frank Ellis.

His fellow Naval Aviator was jubilant. "God bless you, John!"

"Thank you, sir. No man walks alone!"

In the auditorium, Colonel Tommy Hull opened a bottle of champagne in the middle of the joyous chaos. Tommy smiled as he handed John the bottle. "Don't you love it when a plan comes together?"

John laughed at his squadron's own undefeatable Hannibal.

"Enjoy it, Alvarez. Hey, take the rest of the day off," Hull told him. "But you got duty on Monday."

30 JUL 1997 // HURLBURT FIELD AFB, FLORIDA // 0800L

Tommy Hull didn't bother knocking. He pushed the office door open with his shoulder, a folder tucked under one arm, the other hand pressed to his temple as if he were physically holding his brain together. John stood and almost saluted.

"Johnny A," Hull said. "You got a minute?"

John gave a faint smile. "Any minute for you, sir."

Hull let out a humorless laugh and tossed the folder onto the rolling tray table with a slap.

"I just got off the phone with someone from the Chief of Naval Operations office. It's about your waiver."

John blinked. The scale of it felt surreal. "That seems... above my pay grade."

"Oh, it gets better," the colonel continued. "After that, I had to call the Chief of Staff of the Air Force's office and the Surgeon General of the Air Force. So now I've got two services, two four-stars, their staff, and one pilot who's been turned into a science project."

John couldn't argue with that. After the endless tests, evaluations, fittings—being measured, scanned, prodded—he sometimes felt less like a military officer and more like equipment under development.

Hull leaned back, irritation sharpening his voice. "Here's the problem. The Navy tells me they'll approve your waiver if the Air Force approves first. Since you'd be flying Air Force helicopters." John nodded. *And...*

"And the Air Force," Hull continued, "says they'll consider it only once the Navy approves it first. Since you belong to the Navy."

John stared at him. "You're kidding." *Catch-22.*

"I wish I were. It's like watching two kids argue over who has to jump in the pool first."

John felt a flicker of disbelief give way to something close to amusement. "So what happens now?"

Hull's frustration shifted into something else; a quiet, deliberate resolve. A familiar look John had seen before. Hannibal with his plans for his A-Team. Plans that the brass didn't always take kindly to.

"I decided I don't care who jumps first," Hull said. "The Wing here prepared your waiver package after your flight physical. The docs here were chomping at the bit to do so. And the Commander at NAMI pushed this through on his end. So Colonel Comer, Colonel Connors, and I decided to cut to the chase and endorse your waiver 'on behalf of the Air Force' and just submitted the package to the Naval Bureau of Personnel through NAMI. First time ever that this has happened between services, so we took charge."

"That didn't sound remotely complicated," John said wryly.

Hull confirmed. "And then...I was told higher headquarters are both navel-gazing to figure out who should approve it first."

A slow laugh escaped John before he could stop it. After months of surgeries, pain, and uncertainty, it was almost absurd that the breakthrough came down to a pissing contest.

John laughed again. "Don't you love it when a plan comes together?"

The humor faded, and the weight of reality settled back into the room.

"Now," Hull said, tapping the folder, "let's hope no admin or risk-averse puke says no."

John grimaced. He was reminded of Frank Ellis and his fruitless fight against the bias of the risk-averse military. The whole circus of memos, enclosures, and signatures had only bought him the chance to be judged.

"I think," Colonel Hull said finally, "if anyone was stubborn enough to make the Navy and the Air Force sign the same piece of paper, it'd be you."

A faint smile tugged at John's mouth. "With a little help from a colonel willing to channel Hannibal the Great. *'I will either find a way or make one.'*"

Hull pointed at him. "I prefer 'strategically synchronized.'"

"Yes, sir."

Hull moved toward the door, then paused.

"And John, dude?"

"Sir?"

"Don't make me regret the headache. You stay clear of the flight line until all the i's are dotted and all the t's are crossed. I already caught wind that Steve Kelly was going to sneak you onboard his fini-flight. You stay clear, do you understand?"

John nodded. "Good to go, sir."

When the door closed, the room felt quieter.

Hull had forced the pieces into place. But now it was out of his hands.

Then came the phone call Tommy was waiting for. Late in the

afternoon on 4 September 1997, the Air Force Staff informed the commander that John was approved to fly. Signed memo to follow. Tommy then mobilized the squadron and wing to make a last-minute, urgent, high-priority change to the next day's flight schedule.

~

05 SEP 1997 // SECURE FLIGHT LINE, HURLBURT FIELD AFB, FLORIDA // 1200L

John's first official unrestricted flight was on September 5th 1997: fourteen days before the first anniversary of his accident.

After the aircrew brief, John had savored the walk in the Florida afternoon heat to the flight-line. He felt the weight of his helmet bag and his flight gear draped over his left shoulder. He was no longer cursing the Mae West LPUs.

During the pre-fight, John ran his fingers along the side of the aircraft prior to saddling up and strapping in. He was finally again in the right seat of the mighty Pave Low. Tommy Hull was in the left seat beside him, as he promised. John recalled the familiar sounds: the crackling of Automatic Terminal Information Service (ATIS) intercom over the UHF radio. His crew checking in disciplined order with their signature cadence. "Pilot's up."

First Tommy. "Copilot's up."

Then the flight engineer. "Seat's up. Right Door is up."

Then the gunner on the left. "Left door up."

Then the gunner on the tail. "Tail up. Loud and clear, Ahab, sir!"

The ATIS broadcast rang in the background through their helmets.

John pulled his visor down to shade his eyes. A stick of gum dissolving between his teeth, he called for the starting engine checklist. The familiar microphone rested against his lips. Tommy relinquished the flight controls to Ahab for the entire flight, from start-up to taxi and shutdown.

John keyed the cyclic's transmission switch, consciously dropping his pitch into his best 'Chuck Yeager' drawl.

"Hurlburt Ground, Cowboy one-one, spot hotel-one, request engine start."

The response came through. "Cowboy one-one, Hurlburt Ground, engine start approved, runway three-six in use, winds three two zero, five knots, altimeter two-niner, niner-niner."

"Two-niner, niner-niner for Cowboy one-one." John dialed the setting into his altimeter.

"Set co." Tommy dialed it into his.

John inhaled the familiar smell of hydraulic fluid and jet engine exhaust as the mighty Pave Low came to life. First, the high pitch sound of the auxiliary power unit (APU). Then the shuddering of the airframe and the whines of the massive turbine jet engines as each was cranked up. And finally, the rotor brake was released. John watched the tips of the massive titanium blades spin out in front of the nose, under his control.

He pulled back on the radio transmitter trigger with his right forefinger on the cyclic altitude control stick. He called for taxi clearance, then took off, checking in with Eglin Approach Control.

They flew over the beach, and John reveled in its magic. John even flew a tactical low-and-slow approach over Gator Lake, simulating a delicate water infiltration just a couple of feet above the water.

Promptly notifying the crew, he began to turn the aircraft tightly into a final approach line-up, and with his left hand lowering the collective (power grip handle) to begin the descent.

"On approach."

The 'seat' started the disciplined cadence calls: "200 feet, 100 knots, sink 5," instantly followed by the flight engineer in the right door, extending to the aerial gunners in the left window and tail positions. "Bearing one-eight-zero degrees, 100 ft, 80 knots, Sink 3, good descent."

"Clear forward 500, clear down; right." "Clear forward and down; left." "Clear down; tail."

"On final," John reported. The verbal sequence of each scanner continued, starting with the right scanner. "Continue forward, clear down; right", "left", "tail".

At 50 feet, the tail gunner then called, "Spray at the tail", as the aircraft continued to descend to the desired threshold of "five feet, five knots."

Looking through his forward-looking infrared monitor, John used the same symbology required to maintain heading, ground speed, altitude, and vertical velocity indicator, all calculated and displayed from readings of the Inertial Navigation System (INS). Then came the call from the flight engineer in the 'seat' checked in the precise measurements from their radar altimeter and GPS, which was coupled with their INS: "Five feet, five knots."

The entire operation was intense. Precisely maintaining a constant speed, altitude, and drift of the MH-53J/M Pave Low—even in a daylight scenario—is extremely difficult for any pilot.

John again reveled in the mist's smell creeping into the cockpit as the upside-down rain created by the massive rotors washed over the windscreen of his steel horse.

John lowered the collective gingerly with his fingertips and inched the aircraft closer to the undulating surface of the ocean. His six-foot-six tail gunner, "Meat", also reveled in riding the open ramp as the Pave Low glided along the wave tops.

John calmly commanded, "Boats, boats, boats." That was the signal for the tail gunner to help deploy a simulated combat rubber raiding craft with swimmers off the tail ramp.

Meat systematically verbalized each simulated swimmer jumping into the water and finally declared, "Boats away, swimmers away, all thumbs up."

The crew made their calls in exact sequence as the insertion was completed. With a final "tail cleared out," they followed the command to safely climb to altitude.

"Clear up and forward right."

"Left."

"Tail."

Just as smoothly, John pulled the lumbering beast up through the giant water cloud it had churned up. It created a spectacle over the golf course lake.

Before returning to the airfield at Hurlburt, the copilot usually called ahead to Cowboy maintenance. They were to report the status of the aircraft's condition, and the controller on the other end provided the parking spot: the letter for the row and the number for the spot. Tommy purposefully had John make the customary maintenance status radio call and ask for their parking spot.

The controller's response was priceless.

"Cowboy one-one, expect spot Hotel-One...designated *disabled parking*."

When they came back to the flight line and parked, there was a massive crowd waiting for him. Also waiting for him was a Marine Corps CH-53 pilot chair with armor plating—gifted to the squadron —strapped to an ATV; a "gator." Meat, his tail gunner, had *acquired* a disabled sign from a nearby parking lot to complete the throne.

Shelley, still in her hospital scrubs, and his little Nicole ran over to embrace him. He lingered in Shelley's kiss and breathed her in, and hoisted Nicole into his arms. She was holding yellow wildflowers in her hand; she had picked them from the grass outside the hangar.

"Where's Setty?" John asked Shelley over the chaos.

"There hadn't been time to pull Lisette out of her kindergarten class when I got the call!" Shelley told him. "I had to dash from work to make the drive from Pensacola to Hurlburt in time! But you know how proud she is of her daddy. Just like I am. Just promise me one thing, Johnny A."

"Anything," he told her with a grin.

"Every time you fly, as soon as you land, call me," she requested. "I don't need conversation, I just need confirmation. Just call, leave a message and say you've landed, and hang up."

John looked at his darling Shelley, never again wanting her to feel that same helplessness she had suffered. He made his promise just as he prayed to God that he could keep it.

"As you wish," John pulled her close into an embrace. They touched foreheads and John kissed Shelley again.

Tommy then popped the cork of a bottle of champagne and sprayed John down. Colonel Rich Comer, his wing commander, was next in giving John a bear hug. The group commander, Colonel Wurster, came up and did the same. The rest of the Green Hornet squadron mates followed. Shelley and Nicole were again in John's sights as he grabbed her and kissed her and Nicole. Shelley then took hold of the champagne bottle.

John was loaded onto the gator and was triumphantly paraded around in his makeshift chariot.

Tommy Hull gave the following statement for an article in the local base newspaper: *"Lieutenant Alvarez represents the warrior spirit, the special operations spirit in the 20th. He has the right attitude, outstanding motivation, and continuous drive—the stuff it takes to be a special operator. The country gets a valuable asset back."*

Despite Colonel Hull's words to the newspapers, he ran John through the wringer. Hull pulled him aside after the celebration.

"Dude, you know this flight was just for show," Hull told John, deadly serious. "You're still going to have to prove to me you can fly in combat. I'm going to give you your check ride."

"Alright," John replied, his 'fangs' out for the world to see. "Good to go, sir."

And he was. He had faith in himself, his training, his family, his community, and in the path the Divine had laid before him. He found grace and joy in the life he fought for and shed blood for.

No one could take the sky from him now.

EPILOGUE

A blazing fire makes flame and the brightness of everything that is thrown into it.
– Marcus Aurelius

Not until you spread your wings; will you know just how far you can fly.
– Mathew James Elliott

BIEBERE EX CRURIS

They've been on the run for over 48 hours. They were what was left of the OAD-A. They moved silently and deliberately through the thick pre-dawn fog. They could barely make out anything beyond arm's length. They were running on no sleep, hardly any food, and shouldering the relentless burden of knowing their host-nation base was overrun and other teammates captured. Their faces hollowed by fatigue, uniforms soaked and dirty. Now, with just over a mile to their extraction point, their world feels painfully close and dreadfully remote.

It is eerily silent as they tread through deep sand, wire-grass, and palmetto brush. Quiet yet unnerving. The team moved swiftly, in a loose formation, eyes scanning through the pre-dawn mist, weapons lowered but at the ready. The sound of automatic fire ripped through the fog from the left flank. Their world suddenly ignited into chaos.

"CONTACT LEFT!" the team leader shouted, voice cracking from adrenaline.

The team dropped instantly, muscle memory overriding fatigue. Dirt and wet pine needles sprayed as they scrambled into defensive positions. Another burst—this time from the right.

"CONTACT RIGHT! Multiple shooters!"

The fog turned into a wall of confusion, shapes moving, muzzle flashes *strobing through the mist. The team returned fire in coordinated, controlled bursts, calling out sectors. 'Keep moving.' Desperately trying to keep from being out-flanked. Their hearts thumping, their hands shaking. They were running on fumes and instinct.*

The firefight lulled for a moment; the woodland went eerily quiet again. No one had been hit yet. The mist, now being lit by dawn, was still swirling, thick and ghostlike.

Then they see them. Dark shadows emerged—slowly, deliberately, from all directions. Silhouettes of armed men moving towards the team through the haze. One team member cursed to himself, "We're not gonna make the last mile..."

Another gripped his M-4 carbine and reached down to the location of the extra magazines in his vest. Trigger finger at the ready. They braced. They breathed as quietly as they could.

Ready for a final push, or their last stand.

12 SEP 2018 // RANGE ROAD RR 211 – EGLIN AFB, FLORIDA // 0630L

"Cease fire! Cease fire! Cease Fire. Endex! Endex! Endex!" A calm, barreling voice cuts through the mist and chaos.

The advancing figures now become familiar faces. It's the cadre of instructors stepping out of the fog, and all available CAAs that are not deployed. The sudden shift from combat adrenaline to dawning realization leaves them momentarily frozen. The cadre and CAAs fall in around them, not as evaluators, but as guides and brothers. They moved down the line, lifting the heavy rucksacks from the A-Team's shoulders, offering quiet nods of respect. Together, bearing each other's burdens, they walked the final mile toward the RV.

Col A? Is that really him? *A few of the graduating students silently recognized him. Dressed in garb, retired Colonel "Johnny A" Alvarez CAA # 72 is not merely setting pace among them but, like all other CAAs, is himself carrying the burden of a new teammate. The rest of the cadre and support teams were waiting in the clearing for their field ceremony, morning light now breaking through as the truth settled in. They had passed the final test. Their world feels strangely peaceful after the anarchy.*

As they come on to a dirt fire road in the pine and palmetto brush swamp in the Eglin Air Force Base Range, the rendezvous (RV) point comes into view; a clearing marked by vehicles, a few field tables, and the rest of the instructor cadre waiting in a loose semicircle. Some operators stand with arms crossed, others with steaming coffee in hand, all of them looking on with solemn respect. All on the team are about to be presented with the CAA tab they worked so hard for.

Many had seen it before; the distinctive 6th SOS Commando emblem on it, sitting on a sacred shelf behind the squadron's bar alongside the over-turned mugs bearing the names of two fallen CAAs. Major Mark Todd and Major Brian Downs. They were about to be toasted and initiated by drinking from the legendary socket.

The leg LT Alvarez, CAA # 72, first walked on.

THE GRADUATION EXERCISE, called Raven Claw, was the culmination exercise for the Combat Aviation Advisor's Operator Qualification Course near the Army Ranger's training camp. This grueling and challenging exercise was modeled after the Special Forces Selection final exercise known as Robin Sage. In 2003, then Lt. Col. Alvarez approved and presided over the first iteration of the qualification exercise. Through the ingenuity and hard work of the architects of the course, legendary CAA's Master Sergeant Vince Milioti and Senior Master Sergeant Hale Laughlin, the course was further formalized and then certified by USSOCOM.

Immediately after Ecuador, John's teammates from the 6th SOS adopted the Alvarez family, even though he was formally assigned to the 20th. From bringing meals, workout gear, to modifying his home for his wheelchair. John was issued a numbered Combat Aviation Advisor (CAA) coin—coin #72. Meaning he was the 72nd CAA accepted into the unit. He later returned to the 6th as a Latin American OAD-A team leader and assistant ops officer, and again as the operations officer, and finally as the commander. The first leg socket he walked on lived in the 6th SOS Air Commando CAA bar for almost twenty-five years. It travelled the world for promotion and retirement ceremonies. Until the program was closed in October 2022, it was a rite of passage for all CAAs upon completion of their CAA Qualification Course field exercise. All graduates of the grueling course drank Johnny Walker Blue Whiskey from the leg, in the field, and together they had to buy a bottle of the same for the next class.

The socket of the leg he first flew with on his tactical checkride administered by Tommy Hull was fitted with an ivory handle from a 20th SOS Green Hornet's Vietnam era mug. Lieutenant Colonel Johnny A presented it to Colonel Tommy Hull at Hull's retirement.

A third socket, the one he first flew with, resides at the 20th SOS alongside a canoe LT Alvarez 'liberated' (and paid for) in Sierra Leone.

The leg-drinking became a tradition, along with an official "A Flight" aircrew patch and motto "Biebere ex Cruris," and a rite of passage. As the legend spread, even the Air Force Chief of Staff would drink from it. But to this day there is an argument in the Air Force Special Operations Command on who was part of the "first-time" the leg was passed around.

In the early spring of 1998, as part of his tactical requalification, Ahab flew out to NTU Oceana Naval Air Station again, this time leading the flight of MH-53J Pave Lows alongside his flight ADO Major R.K. Williams. He could reunite and conduct training with the SEALs of SEAL Team 4. While he was not technically supposed to do any shipboard tactical maneuvers yet, he flew while the SEALs from the platoon that helped save him parachuted out of the Pave Low. Later that evening, with night vision goggles on, John went out to a Navy ship again as the tower flower.

He flew with instructor pilot Captain 'Little Rob" A. and circled around to land on the ship. A plastic chemlight was placed on the deck where the Pave Low nosewheel needed to land on. Rob let John fly the approach. He was so technically precise that he cracked the chemlight with the nose landing gear. Afterwards, they realized John wasn't *officially* allowed to fly the shipboard landing just yet, especially at night. They returned to Virginia Beach, where they celebrated at the Oceana Officers Club. Marine Major Brooks Gruber, Air Force Captain Jimmy Cardoso, R.K., and other pilots joined John as they drank and swapped stories. At some point in the night, John took off his leg and filled it with beer. He raised it and declared a toast to their fallen brothers.

As the group ramped up and became more rowdy, a Navy Captain who was having dinner with his wife seemed to get a little upset about noise. The bartender walked over to their group and approached John, who was the only sober one. John was sitting on the barstool without his leg. They were all still in their flight suits.

Great, he's going to kick us out or berate us or something. John was ready to apologize and promise to control the boys.

As the bartender came up to him, John noticed his watch. The watch included an explosive ordinance diver (EOD) badge, identifying him as having one of the most dangerous jobs in the military. The bartender was also missing a finger.

"Sir, are you on active duty?" the bartender asked, noticing his flight suit.

"Yes, sir."

"Is that your leg they're passing around?"

"Yes, sir."

The bartender reached over to shake John's hand.

"I have too many friends who've lost limbs—"

"—thank you for your sacrifice, too, sir," John added.

"No, this is awesome. Give me that leg. You guys are drinking out of it for free for the rest of the night."

It wasn't the last time John's leg became a beer mug. In the spring of 1998, John was in Asheville, again for night mountain training. John was one of the senior ranking officers during the training. It was early spring, and they were shut out from training during a freak snow storm one night. Since they couldn't fly, they went to a nearby Irish pub. John noted a group of enlisted "crew dogs" at the bar while he and another officer, Steve Moss, had dinner. John and Steve finished and were getting into the car when one of the waitresses came out.

"Hey, one of you forgot your wallet," she told them. John checked his pockets and sighed. His coin, of course, was in his wallet. When he re-entered the bar, all the enlisted guys were smiling. They all coin-checked him.

"Ha-ha," John said and agreed to buy them all a round of drinks.

He decided to stay a bit longer than he expected. John took his leg off and they all began to drink out of leg. At some point, one of the guys tried to hand it to the lady bartender for a refill. "Sorry, I can't. It's unsanitary. We have laws..."

Meanwhile, at the end of the bar, there were a few older guys drinking. Several were clearly vets. One walked up to John.

"Are you with these guys?"

"Yes, sir. I am," John admitted.

The enlisted guys jumped in.

"Yeah, he's our senior officer!" one said.

"He's in charge!" another yelled.

The older man raised a brow. "You're a pilot?"

"Yes, sir."

"And you fly with that?" he asked, pointing at the leg on the table.

"Yeah, he's the first guy to go back on combat duty after losing his leg," one of the crew answered.

The man smiled at John. "Well, I'm proud of you, let me buy you a drink." He walked around the bar and filled the socket of his "bad-ass robot leg". The old man was, in fact, the owner of the bar. "You're all drinking out of this for free the rest of the night."

In December 1998, the 20th SOS had a Christmas party at the Crab Shack in Destin, Florida. Shelley had brought their newborn, Jake. After a round of the squadron's theme song—Bon Jovi's "Wanted Dead or Alive"—Lt. Col. Jack Hester, the Hornet's new commander, went to the mic in the venue.

"Johnny, get your ass up here, take off your leg!"

John obliged while Shelley laughed and rolled her eyes. There were some new folks who joined the squadron since John had returned. Hester pointed to them with the leg. "No one gets to fly in my fuckin' squadron unless you drink from the leg." He refused to give the new aircrew their unit coins until they did.

John also never showed up to a gathering without a spare or decoy leg. Later, Jack Hester would assign John to fly the Air Force Chief of Staff in a live-fire demo. The AFSOC commander arranged the demo to highlight the command's war-fighting capabilities. When asked why he chose Alvarez, Hester stated: "Because Johnny is my best damn pilot—that's why!"

But as to the "first to drink from the leg"? John bestows that honor to Brooks Gruber and nobody can dispute it. In 2020, Marine Corps Major Brooks "Chuckie" Gruber was among those tragically lost in the operational testing of the fledgling MV-22 Osprey program. Brooks's infectious smile, grit, and legacy endure not only with the Marines and special operators he served with but in John's and Shelley's hearts, who honor his memory.

No man walks alone.

TAG, YOU'RE IT: THE ELITE CLUB

John kept his promise to the Navy SEAL who told him to pay it forward. John and his family were stationed in Italy at the start of 2001. John worked as an action officer assigned to NATO South Headquarters in Naples, Italy. After the attacks on September 11th, John's priorities changed as NATO forces deployed to Afghanistan. Soon, multiple people would be invited into the "network" of Special Operators and "elite club" of amputees. John would mentor some of the first medevacs from operations in Afghanistan post-9/11.

Camp Rhino was the coalition foothold in the opening months that followed. Marine Lance Corporal Chris Chandler was first. He was young, only in his early twenties, and had his leg blown off while clearing mines. Next was Army Specialist Matt Hess. Married and a little older, Matt was also an explosive ordnance disposal (EOD) specialist and also ended up losing his leg. Both were being brought back via C-17 cared for by CCATT medical while in-flight to Landstuhl Regional Medical Center located near Ramstein Air Base in Germany. John got a call from Major Brett Hartnett in Iceland while on a NATO bombing range in Sardinia. John scrambled back to Naples Italy, gathered his little family, and they flew to Landstuhl via a C-21 executive transport re-purposed on the spot at the Naval Support Activity (NSA) Naples Passenger Terminal. They made it a family trip as it was days before Christmas and to allow for Shelley to be there for Matt's wife.

Upon their transfer stateside, Mr. Francis was also brought in to intervene and ensured the two were properly equipped so they could go back to work on their respective specialties. Chandler also became the first service member and amputee to complete Army Airborne (parachute school) and a honor graduate. He went on to complete two more combat deployments. Matt went on to work as a civilian EOD specialist in countering the threat to our troops and later moved to the Pacific atolls with his family.

John would mentor many other 'firsts' in the military. He supported and mentored Chief Warrant Officer Three (CW3) Dana "DJ" Jones, a former fellow joint special operations planner and friend. More importantly, he introduced DJ to Mr Francis. Through the network, DJ became the first Army pilot to go back to flying in the elite 160th Special Operations Airborne Regiment (SOAR) Night Stalkers; just seven months after losing his leg. DJ almost immediately deployed back into the fray, serving in six combat deployments to Afghanistan and Iraq. He retired as a CW5 and traveled the world as a defense contractor. DJ is the chief flight safety lead and program manager for a world-renowned aviation company. John stood up and poked at an Army Four-Star General when informing him about DJ. "Does the Air Force always have to lead the Army in how to get things done?" In turn, DJ and John would welcome and support two more Nightstalkers into the elite club, an MH-47G pilot and a developmental test pilot. Both are thriving and inspiring others.

Air Force pilot Lieutenant Colonel Andrew Lourake was assigned to the elite and prestigious 89th Airlift Wing (also known as the "Presidential Air Wing") when he was injured in a motorcycle accident. He became the first above-the-knee amputee to go back to flying. Afterwards, Andrew and his wife made it their mission to regularly visit and volunteer their time at Ward 57 in Walter Reed Hospital, which served severely injured service members.

First Lieutenant Ron Boisvert was going through the U-28 qualification course at the 19th SOS training squadron when he was hit by a car while on a motorcycle. First Shelley, then John intervened, both going to Pensacola's Sacred Heart Hospital to counsel Ron, his parents, and his fiancée. John just happened to be scheduled for his yearly flight physical at Hurlburt and flew in from Bolivia. Ron went on, with the assistance of Andrew, in becoming the first-above knee combat pilot in AFSOC. He's since been promoted and is still serving as of 2026.

John and Shelley also arranged for specialized simulator training for the first female military pilot to go back to flying duty as an amputee, and with an above-the-knee amputation on top of that. Captain Christy Wise (now Kinsey) received unwavering support from her wing Commander Chad Franks. Chad was around to witness John's recovery and return to the cockpit. He was also a fellow helo pilot, deployed with John as part of Operation Allied Force (OAF). John handed off the reins to Major Al Brown—the first amputee National Guard C-130 pilot and one who held the record for the most combat missions flown as an amputee—as well as Andrew and Ron. They all took turns in mentoring Christy. She went on to requalify in the HC-130 as a combat rescue pilot and also was captain of the US team at the 2017 Invictus Games in Toronto, Canada. Christy has since been promoted and continues to serve in the US Air Force.

In another twist of fate, John was not just asked to advocate for amputee warriors in the United States. John personally intervened on behalf of a Uruguayan pilot injured in a motorcycle accident. He happened to be in Uruguay for work when Andrew Laurake called him about a pilot he was hosting in St Petersburg to have a state-of-the art leg made for him. With this twist of fate, John changed his itinerary in-country and briefed the Uruguayan Air Force commander and his chief surgeon, showing them the pictures of one of their own pilots jet skiing, flying, and rollerblading in Florida with his high tech leg Andrew Lourake arranged for. John decided to raise the stakes during his presentation by declaring, "There is no reason why he couldn't become the first *Latin American* pilot to go back to flight status."

John also reached out to Ross Perot, twice, to intervene on behalf of two severely wounded Pave Low aircrew. A former Nightstalker, Bruce, was commissioned into the USAF and was stationed at Kirtland AFB to transition to the Pave Low. He was in the back of a Pave Low that crashed, taking his ear and eye. Ross Perot sending him to a specialist in Dallas actually saved Bruce's life. Later, MSgt Chris "Mack" MacKenzie, a former FE and planner assigned to John, was in a Pave Low that was downed by a rocket propelled grenade (RPG) during a raging battle in Fallujah, Iraq. Mack went on to fly again as an aircrew with the Presidential Wing before he decided himself to go back to the warfighter community and "pay it back". He became the first AFSOC representative of a newly formed groundbreaking program called the Care Coalition. John had the honor of presiding over Mack's retirement from the Air Force.

John has also worked with civilians. On September 20, 2015, John received a call from his sister Cuqui. Her neighbor had a friend in South Florida who was on the verge of losing his life due to diabetes. It aggressively progressed over three years. Stephen Cummings was a successful financial manager who was desperately trying to save both his legs but it was draining the life out of him. John called Stephen the night before his surgery to encourage him. Steve at first hung up on him. John called back and eased his mind about having the surgery the next day. John also promised he would follow up with him and let Stephen know that there was a network standing by to assist. Stephen provided this testament to what it meant for him to hear from John and such a crucial time in his life:

"The surgeon informed me that he estimated that I had four days to live if I did not have the surgery and if the infection entered my heart, I would die. Shaken, I would spend another 18 days in the hospital in total, but two days until the amputation takes place... Upon losing my leg, the pain was excruciating for three days, but the infection was rid of my body.

When he called back, I was horrified that I was so rude. He told me that as an amputee, I could still live a very full life and he gave me great confi-

dence. John was so supportive to me as I was retrained on how to walk again.

I read about John's story online, but had the opportunity to meet him in Miami on a visit he made to Homestead Air Force Base. He was everything you would expect from a military pilot. Incredible physical condition at 51 years old and exuded great confidence.

Although I cannot run marathons like John, his determination and caring for other amputees is heartwarming and inspiring. In summary, I have learned that one can live a very full life as an amputee and a positive attitude is everything."

Stephen continued to pay it forward himself and is a motivational speaker at nursing homes and schools in the South Florida area. Stephen is a full fledged member of this Elite Club.

The unofficial "Tag-You're-It" military amputee network could not list all of the men and women that were touched by their mentorship here or anywhere else.

In 2005, the USSOCOM Commander, General Doug Brown was moved by the 'network' of operators set on creating a Special Operations program called the Care Coalition, also known as the US Special Operations Command Warrior Care Program.

"They made a promise to the U.S. when they joined, whatever service they joined," General Brown said, regarding his motivation. "And then they made another promise to us when they came in as Special Operators. We are making a promise to them that we are going to be with them for the rest of their lives if anything happens to them. We are going to take care of their families as well." General Brown also made it clear he was tired of getting calls from Ross Perot in the middle of the night asking, *What they were to do with so-and-so?* and how Mr. Perot was already taking care of them.

Today, US SOCOM's retention rate after illness or injury is 73%. The services are generally at 10%. This work embodies the most important of SOF truths: "Humans are more important than hardware." John knows that offering a hand makes a difference, as it did for him. By keeping the faith, he recognized that everyone deserves the chance to walk, run, and fly again.

LEGACY

John's Special Ops Career

John kept his faith in his military community throughout the rest of his career. John told the author of the compendium of the 20th Special Operations Squadron, *On A Steel Horse I Ride*, "I truly believe that if I were not in Air Force Special Operations Command and not part of the 20th Special Operations Squadron, I wouldn't be flying again. It was amazing to see all these people from the special operations community, many of whom I didn't even know, just come out and help me. What we really have here is a brotherhood, not just a job."

John indeed passed his checkride with Tommy Hull and then a multitude of tactical qualifications such as flight lead, shipboard ops, and others. He re-qualified as an instructor then evaluator in multiple US and Russian aircraft. He flew over 200 hours in combat and operational missions. He went on to get additional qualifications in both fixed-wing and rotary-wing aircraft and flew over thirty different aircraft throughout the globe and logged over 3,300 hours before retiring.

Many additional 'firsts' followed. A month after pinning on Lieutenant Commander, John completed an inter-service transfer to the US Air Force as a Major in 1998. The only downside was that John could never become *Captain* Ahab. Tommy would joke about it: "We broke you so now we have to keep you."

In early 1999, Major Ahab shared a unique 'first' with Senior Chief Rat. Rat and a small group of SEALs showed up to Hurlburt Field for pre-deployment air-to-ground training with AFSOC assets as the conflict in Kosovo ramped up. John flew the small team out to the USS Baylander (India Xray IX-514). dubbed the "World's Smallest Aircraft Carrier". The small Navy boat out of NAS Pensacola was the dedicated platform for initial helicopter shipboard landing qualifications for Navy, Marine, and Coast Guard aviators in the tiny TH-57 Bell Jet Ranger helicopter. AFSOC Air Commandos and the 160th Special Operations Airborne Regiment Night Stalkers would occasionally hijack it for more nefarious reasons at night. The massive Pave Low was too large and heavy to land on it. However, hovering over it for assault training in what was known as Visit, Board, Search, and Seizure (VBSS) operations was doable. Navy SEALs could also rehearse small-team boarding, hook and ladder drills, and close quarter combat tactics while the boat was underway in the Gulf. Senior Chief Rat was the first off the tail ramp of the Pave Low to slide down the thick two inch thick braided *fast rope*. This fast rope insertion technique is the fastest way to get a full SOF team from a hovering helicopter onto a small, moving deck. Untethered. Unattached. After their combat training on the cramped boat, Rat was the first to climb up an undulating rope ladder known as a "Jacobs Ladder", dangling from the tail of the Pave Low approximately ten feet over the deck of the Baylander. Over a couple drinks afterward, Rat would joke that he was the "first pegleg pirate to fast rope from a helo flown by a pegleg pirate pilot."

John's first operational deployments as an amputee aviator included participating and commanding combat rescue and Special Operations missions and units worldwide, including Operation ALLIED FORCE (OAF) in Serbia and Kosovo where his team rescued the future chief of staff of the Air Force. He went on to NATO AIR

SOUTH after the Kosovo conflict and helped establish the first combined Special Operations training and collaboration in NATO after 9/11.

He went back to the 6th twice, first as an Assistant Director of Operations (ADO) and Latin America lead and then finally as the Operations Officer and Commander. He participated and led teams in operations worldwide during the Global War on Terror and ENDURING FREEDOM. During Operation IRAQI FREEDOM Alvarez commanded the first combat direct-assistance aviation advisory mission since Vietnam through rebuilding the new Iraqi Air Force.

The SEALs of Golf platoon had given John his new callsign - Ahab. John reunited with Howard "Rico" Lenway several times and collaborated with him over the years. John was witness to Rico's reception of the Bull Frog Trophy in 2014. Rico was designated the 16th Bull Frog, the 'senior' longest continuously serving SEAL on active duty. It was passed to him by Admiral William McRaven, who was the 15th. Captain Lenway retired after 40 years in uniform. He is an accomplished pilot, and still flies.

Matt, who had been in the helicopter crash with John, completed the mission in Ecuador despite a cervical injury. Later, Mr. Francis offered to get Matt to his ortho surgeon. Matt decided to get out of the military because of his neck injuries since he could no longer parachute. John later wrote a recommendation letter for Matt to law school. Matt went on to bigger and better things.

John also reunited with Navy SEAL Jeremy Trump and his family in his mom's home in Tampa, Florida. There, Jeremy got to meet Shelley and Jake, John's youngest. Later, John proudly attended Master Chief Jeremy Trump's retirement at the SEAL Heritage Center in 2018. This is the first book Master Chief Trump has agreed to have his name mentioned in.

Petty Officer David Barrett "Dave" Scott, later was commissioned as a SEAL officer but was lost in a diving accident in October 2002. Petty Officer James Martin, on that same deployment, was later injured in Colombia. He confided in John that despite being one of the most experienced SEALs on the team he was shaken by working on John in the canoe. James went on to finish formal corpsman training in part because of his experience that day and what he witnessed his two youngest SEALs Jeremy and Daisy do under pressure. He especially had a newfound respect for his 'problem kid' Jeremy. Perhaps he saw part of himself in Jeremy. Sadly, he was lost in a commercial diving accident after he left the Navy.

Mike Hargis went on to fly Pave Lows, and was part of the initial cadre operationally certifying the CV-22B Osprey that replaced the mighty Pave. After retirement, he still flies overseas in a discrete capacity.

Master Sergeant Ramon Acosta and John continued their brotherhood in Pave Lows and at the 6th SOS when John was the SOUTHCOM ADO and again as operations officer and commander. Upon retirement, Ramon became a contractor and CAA integrated skills instructor.

TSgt Frank Rivera built ramps and widened the doors to John's bedroom to fit his wheelchair. Their special relationship continued into retirement as Frank worked on the non-standard, one-of-a-kind aircraft the 6 SOS flew, and later he travelled the world as a defense contractor.

Senior Master Sergeant Dan "Labby" Labrador was also still at the 6th upon John's return and deployed with him overseas multiple times. After 22 years of service to the Air Force, Labby became a beloved elementary school teacher in Navarre, Florida, at the same school where all the Alvarez children attended. Sadly, Dan was lost to cancer in 2015.

The amazing Critical Care Air Transport Team (CCATT) concept was born in 1988 when then Colonel P.K. Carlton and Major J. Chris Farmer, both trauma surgeons, developed an expeditionary and airborne surgical Intensive Care Unit (ICU) to address a critical gap that existed in long-range aeromedical evacuation. They honed their capability in the early 1990s at Wilford Hall. Lt. Col. Stephen Derdak along with Lt. Col. Steven M. Josephs were in the first wave of doctors to validate this capability during the Balkans conflict and later in Latin America. JSOC was an early proponent and adopter to rapidly recover severely wounded SOF operators from remote or politically sensitive environments with ICU-level care. Its early operational funding pressure helped accelerate CCATT's growth by the late 1990s into a global, combat-tested organization that is the flagship medical evacuation capability for the U.S. military to this day. One of the earliest real-world tests of the entire concept happened in Ecuador.

LT Alvarez's evacuation set precedence when that C-141 was diverted, reconfigured overseas, and launched with a CCATT team to bring him home alive.

$$\sim$$

Doctor Joe Basinger

Doctor Joe Basinger now works as the deputy at the Medical Center at Fort Sill and a part of the Military Entrance Processing Station (MEPS) network. He conducts examinations and follow-ups for all branches of incoming military members. Someone, after John's accident, helped tip the scales to keep Joe's commander from doing anything to retaliate against Joe for insubordination. This someone leaked the story to the local chamber of commerce. Almost as soon as he got back to Fort Walton Beach, Joe was presented with a plaque of honor, with the intent of forcing the chain of command to recognize his actions as a success. Doc Joe remains a close family friend and is the godfather of John's youngest child, John "Jake" Raymond Alvarez. One of their funniest memories is when Joe received a call from John a few months after beginning his recovery.

"Hello, John!"

"Hey, doc," John said. Joe thought he heard kids' voices in the background, maybe Shelley's...

"What can I do for you?" Joe asked. It was an early Saturday morning, and Joe planned on getting a few errands done before spending some time on the beach. The Gulf brought in a hazy spring warmth. While it never truly got cold, it did get chilly. The warm, salty breeze was a welcome change.

"Well," John huffed, and Joe thought he could hear a slight strain in the Lieutenant's voice. "Okay, so the girls were probably playing outside for a bit after school. We didn't see anything last night, or maybe she just—anyway. Nicole's got a...tick in her bellybutton. Shelley's tried to get it out, but it's, uh, stuck in there. I thought maybe—"

"Yeah, I can head right over," Joe chuckled. "I have to see this!" He did, and got out the tiny bug from the similarly tiny brunette, and John clapped him on the shoulder. Shelley teased her husband for his apparent overreaction, but also thanked Joe.

Colonel Tommy Hull

As for Col. Tommy Hull and the Alvarez family; they remained close. When Shelley received her US citizenship, she asked if Tommy would swear her in again during the celebration party, to make it all officially official as he had sworn John into the Air Force. Tommy Hull considered it the second highest event in his career...aside from John's recovery.

Additionally, just as Tommy was getting ready to retire, John decided to kidnap him for his "fini" flight, his final flight. John recruited a bunch of guys from the squadron and called Hull down for a briefing. All of a sudden, two guys busted in with guns and put a bag over Tommy's head, tied hands, and dragged him to a van. But they had not tied Tommy's hands very tight. He got his hands free, jumped the two would-be kidnappers, and took control of the vehicle. He let them continue to drive on the flight line (for which they could have been arrested). In the end, they were supposed to deliver Tommy to John in the helicopter, but in fact Tommy delivered *them*. John thought it was hilarious. Well, that's Tommy's version of the story.

In the end, Tommy was doused with the fire truck hose and

champagne; reminiscent of John's first flight back and therefore "payback". In 2010, Colonel Tommy Hull (retired) presided over John Alvarez's retirement ceremony.

Major Brian Downs

Brian "Downer" Downs left the active duty Air Force in 2000. He came back on September 12, 2001, and went on to serve in the 6th SOS as a CAA. He led missions across the planet during the Global War on Terror. He also became the youngest lay pastor in his church and he and his family attended John's first public "testimony" at the Navarre Methodist Church on the Panhandle of Florida. Downer deployed alongside John to the Philippines, Colombia, and in 2005 to Iraq.

On Memorial Day May 30, 2005, an Iraqi Air Force Comp Air 7 crashed while in the eastern Diyala province. Major William "Brian" Downs, 40 years old and then assigned to John at the 6th SOS, was in the aircraft. Major Downs, who played a critical part in saving John's life in the jungles of Ecuador, died along with all other occupants onboard; U.S. Air Force Captain Jeremy Fresques, 26, of Clarkdale, Arizona; U.S. Air Force Captain Derek Argel, 28, of Lompoc, California; and U.S. Air Force Staff Sergeant Casey Crate, 26, of Spanaway, Washington, and Iraqi Air Force Captain Ali Hussam Abass Alrubaeye, 34.

John, as Major Down's commander, had the heartbreaking but solemn task of notifying Brian's wife Beth and their three young children; Bailey, Ella, and Chandler. Since then, John maintains his support of their family and in upholding Brian's memory.

Lieutenant Commander Frank Ellis

Lieutenant Commander Frank King Ellis went on to attend John's change of command ceremonies as a special guest of honor each time. He passed away in December 2016 and is interred at Barrancas National Cemetery in Pensacola, Florida. His legs and his trailblazing story are on display in the Naval Air Museum in Pensacola.

Ross Perot

In 2004, Ross Perot finally accepted the Eisenhower Award for his over 40 years of unwavering support to the US Military. All the Services Chiefs, Chairman General Richard Myers, Vietnam POWs, Medal of Honor recipients, and more than 1,500 others attended the ceremony. Each Service Chief presented a video story of Ross Perot's assistance to one of their Service members. General John P. Jumper, the US Air Force Chief of Staff presented Lt. Col. Alvarez's story. Mr Perot passed away in 2019 at the age of 89 after a lifetime of faithful service to his nation and those who served.

Raymond Francis

Mr. Raymond "Pops" Francis, before he retired he convinced his team at the WillowWood Company in Mt. Sterling, Ohio to allow him to mentor aspiring prosthetists. He was also an advocate of the Ertl procedure, which unfortunately has been sporadically adopted as a practice. He believed in creating a better, more sustainable model of prosthetic support for both civilian and military amputees. He continued to fly well into his late seventies and mentored hundreds of aspiring pilots at no cost to them. He was the recipient of numerous awards and decorations, including being presented the FAA Wright

Brothers Master Pilot Award in 2018. This award recognizes pilots who have conducted 50 or more years of safe flight operations. As for his relationship with John, Mr. Francis saw the pilot like his son. John named his own child after Raymond. They continued to meet on a regular basis. In fact, as Mr. Francis remarked, "I will continue seeing John until I can no longer see anyone."

Pops passed away in January 2025 at the age of 86. Months later John, retired Senior Chief Rat, Lennie, and Steve (Callsign Flounder) laid Raymond's ashes to rest in the Atlantic at a GPS coordinate location named Point ROMEO FOXTROT, and known only to them. Two SOF amputee veterans, a retired school teacher, and a US Air Force fighter pilot. All brothers because of Raymond Francis.

～

Unsung Heroes

That Navy SEAL who first reached out to John after the accident also presided over John's promotion to Lieutenant Colonel in Norfolk, Virginia in 2022. There are additional heroes in this story whose identities cannot be shared that had a direct hand in saving and mentoring John. Their names remain unspoken for *now* as some continue to serve in the shadows. One day we hope their extraordinary stories can be properly told.

In the years to come, John would lose friends, squadron mates, and other brothers in arms. In addition to Labby, Commander Len King and four others were lost to aggressive cancers, most likely caused by their exposures during service. He also lost friends to emotional and mental demons, where the weight of their service took its toll.

～

JOHN PARTICIPATED in all kinds of distance runs and several sprint triathlons. Later, in part, to heal himself. In 1998, John also won the coveted Pave Low Beer and Taco Run, a full-contact event thanks to captains AJ Gaston and Stan Allen. He placed first in his category for the Destin Crab Trap Sprint Triathlon (he was then the only one in this category). After his 'experimental' Ertl revision in 2001 that also removed significant bone spurs, he was able to finally experience the "runner's high" he had missed for so many years.

John always kept a laminated card on a plastic lanyard around his wrist for all the marathons (including the Marine Corps and Air Force Marathons) and Army ten-milers he would run as an amputee. On one side a list of his fallen comrades, and on the other a verse.

Isaiah 40:31

The Journey Continues…

John's final assignment in the Air Force was as the Defense and Air Attache to Bolivia. Never one to shy from tough missions, he continued to advocate for the military and for American values through his time in Bolivia. After only a month on assignment, then-Ambassador Philip Goldberg was declared persona non-grata in the early days of September in 2008. Shelley, Lisette, Nicole, and Jake had to be evacuated back to Navarre near Hurlburt Field. The SOW commander, Colonel Brad Webb at the 1st Special Operations Wing, took care of them and was on call to execute a Non-combatant Evacuation Operation (NEO) John had to plan for himself and what had been left of the embassy staff.

Thankfully, the situation de-escalated and his family was able to rejoin him in La Paz. Despite the political unrest, John did the job to the best of his ability. Even when that meant antagonizing the Bolivian and Venezuelan governments from time to time and being accused of supporting a 'coup'. But that's another story.

Colonel John Alvarez retired in September 2010 at Hurlburt Field on the Emerald Coast. He sent Jimmy Buffett a formal invitation letter, and signed his Ahab pirate pilot photograph for him. Jimmy could not attend, however replied with a picture and guitar pick signed '*To Colonel Alvarez, Retirement is a Beach,*' and a letter stating John was his official "pirate pilot." Years later John and other wounded warrior veterans would go on fishing excursions on Jimmy's personal boats the "Margaritavich" and "Last Mango II." A fellow disabled veteran was awed when he saw the pirate pilot picture of Ahab over Jimmy Buffett's desk at his Key West office.

John served as a Senior Fellow at the USSOCOM Joint Special Operations University in Tampa, and was later part of their adjunct faculty. In 2013 he transitioned into industry. He was inducted into the Air Commando Hall of Fame in the summer of 2014. John supported Shelley as she finished her Bachelor's and Master's degrees in Nursing.

As of 2024, John retired as an aerospace executive and Shelley retired as a nurse practitioner. John and Shelley are officially splitting their time between New York near their Canadian family, and their home base on the Space Coast of Florida. John also enjoys time with his lovable service dog, courtesy of Dogs Inc!

All three of their children are graduates of Florida State University (to John's dismay, as a University of Miami alumni).

Lisette is now an award-winning storyteller and podcast producer, married, and a co-parent of two cats. Lisette also became close friends with Brian Downs's daughter, Ella, when they connected while living in the Washington, DC area. After spending a few decades listening to various versions of John's story, Lisette decided to take a crack at it, interviewing many of the people involved. The very first draft of this memoir was gifted to John in 2016. If you're reading this, it's because Lisette inherited some of John's stubbornness.

Nicole obtained an Ivy-League engineering degree after FSU, working for major defense industry and consulting firms. In 2025, she welcomed her first child with her husband and made John and Shelley grandparents. "Forrest John" is currently the light of his Nana's and Papa's lives. His favorite song is "Volcano"—by Jimmy Buffett, of course.

Jake, the promised 'miracle' third child, was still in middle school by the time John retired. During their time at FSU, Jake worked summers as a Park Ranger in Washington State and Washington, D.C. Jake now serves as a communications staffer and supervisor in the US Senate. Jake is also currently attending Duke University, pursuing a master's degree in Christian studies.

The *Alvari Parrotheads,* as they call themselves, finally attended a Jimmy Buffett concert together in December 2021. It turned out to be Jimmy's last concert in Tampa.

By sheer grit, love, and faith—and perhaps some divine grace—John Alvarez is still around to see it all.

ACKNOWLEDGMENTS

This book's publication was made possible by the unwavering support and decades of diligent effort from numerous individuals within the extensive Alvarez network.

Thank you to Randy and Laura from Story Ninjas, our editors, who helped shape this from an internal family legacy memoir to getting us to the finish line as a truly inspirational memoir.

We would also like to thank Dominic for a powerful book design that captured the emotion and depth we hoped for this project.

Thank you Eric Huppert and Randy Anderson for your aviation expertise and technical advice. Thank you to Max Sears for your thorough review and insight as an author and accomplished aviator.

Thank you to Nicole for your visual layout and photography skills, and for your support throughout the end stages of this book... while also being a new mom!

Thank you to Jake; you were not just the miracle child, but you also offered spiritual and editorial guidance to your dad and eldest sibling, which is a miracle in itself.

Thank you to Danny, who offered continuous praise and a tender ear as both a spouse and a philosopher.

Thank you to Pastor Dan Morris for encouraging John to share the truly powerful part of his journey.

Thank you to General Norton A. Schwartz, General Charlie Holland, Admiral William H. McRaven, Lt Gen Tom Trask, Lt Gen Marshall "Brad" Webb, CMSgt Greg Smith for giving your heartfelt endorsements ahead of this book's publication. Your encouragement is humbling.

We give thanks to everyone who allowed us to pry into their feelings about this story; Carmen, Juan, Cuqui, Joe, Tommy, Butch, and so many more. We are also so, so grateful to those we managed to interview before they passed; Pat and Raymond. Their stories helped bring more color and texture to the tapestry of this book.

Thank you to Shelley, whose perspective, heart, and struggle also epitomized the faith, grace, and love we wanted this story to embody. You are an amazing woman, wife, soulmate, mother, and badass (retired) nurse!

Finally, Lisette and John would both like to thank the greater SOF and military communities for teaching and supporting us throughout this story. May you all find the same grace and love you have poured out to us.

COYOTE'S RULES

~

1. If you run with the pack, play by pack rules, but keep your options open.

2. When you hunt alone, stealth is your best hope. You may only get one try.

3. Know the terrain cold, especially the escape routes.

4. Do not depend on others for ideas; they are rarely available.

5. Have your own ideas and keep plenty of them in reserve. Develop instincts.

6. Where instinct fails, build plans. Define your objectives. Refine your methods.

7. Success has three phases: extensive planning, exhaustive rehearsal and swift execution.

8. If you're in a fair fight, you didn't plan it properly.

9. Don't take stupid chances. Surviving is a professional endeavor.

10. Consider the consequences of your acts. Survival of the pack may be at stake.

11. *Have a back-up plan if things go wrong. Keep it simple.*

12. *Know your limits and when to quit. If you can't kill two geese, kill one and make it home.*

13. *Most of us come to grief because we want too much.*

14. *If you run with bad dogs, you get shot with them.*

15. *Most traps are set on trails that are already out of bounds.*

16. *If you suspect you're out of bounds, you probably are.*

17. *Give quarter where it's due. You may need it yourself someday.*

18. *Never assume that no one wants you dead.*

19. *Threats rarely announce themselves. Stay alert. Anticipate the unexpected.*

20. *Be ready to move on if the game gives out.*

LISTEN TO THE PLAYLIST

"Every life tells a story. Every story has a soundtrack."
— PJ Wright

"Where words fail, music speaks."
— Hans Christian Andersen

Scan to access the full curated playlist.

Available on Apple Music, Spotify, and Amazon Music.

www.ingramcontent.com/pod-product-compliance
Lightning Source LLC
Chambersburg PA
CBHW040729120726
48010CB00019B/389/J